D0891829

Getting Computers to Talk Like You and Me

Getting Computers to Talk Like You and Me

Discourse Context, Focus, and Semantics
(An ATN Model)

Rachel Reichman

A Bradford Book
The MIT Press
Cambridge, Massachusetts
London, England

This book was set in Palatino by Village Typographers, Inc., and printed and bound by The Murray Printing Company in the United States of America.

Library of Congress Cataloging in Publication Data

Reichman, Rachel.
  Getting computers to talk like you and me.

  "A Bradford book."
  Bibliography: p.
  Includes index.
  1. Discourse analysis—Data processing. 2. Artificial intelligence. I. Title.
P302.R45 1985   401'.41   85-7183
ISBN 0-262-18118-5

Contents

Acknowledgment

Over the course of years I have become indebted to many people for their intellectual stimulation and help in preparing this manuscript. First and foremost, I would like to thank Bill Woods whom I met when I began my work on natural discourse at Bolt, Beranek, and Newman, Inc., in 1977. Bill's encouragement, ideas, and thorough reading of my works over the years have made this book a reality. I would also like to thank Cheri Adrian whose comments and suggestions have elucidated the theory presented here and whose clarifications have hopefully made this book easy to read. Last, I'd like to thank David Adar, Allan Collins, Brad Goodman, Yorick Wilks, James Allen, Don Norman, Sonvra Buffett, Marlene Vigel, and individuals at the Institute for Semantic and Cognitive Studies in Geneva, Switzerland, who over the years have been good friends and supportive colleagues.

This work was supported in part by the National Science Foundation Grant IST-81200018, under the auspices of the Institute for Cognitive Science at The University of California, San Diego.

Introduction

Artificial intelligence is an area of computer science whose thrust is to build computer programs capable of modeling or simulating intelligent behavior. To do that, computer scientists first had to agree on some metric of intelligence. To measure intellience as it relates to computers, they chose human intelligence.

Artificial intelligence came alive in the early sixties, mainly deriving from chess-playing programs, algebraic word-problem solvers, scene analyzers, natural language translators, and parsers. Many of the same problems that confronted scientists in the sixties and seventies still confront us today. There is just so much more knowledge used by humans in the performance of even the simplest tasks than we can get into a computer and retain some sense of efficiency and response. How do we shy away from exhaustive searches of lengthy lists of facts and rules? Are there some *general* strategies or principles that people use in their cognitive performance of everyday tasks?

This book is about one particular task that we'd like a computer to do. Wouldn't it be nice just to sit down at some computer terminal and tell the computer, in whatever language you speak, some task that you want done and have the computer do it? Of course we cannot yet do this. Today, rather, managers of some company may know their company's problem, but they do not know "computer talk." They therefore hire a computer programmer to whom they try to explain their problem. The programmer in turn tries to explain it to the computer in computer talk. Needless to say, much is lost in the translation.

So we want a computer that can understand our everyday language. It will probably take many more years for this to become a reality because language communication is a verbalization of thought. There are two problems confronting us: (1) getting a computer to think and (2) getting a computer to know the rules of a particular language.

Current and previous works on how people think have been forced to reckon with the vast amount of knowledge used in everyday thought. A linear list of everything we know cannot work. It would simply be too exhaustive and time-consuming to search through such a list. Additionally, having to list explicitly everything we know does not account for the vast amount of inferencing and deducing people seem to do all the time. Therefore a great deal of work has gone into organizing knowledge in some cogent manner to reflect the interrelationships among the things that we know. Having these interrelationships, we can then specify some logiclike rules that would enable the computer to draw inferences and deductions much like a human would.

In the sixties and seventies work on natural language (the language of any given society) focused on the rules of sentence construction. This type of work is called sentential linguistics and researchers in artificial intelligence, in the area of computational linguistics, tried to incorporate and develop the findings of sentential linguists to build computer programs that could *parse* and *generate* single sentences. But most language interaction spans many sentences. As such the difficulty and complexity of the language part of "talking" computers multiplies and explodes. We must now worry more carefully about elliptical utterances, utterances like "Did he really?" where what it is that he did or said must be retrieved from some earlier part of the discourse. We also get a proliferation of anaphoric and deictic references, both of which usually require binding to an entity mentioned earlier in the discourse to find out who or what is being talked about.

In sentential linguistics we not only have the "ordinary" rules of grammar like *third person singular requires an S ending on the verb*, we have in addition selectional restriction rules that are much more semantic in nature. For example, it is *ungrammatical* to say "The pebble thinks" because the verb think must have an animate subject. When we get into discourse, rules of a more semantic, pragmatic, and logical nature predominate. We get more fully into the marriage of language and thought. The following discourse between two people is incoherent: A: "I'm going to the store to buy a newspaper. Do you need anything?" B: "I sure hate Max." Our computer, to be able to talk *coherently* to a person, has to know how and why an exchange like that doesn't work too well. It can no longer be just a grammar parser; it has to "understand" what's being said to respond appropriately. In most of our conversations much of what is said is not explicitly stated. It is implicit in the communication, and our computer needs some general rules of inference and logic to ferret out implicit communication.

In this book we shall study extended person-machine communication. We shall begin by looking at person-person communication to understand the problem we're dealing with. Later in the book, only after formulating rules of discourse engagement for people, we shall describe a computer module that embodies these rules.

As will become evident in reading the first few chapters, there is a great deal of subtlety and complexity underlying person-person conversation. Much of this complexity transcends sentential linguistics and any particular facts people know about the world. Consequently we focus on one major aspect of person-computer extended communication—the conversational flow itself. What makes for coherent discourse? How do we follow the twists and turns of another speaker? When, where, and how are references to preceding parts in the discourse "well formed"? These aspects of communication seem to occur effortlessly in the person-person forum. We show, however, that much underlying subconscious work is actually being done. Discourse engagement is learned. It develops over time and in this book we show why.

The computer program in later chapters similarly is limited in scope. It describes the "highest level" of the communication process. It tracks the conversational flow and the underlying *model building* that each conversant performs as a conversation progresses. Rules and mechanisms described in the first part of the book are formulated into this program. The rules as well as the system itself presuppose other computer modules in a full natural-language computerized system. For example, abstract characterizations like "Speaker Express A Instance B" are part of the conversational computer module. "A Instance B" is a function call onto some other computer module which, given B from the discourse module, could retrieve a proposition A from memory that was an instance of B. Similarly, "Express" is a function call onto some syntactic module which, given a proposition of the form "A Instance B," could realize that into its given natural language form. In our current state of research such other computer modules are not quite developed. It is vital, however, that as developments proceed in these other areas, we simultaneously work on the more global aspects of person-machine interaction. The analysis presented here is a step in that direction. This process provides a context and a direction for development of lower level computer modules.

Getting Computers to Talk Like You and Me

Chapter 1

The Need for a Theory of Discourse

Everyone knows that clear communication requires a speaker to follow certain rules in selecting and ordering the elements of sentences. In English, for instance, we do not demand that someone "Dog the out put" or ask "If dog the came the yet in back"; English grammar does not permit such orderings. Though particular rules vary from language to language, most every language has ordering rules of this kind. Language users are not ordinarily aware of the rules they follow as they speak, but it is in large part the grammatical rules they share that permit mutual understanding.

Beyond the sentence level we do not usually think of our communication as governed by rules. Spontaneous, natural conversations are generally thought to be "rule free," with speakers selecting and ordering their utterances without any necessary consideration of what has gone before. Though as participants in conversations we take for granted this apparent freedom, to the observer it presents a puzzle; indeed, one who looks closely at natural dialogues must often marvel that communication occurs at all. Consider, for instance, the following portion of a spontaneous conversation between three friends, F, C, and R; the excerpt begins as F enters and notices a burn on C's leg:

F: 1. Oh my God, how did that happen?

C: 2. Well, I don't want to go into this again.

F: 3. Tell me briefly.

C: 4. You know I can't tell anything briefly.

F: 5. Wow, right, I have to think about this. All right.

C: 6. Well, starting at the beginning. Ummm. Arthur has
    7. a box, it's called a "hot box," okay? It's
    8. insulated and you open it up and you put like a
    9. tricket, special tricket, in it and you close it.
    10. And it's very cold in our room, so Arthur and I
    11. sometimes use this in bed, between us when we're
    12. snuggling, when we're ready to go to seep. And—

R: 13. Don't get too risqué here.

F: 14. Don't get too graphic.

C: 15. You notice the way I use the word "seep"?

F: 16. Huh? "Seep?"

C: 17. "Seep."

R: 18. "Seep?"

C: 19. That's how we say "sleep." "Let's go to seep."

F: 20. Oh, I didn't see that.

C: 21. So that's getting pretty intimate right there, but
     22. that's as far as I'll go. And normally—

R: 23. To sleep.

C: 24. Right. And normally it falls out of bed, you know,
     25. and I wake up in the morning and I go, "Gee, it's too
     26. bad that fell out of bed." Well, the other night it
     27. didn't fall out of bed, and I woke up with this burn.

Because we all manage conversations such as this one every day without undue difficulty, we take for granted our ability to follow the point of another person's remarks, and to choose responses that fit coherently into the discussion. A little thoughtful scrutiny reveals, however, that managing even the most ordinary conversational engagement is quite a remarkable feat. The means by which speakers follow each other in spontaneous conversations are far from obvious.

Notice, for instance, that the telling of the story about how C got the burn does not proceed in any simple, straightforward way but is interrupted by several tangential discussions—about whether the story can be told briefly, about whether in the telling the speaker is getting too risqué, and about the speaker's use of a private expression, "to seep" (in fact a metadiscussion about whether her listeners understood the meaning of her language). Though each speaker grasps the other's points and makes her own understood rapidly and easily, such mutual understanding requires a considerable amount of internal interpretation and analysis—clearly much is left unsaid. A most interesting instance occurs in C's next to last utterance, in her statement "And normally it falls out of bed." Given all the interruptions that have gone before, how is it that her conversants understand what "it" means? Earlier in the conversation, understanding at one point gets off track, but even the clarification requires considerable inference ("So that's getting pretty intimate right there") and proceeds with remarkable efficiency. Clearly, in order to follow each other through the twists and turns and jumps of their conversation, the conversants must share a number of implicit assumptions, a common ground, that allows their conversation to flow. But what is the nature of these implicit assumptions, this common ground? What kind of knowledge do conversants need to share in order to engage in coherent discourse?

Mutual understanding depends in part on the fact that participants in a conversation share in external, situational context. The extent to which they share such a context partly determines, for instance, how much and what kind of detail is (and is not) stated. In our example, the friends know each other well enough to interpret F's remark, "I have to think about this," as teasing. F and R evidently already know who "Arthur" is and the nature of C's relation to him, so neither is explained; the shared knowledge that the conversation is being taped motivates (and allows C to understand the motivation of) R's comment, "Don't get too risqué here"; and so on. The prior knowledge of conversational participants about each other and about the subjects of conversation are factors external to the talk itself that help determine the course of conversation and permit the talk to be understood.

Another kind of knowledge that conversational participants share is semantic knowledge: because they share a language, they can understand not only the meaning of each other's words but the particular meanings those words take on in the immediate semantic context. If, for instance, in a discussion about cars one speaker said, "A loose hood can be deadly," "hood" would no doubt be interpreted as the hood of a car; if the Mafia were under discussion, however, a "loose hood" would be interpreted in quite a different way. The power of semantic context in aiding interpretation of meaning is illustrated strongly in our example by the discussion of "to seep." Neither R and F noticed C's use of "seep" for "sleep" until C pointed it out. Because the scene was already set with C and Arthur snuggling in bed, the semantic context directed not only the semantic interpretation of "sleep" rather than "seep" but evidently even what word R and F heard. An assumption conversants typically make, then, as they interpret the meaning of each other's remarks, is that speakers will not shift semantic context without some warning or explanation.

This last point is tied to a third kind of shared, implicit knowledge that is required if conversation is to flow: identifying a current discourse context. The most remarkable feature of natural conversation, which we do not experience as remarkable since we manage it so easily, is that topics are typically developed, suspended, and resumed without need of explanation or even comment. With every utterance a listener must grasp the relevance of what is being said to

what has been said before—whether, for instance, the current statements are said in illustration, support, agreement, or disagreement,
or whether they are tangential, represent a shift of topic, or a return
to an earlier subject of discourse. Without the ability to grasp the role
served by a speaker's utterance in a conversation, a listener is lost,
confused, forced to ask: "But what does this have to do with what we
were talking about?" Such questioning illustrates a clear presupposition that operates in discourse communication: we expect speakers
to select and order their comments so that the relation of the remarks
to preceding discourse can be easily understood.

Notice, however, that most conversations consist of several sub-
conversations—in our example, four: about the burn, about the
brevity of telling, about being risqué by revealing intimate details,
about the use of "seep." Notice further that at any given point in the
discussion only a small portion of the preceding discourse is selectively focused on at any one time. In our example, F's "I have to think
about this" clearly refers only to the question of whether the story
can be told briefly; R's "Don't get too risqué here" focuses only on
the fact of C and Arthur being in bed; and so on. The main focus of
the conversation is the burn, and the conversation isn't "finished"
until how it happened is explained. But along the way, how is it
that the conversants manage their frequent shifts of focus without
confusion?

For conversants to follow a conversation, they must share not only
common situational knowledge and common semantic reference,
they must also share considerable knowledge about the structure of
the conversation itself. Conversants must share compatible assumptions about, or models of, the identification of the current topic, the
current focus of attention, and the relevance or role of each discourse
utterance in the ongoing exchange.

This complex feat clearly is not accomplished by conversants' continually verbalizing their underlying models to one another. We do
not continually interrupt ourselves to say things like, "Now I'm
going back a minute to what you said about . . . ," or "I'm going to
change the subject here and we'll get back to what you're talking
about in a minute." If such verbalizing were necessary, there would
be little time for substantive discussion—only time for metadiscussion. Effective, efficient communication occurs because participants
share implicit knowledge about the shifting of conversational reference frames and even about shifting between different levels in a
conversation (as when, as occurs twice in our example, talk about a
subject is suspended for discussion of the conversation itself).

When we consider the knowledge that conversants must share about the structural development of a conversation, we are led to the possibility that conversations do indeed, like sentences, have a kind of grammar: a set of implicit rules that speakers and listeners assume, that help govern the selection and ordering of elements in a discourse and that make our seemingly randomly organized conversations understandable to one another.

Though in the field of linguistics there is wide acceptance of the notion that sentence generation and interpretation can be described by grammatical rule systems, there is much disagreement among linguists about the possibility of describing a set of structural conventions or rules for the generation and interpretation of extended discourse.[1] There are, however, a number of reasons to suspect that conversations may also be governed by implicit linguistic rules. One reason we have already suggested: since we are able in conversation to follow complicated twists and turns, suspensions and resumptions, without elaborate metadiscussion to keep each other up to date on this topic shifting, there must be some implicit means by which we know how to follow along.

Second, though we have a great deal more freedom in our selection and ordering of elements in conversation than in single sentences, not *everything* we might wish to add to a conversation is "legal" or "allowed." In our example, for instance, if one of the speakers had suddenly said something like, "There are children starving in Bombay," the others would have had to ask what this had to do with anything. Consider this sequence:

F: Tell me briefly.
C: You know I can't tell anything briefly.
F: There are children starving in Bombay.
C: Well, starting at the beginning. Ummm. Arthur has a box . . .

This is not a "conversation" in our ordinary sense of the term. The fact that some elements or orderings are not regarded as appropriate in discourse suggests assumptions or expectations we have as to what is appropriate; and when these are violated, conversation becomes, like ungrammatical sentences, incoherent.

A third reason to think that there may be rules underlying our conversational engagements is that just as children in their language development must learn how to construct "legal" sentences, children must learn how to converse coherently. When children begin talking, they tend to carry on their "conversations" quite independently of anyone else who may be talking. Later, though they engage in dialogue, they tend to confuse their listeners by shifts of topic and ambiguous references that are clear only to themselves. It takes considerable time and practice for children to learn the conventions of *shared* topic identification and focus which allow clear and efficient communication with others.

In the following chapters we shall examine many natural, spontaneous conversations in an effort to identify and characterize formally some of the structural conventions that allow us to generate and interpret understandable conversations. We shall explore many different kinds of conversing—instruction, debate, storytelling, social interaction, and so on—to identify those linguistic features that are common to all forms of effective discourse, regardless of its purpose or subject matter and regardless of the situational context that motivates the discourse. As Sacks, Schegloff, and Jefferson (1974) state:

> Since conversation can accommodate a wide range of situations, since it is a vehicle for interactions in which persons in varieties of identities and varieties of groups of identities are operating, since it is sensitive to the various combinations, and since it is capable of dealing with a change of situation within a situation, there must be some formal apparatus (in conversation) which is itself context free . . .

It is not obvious, however, what form this "formal apparatus" should take: what aspects of discourse structure and what features of conversational interaction might be amenable to formal analysis. Even less is it clear to what extent one might expect rules or conventions identified for conversation to operate with the force of linguistic rules—that is, to operate such that the introduction of one element of discourse predicts and constrains the subsequent development of the conversation. Our first task, then, is to understand what specific aspects of discourse need to be explained and what kinds of conventions or rules may be necessary for an adequate explanation.

Is a Linguistic Theory of Discourse Necessary?

A number of attempts at structural and functional descriptions of extended discourse have previously been attempted. These will be examined in chapters 9 and 10 in considerable detail. It is useful at this point, however, to consider the theories that have thus far been offered to account for discourse phenomena.

One common approach has been to characterize and differentiate between different discourse forms. Each such categorized form is treated as a distinct discourse genre or schemata with its own special and predictable structure. Various analysts have generated a profusion of genre classifications, based on widely varying criteria for distinction, and delineated different conventions applicable to each type. Some classifications are based on the purpose of a set of utterances and result in classifications like "narratives," "arguments," and "descriptions." Other classifications are based on the style of presentation and result in distinctions like "poetry" or "verse." Still others are based on content and result in classifications like "drama," "fiction," and "riddles." Whatever the classification scheme, this approach assumes that genre dictates structure, that shared rules of discourse development depend on these various possible "structures."

It is certainly the case that we have different expectations of what someone telling a story and someone making an argument will say and of the order in which the different kinds of elements will be arranged. Our analysis of discourse must therefore incorporate these distinctions. However, the "genre dictates structure" approach leaves some fundamental questions about discourse unanswered. Since it is clear that in any ordinary discourse or conversation, speakers use a number of different "genres"—stories, descriptions, arguments, for instance—what conventions govern the development of the whole conversation that includes these subparts?

An adequate theory of discourse would need to specify the conventions or rules that apply across as well as within discourse forms: rules that describe our discourse processing regardless of particular discourse developments.

An approach that has attempted to include such general rules of discourse is that of the ethnomethodologists, which focuses on the universal and context-free conversational phenomenon of "turn taking." This focus has resulted in descriptions of rules that define "legal" points of transfer from one speaker to the next. In this view conversations develop as speakers take turns completing conventional paired forms such as greeting/greeting; offer/acceptance or refusal; question/answer; and so on. Though this scheme has the advantage of identifying some general conversational rules that pertain to the function of different conversational elements, the rules are less linguistic conventions than simply conventions of general interpersonal behavior. More important, because the emphasis is on paired forms in discourse, the analysis is restricted to linear conversational development. It has no way to explain (except as exceptions to the rule) the large proportion of discourse that is nonlinear and nonsequential—the frequent shiftings, suspensions, and resumptions of topics that we find in natural dialogues. Accounting for these must take a central role in any adequate theory of discourse structure.

More strictly linguistic attempts to show how conversants follow each other through discourse have taken two approaches. In the first, analysts attempt to explain how discourse "hangs together" or "coheres" by attempting to identify surface linguistic cohesion devices. Halliday and Hasan's work. *Cohesion in English* (1976), exemplifies this approach. As will be described in much more detail in chapter 9, Halliday and Hasan divorce their claims about the surface linguistic evidence for text "cohesion" from any notion that a text may have a rich, underlying deep structure. The linguistic claims, then, though general in form and specific to language use, are of a very different sort than the type of analysis attempted here. As to be amply illustrated, one of our main conjectures is that "lexical cohesion" can only be properly understood and identified given a rich and careful description of a text's underlying deep structure. Halliday and Hasan's evidence of lexical cohesion, on the other hand, includes the observations that (1) in "cohesive" text we find an abundant appearance of related words in close proximity (e.g., key and door appearing within short distance of each other) and (2) we find pronouns following nouns. Most "ties" like these, however, are artifacts of the talk content and are found in the single sentence as well.

In the second discourse-linguistic approach, of which we are a part, identifying a conversation's "deep structure" in terms of structural relations between discourse elements precedes linguistic analysis. Among this class of researchers we find the works of Linde (1974), Hobbs (1976), Grosz (1977), Longrace and Levinsohn (1972, 1976, 1977), and Weiner (1979). Let's briefly consider the works of Linde and Grosz. Both researchers, studying task-oriented dialogues, show that we can parse a discourse into a treelike structure where each node of the tree represents a distinct discourse element. They then demonstrate how, given this structure, we can explain and even predict the appearance of many "surprising" surface linguistic forms found in a discourse. Grosz, for example, studying the transcripts of experts teaching laymen how to assemble a water pump, shows that in the water pump world distinct discourse elements corresponded to the particular subtasks involved in such an assembly. Grosz demonstrated then that when conversants complete discussion of some subtask and return to the larger task in which the subtask is embedded, they will often use a pronominal form to reference something in this larger task even in those cases where a seeming contender for this pronominal is found in the linearly closer discussion of the subtask. Grosz notes that it is the underlying hierarchical structure of the dialogue that explains why no ambiguity arises—after completion of a subdiscussion its elements are no longer available for pronominal reference. Here you notice we have a truly discourse-linguistic phenomena, not something explainable by or an artifact of the external world of talk.

Despite indications of this type of structural linguistic approach, some schools of thought working on discourse processing have abandoned "the linguistic approach" as fundamentally wrongheaded and misdirected. These analyses proceed from the assumption that it is not specific linguistic conventions that guide discourse development and interpretation; rather they assert that it is the "world knowledge" conversants share that accounts for mutual understanding. Morgan and Sellner (1980), for instance, in a review of linguistic approaches, conclude that "as far as we can see, there is no evidence for cohesion as a linguistic property, other than as an epiphenomenon of content."

The world knowledge school has offered an alternative explanation of discourse processing based not on a structural linguistic analysis but on a psychological one. In this view the primary, prominent feature governing discourse processing is a listener's identification of a speaker's *intention*. It is this knowledge, quite external to the discourse, that allows conversants to interpret each other's meaning and follow the discourse flow. If conversants apprehend each other's intentions, they can on the basis of these share compatible models of the current topic, focus, and role of discourse elements. As Spiro (1980) states:

> When comprehending utterances in conversations, the speaker's intent is all that is attempted to be communicated. If that intent is apprehended, the goal of communication is met and the communicative act is "understood."

There are, however, important difficulties inherent in this approach to discourse analysis. The determination of a speaker's intent or goal is certainly a part of grasping meaning, but it is of utmost importance to distinguish between a conversant's intention for an utterance and the communicative effect of that utterance in the conversational context. Though not intending to inform, a speaker may yet inform; though not intending to persuade, a speaker may persuade; though not intending to support, an antagonist's remarks may be shown to support the position the antagonist intended to dispute. This last case highlights the fact that not only can an utterance have an effect or force independent of a speaker's intent, but even when a listener knows that the force of an utterance does not necessarily correspond to a speaker's intent, the effect of that utterance may remain the same.

This differentiation between structural relation and intent is a distinguishing feature between the theory here and a speech act analysis of language (Searle 1969). Perhaps illocutionary acts cannot be unintentional, but we need a level of discourse analysis that is directed by intention-free means. This level of analysis is being given in the approach presented here. Because of this fundamental difference we do not call the discourse actions here illocutionary acts but rather simply conversational moves or communicative acts. Both analyses are necessary as discussed later in the book.

There is a more fundamental logical difficulty with the enterprise of understanding a communication by inferring the communicator's goal or intent. Consider the following example by Bennett (1976) in illustration of how an individual comprehends through building a private model of a communicator's intent: Bennett and a friend watch a performance in an opera house; their eyes meet, and the friend "grimaces in an exaggerated manner while holding her nose." Bennett explains how he recognizes the grimace as a communication that his friend dislikes the opera as follows:

> My friend's gesture led me to believe that she hated the performance because this is what I thought she was trying to get me to believe. She intended to get me to think that she hated the performance, intending this to be brought about through my realizing what she was up to.

In addition to the fact that this analysis is quite unwieldy, and that any stranger in the same audience would have been able to reach the same interpretation based on understanding the conventional gesture of disdain, such an approach is logically circular. To comprehend, an interpreter first must know what the communicator intends—so what is it that the communication accomplishes? If the interpreter knows what the communicator intends, communication is redundant.

An analysis by Clark and Carlson (1982) of a single line of Shakespearean dialogue, Othello's "Come, Desdemona," illustrates the rigor with which the world knowledge theorists apply their method to explain the processing of verbal communications:

> Othello intends to get Desdemona to understand that he wants her to go with him. He gets her to understand this by getting her to recognize his intention to get her to understand this.

It is easy to see how this kind of purported explanation could be applied to the analysis of extended conversation. But even in such a simple case, if a communicator's goal could not be inferred until a message were grasped, and if a message could not be grasped until the communicator's goal was inferred, prospects for communication would not be good.

There is really another issue here: *mutual knowledge*. We would argue that the world knowledge theorists' focus on intentional accounts of discourse has become so radical as to obscure the obvious: it is often the case that understanding necessitates some mutual or privy knowledge between conversants. We have included this earlier in our discussion of the "situational context." So, for example, perhaps Bennett's friend really does like the opera; however, she does have an allergy. Then, yes, given the seeming conventional gesture of disdain, an onlooker would incorrectly infer the woman did not like the opera. Bennett, on the other hand, with his added knowledge of his friend's allergic state, would correctly interpret the gesture as some kind of allergic twitch. Intention? No. *Mutual Knowledge?* Yes. For example, consider the following scenario and analysis presented by Clark and Carlson (1982):

Scenario
1. Ann and Barbara went to both the Tate and British Museums.
2. Barbara had discussed with Charles her going to the Tate Museum.
3. Barbara does not know what museum plans Ann and Charles have discussed.
4. Charles to Barbara in front of Ann: "Did the two of you go to the museum?"

Analysis

Charles could expect Barbara to recognize that the museum he was referring to was the Tate, since it was the only museum they had discussed together; that is, he could expect her to pick out the Tate by means of her recognition of his *intention*.

We agree with Clark's analysis up until the last phrase "her recognition of his intention." Substitute "mutual knowledge" here, and we have a winner (Clark and Marshall 1981).

In sum, though a speaker's intent may well be reflected by a communication, grasping that intent cannot be a necessary precondition for understanding. A "pure" world knowledge theory is simply unable to account for how communicative goals are in fact apprehended.

Some world knowledge theorists allude to the inadequacy of an intentional account alone. Searle (1971), for instance, points out that our use of language does not vary arbitrarily because we decide to intend new meanings; that "meaning is more than a matter of intention, it is also a matter of convention":

> In the performance of an illocutionary act the speaker intends to produce a certain effect by means of getting the hearer to recognize his intention to produce that effect, and furthermore, if he is using words literally, he intends this recognition to be achieved in virtue of the fact that the rules for using the expressions he utters associate the expressions with the production of that effect. It is this combination of elements which we shall need to express in our analysis.

In general, however, Searle does not explicate these rules of linguistic convention which must operate to associate particular expressions with the production of particular effects. It remains then to explain how communicative goals among conversants are understood.

Now, though some researchers (e.g., Bennett 1976, Clark and Marshall 1981, Lewis 1969, Schiffer 1972) do recognize that "mutual knowledge" and "convention" underlie much of communication, these researchers are still bound to the notion of "intention" and "belief." For example, Schiffer (1972) states:

> x(w) means "p" in G iff it is mutual knowledge amongst the members of G that
> (1) if almost any member of G utters something M-intending to produce in some other member of G the activated belief that p, then what he utters might be x;
> (2) if any member of G utters x M-intending to produce in some other member of G the activated belief that p, he will intend the state of affairs E (which he intends to realize by uttering x) to include the fact that there obtains in G a certain precedent or set of precedents (or agreements) Z such that any member of G utters x in accordance with Z only if he utters x M-intending to produce in some other member of G the activated belief that p.

But this is like saying that each time an English speaker puts the subject before the verb in an English sentence, he is M-intending to produce in the hearer the belief that he put the subject first because of their mutual knowledge that subjects go first in English. And mutual knowledge itself entails what Bennett calls "looped thought"— "thought about someone else's thought about x's own thought" (Bennett 1976).

There are many cases where in fact one needs looped thought of this type. For example, Clark and Marshall (1981) discuss definite reference choices that are governed by one speaker's thinking about what the other person knows which includes what that person thinks the speaker knows which includes what the speaker thinks the other person knows, and so on. Or, for example, consider the coordination problems that Lewis (1969) discusses: A and B are each told to write some number without communicating with one another. If they both write the same number, they will each receive $10, otherwise they receive nothing. Here it is true that A and B's main activity will be to think about what each other is thinking, which includes what they each think the other is thinking about their own thinking, which includes how they are thinking about the other person's thinking about them, and so on. Even understanding this sentence is almost beyond our abilities. Imagine if for even the simplest of statements we had to do this. We feel that in everyday language there is much analysis done that does not involve this type of looped thought. As ordinary language speakers we are quite aware of when we think "Now, I wonder what he really meant by that," and when we engage in thinking about the intentions and beliefs of one another. This is not to claim that thinking about our own intentions and the intentions of others is necessarily limited to conscious thought. Our position, however, is that there is a lot of language use that does not entail complexities of this form. We use the constructs that we do because they are in our repertoire of how our language works. In this work we are trying to formalize this repertoire.

In this work we also attempt to address specific discourse phenomena that cannot be explained solely by a world knowledge approach. In particular, naturally occurring dialogues exhibit a number of different kinds of surface linguistic phenomena that are usually ignored in intentional accounts of discourse but that require functional explanation. These include the use of words and phrases that signal topic shifts or changes in conversational direction ("on the other hand," "anyway") or that effect subtle distinctions in the relation between what is to be said and what has gone before (e.g., what determines whether a speaker begins a contradiction of a previous speaker's point with "Yes, but" or with "No, but"). An adequate theory of conversational discourse must be able to explain speakers' use of such linguistic forms.

Such a theory must also be able to explain and account for reference phenomena in spontaneous discourse, and with respect to these the world knowledge approach sheds little light. Consider, for instance, the use of "here," "this," and the unmodified noun phrase "the potential" in lines 8–9 of this discourse taken from a naturally occurring conversation:

G: 1. It's just a pure electrostatic field, which, between
    2. two points, and the proton accelerates through the
    3. electrostatic potential.
J: 4. Okay.
G: 5. Same physical law as if you drop a ball. It accelerates
    6. through a gravitational potential.
J: 7. Okay.
G: 8. And the only important point here is that the potential
    9. is maintained by this Cockcroft-Walton unit.

According to traditional analyses terms like "here" and "this" are used for items either physically or emotively close to a speaker, or an item most recently mentioned in the discourse; while "that" and "there" are used to refer to items physically or emotively far, or further back in the discourse. Yet G's "here" in line 8 refers to his earlier topic of the proton accelerator rather than to his last topic, and he uses "this" in modification of another reference to this earlier topic, rather than using "that." Additionally G's noun phrase "the potential" in line 8 should be taken to refer to the last potential mentioned, "gravitational potential," or at best should be considered ambiguous. It clearly refers, however, to the earlier mentioned "electrostatic potential." As will be demonstrated, a structural, linguistic analysis of discourse does allow us to explain how such reference choices are made.

As a further example of the kind of surface phenomena that we shall want to explain, consider the seemingly unmotivated non-pronominalizations in the telling of the following story:

P: 1. What happened, her boyfriend from Holland ["her" refers
    2. to a woman named Tammy]—they just left today as a
    3. matter of fact, but we've been spending the past couple
    4. of days together, no just evenings at home—and somehow
    5. they got into this discussion about Americans. And they
    6. were still doing it. And this—his name is Tom—and
    7. he said something, "Oh yeah, Americans are so open. The
    8. minute they meet you they tell you their whole life
    9. history." And I was getting very upset because despite
   10. everyone saying that—and even her own—Tammy's own
   11. saying, "Oh, who said that was right?" or "I wouldn't
   12. tell anyone what to do," they were sitting and
   13. categorizing people.

Why is it that at line 6, P suddenly specifies the name of Tammy's boyfriend? Why does P interrupt herself from, in all probability, saying "this guy said" or not simply say "he said," since "he" is so clearly "her boyfriend from Holland"? And why, in line 10, does P self-correct her initial repronominalization to "Tammy"? There are no other female characters under discussion; Tammy has just been mentioned. There is no danger of semantic ambiguity, which is usually thought to determine whether pronouns are appropriate. So what, in this extended discourse, is the problem? Again we shall require a structural analysis in order to answer our questions.

What we need is a theory of discourse that will account for the suspension, resumption, topic shift, and reference phenomena we find in naturally occurring conversation, a theory that will explain how communicative goals are apprehended and how conversants update their assumptions in an ongoing conversation so that they continue to share compatible views of the relevance of each discourse element to what has gone before and that will elucidate the conventions that govern the generation and interpretation of discourse utterances.

It must be stressed that a linguistic theory of discourse need not, indeed cannot, exclude world knowledge as accounting for much meaning interpretation in discourse. Even at the level of sentential linguistics, it is widely recognized that a purely syntactic analysis often cannot provide a single unambiguous structural description of a sentence, and that the disambiguation of structurally ambiguous sentences often depends on external world knowledge and/or awareness of a preceding discourse context. Certainly our basic elementary objects of linguistic analysis—nouns, adjectives, adverbs, and verbs (or agents, predicates, and instruments [Fillmore 1968])—directly reflect the nature of our external world, or more appropriately our view of it, as consisting of things, with particular attributes, that act and are acted upon. Many linguists would argue that "pragmatic" considerations govern even much of sentential-level construction and interpretation (e.g., choice of tense, placement of adverbs; see Chafe 1973, Comrie 1976, Kuno 1976). Similarly any cogent theory of extended discourse cannot ignore the aspects of our language processing that are not "strictly" linguistic. It is only reasonable that a significant amount of the connectivity between elements in our conversations corresponds to our grasp of causal, temporal, and structural relationships existing in the world beyond our talk. We require a theory that specifies the discourse-specific conventions which, though not alone sufficient for mutual understanding, are necessary to account for those aspects of conversational development that non-linguistic knowledge cannot explain.

A Preliminary Sketch

What kinds of conventions or rules must govern discourse behavior? As a starting point let us consider the useful description given by Grice (1975) of the conversational process as a series of "conversational moves," each of which carries the participants forward to another "stage" of discourse. At any given point in the process Grice suggests, "some possible conversational moves would be excluded as conversationally unsuitable." Grice proposes a set of conversational maxims that are assumed to govern speakers' choice of utterances, defining "inappropriate" conversational moves as the set of moves that would violate at least one maxim:

1. *Quantity* "Make your contribution as informative as required (for the current purposes of the exchange) and do not make your contribution more informative than is required."
2. *Relation* "Be relevant"; take into account the "different kinds and foci of relevance," "how these shift in the course of a talk-exchange," and "allow for the fact that subjects of conversation are legitimately changed."
3. *Manner* "How what is said should be said," e.g., "avoid obscurity of expression, avoid ambiguity, be brief, and be orderly."

These maxims capture some of the dynamic constraints placed on conversants in dialogue. They also raise some crucial questions: How are "the current purposes of the exchange" identified? What does it mean for something to be "relevant" to or in the "foci" of the current discourse context? What influences does the subject of the discourse foci have on the discourse's succeeding semantic development and on the surface linguistic tools used to express developments? How does a conversational move affect the preceding discourse context? How does the discourse context determine what otherwise would be an ambiguous reference or an overly informative utterance? What is "relevance"—can it be formally defined as a set of semantic or logical relationships between utterances? And finally, given a more exact specification of such maxims, how can they be integrated to yield a system capable of describing discourse development as an active, ongoing process?

The description of discourse processing ordered in what follows endeavors to answer such questions. It does so by characterizing a conversation as a hierarchical organization of formally related utterances. From the analysis is derived a set of discourse rules, a formal discourse grammar that can serve as an abstract process module of the generation and interpretation of "coherent" or "maxim-abiding" conversational speech.

The grammar is based on the recognition that in any conversation an utterance's "appropriateness," in both form and content, depends very much on the discourse context that is currently "relevant." Its delineation can be considered a formalization of constructs and operations that are needed to transform Grice's general maxims into a well-defined set of operational rules. It is the conversants' use of these rules that allows for mutual understanding: through our use of such shared rules our surface discourse forms reflect our internal models of a current conversational reference context to each other.

Chapter 2
Relations between Discourse Elements

We have said that for a participant in a conversation to understand the relation of an utterance to what has been said before, the participant must understand the role of the utterance in the discourse. Close examination of naturally occurring conversations reveals that there is a standard set of relational discourse roles that successive utterances play. Knowing this set of roles and choosing those most likely to occur in the current discourse context allow a listener to integrate a speaker's utterances with preceding ones without undue difficulty.

There are two major discourse functions that an utterance can serve: it can be an embellishment or continuation of what has gone before, or it can begin a new communicative act serving a new discourse role. An utterance of the latter kind creates a shift in the discourse and is what we call a *conversational move*. Among the types of conversational moves we can observe are presenting a claim, explaining a claim, giving support to a claim, challenging a claim, shifting a topic, and resuming a preceding subject of discourse.

These kinds of discourse acts are often described as achieving distinct speaker communicative goals. Though it is true that conversational moves frequently reflect speaker goals, it is important to stress that these moves can be identified and interpreted *without* reference to a speaker's underlying intent for an utterance. Rather, conversational moves are defined and understood by their objective, functional relation to other discourse elements.

A conversation is a sequence of such functionally related conversational moves. Consider, for example, the following excerpt from a conversation between four friends, M, R, D, and J, concerning the controversy over whether genetics or the environment is most influential in human development:

R: 1. Except, however, John and I just saw this two-hour
    2. TV show
M: 3. Uh hum,

R: 4. where they showed—it was an excellent French
     5. TV documentary—and they showed that in fact
     6. the aggressive nature of the child is not really
     7. that much influenced by his environment.

M: 8. How did they show that?

R: 9. They showed that by filming kids in kindergarten,

M: 10. Uh hum,

R: 11. showing his behavior among other children,

M: 12. And then?

R: 13. and showed him ten years later acting the same way,
    14. toward, um,

D: 15. Well, of course, that's where he learns his
    16. behavior, in kindergarten.

M: 17. Oh, sure.

R: 18. Now, another thing, it wasn't that he didn't have—

J: 19. What? What's that? What'd you say?

R: 20. The aggressive child in kindergarten who acted
    21. the same way later on.

J: 22. Yeah, he did.

R: 23. Oh, it was twins. The important thing was that
    24. there were two children from the same environment,
    25. whereas only one of the brothers acted that way.
    26. So, you couldn't blame it on the child's home.

D: 27. It has nothing to do with the child's home.
    28. It has to do with the child's environment.

R: 29. Right, but the two brothers have the same environment.

D: 30. They do not have the same environment.

R: 31. Why not?

D: 32. Because you and I are very close in this room right now,
    33. but we don't have the same environment.
    34. Because I'm looking at you, I'm seeing that window
    35. behind you. You're not seeing that window behind you.
    36. You are not looking at you. I am doing it.
    37. Two people can't be in exactly the same place at the
    38. same time, otherwise, they'd occupy the same space.
    39. They do not have the same environment.
    40. They don't have the same friends.

M: 41. And, I mean, they don't even—you know, to say that
    42. two kids come from the same family is really meaningless,
    43. because when you think of the difference in treatment
    44. that two kids can get in exactly the same family, it's

45. incredible. You know, it's the difference between
46. night and day.

Some of the conversational moves in this conversation are R's claim, in lines 6–7, for the genetic side of the controversy; M's demand for support of the claim, in line 8; and R's support, in lines 9, 11, and 13. In lines 15–16 D challenges the support; R presents an alternative support and modifies the original claim in lines 23–26; D challenges in lines 27–28; and R counterchallenges in line 29. In line 30 D counterchallenges; in line 31 R demands support; and D provides support, by analogy, in lines 32–33. Lines 34–36 provide two supports for the claim of the analogy.

What is crucial to notice is the functional relation of each conversational move to preceding discourse utterances. When D begins discussing the fact that he and R share the room they're currently in (lines 32–36), for instance, we recognize that this supports by analogy D's earlier claim (line 30) that the twins living at home have different environments. Therefore we realize that D's shift onto these new discourse elements does not constitute an abrupt end to the preceding subject. A listener would be hard pressed to understand the relevance of D's utterances without recognizing this function that they serve in relation to his preceding claim.

Hierarchical Structure of Discourse Relations

To begin to understand how a listener grasps the relations between discourse utterances, let us consider the analogue of discourse structure in the constituent structuring of a single sentence. It is common knowledge that sentences can be decomposed into noun and verb phrases, each of which in turn is further decomposed into its constituent parts. A noun phrase, for example, is said to be composed of a head noun and its modifiers, whereas a verb phrase is said to be composed of a main verb and its modifiers. Now in the interpretation of a single sentence, given that a noun has just been processed and a relative clause is begun, a listener has no difficulty in recognizing that the relative clause is to be interpreted in the context of this preceding noun. Or, having processed a verb, a listener has no difficulty in recognizing that a succeeding adverb is to be interpreted in relation to this preceding verb. Discourse utterances can similarly be parsed into constituents, which are processed in the context of coconstituents.

In sentences some constituents are independently interpretable— that is, they can appear without the accompaniment of other constituents. For example, we can have a verb without an adverb and a noun without a relative clause. Some constituents, however, necessitate the presence of other constituents for their interpretation and "legality" of presence. We cannot, for instance, have a relative clause without having the noun that it modifies, nor can we have an adverb without the verb that it modifies.[1]

Similarly in discourse some types of constituents can appear in isolation, whereas the appearance and interpretation of others are contingent on the presence of some other constituent. For example, we cannot have purported statements of support without the presence of a claim to be supported, nor can we have an explanation without something to be explained.

A major aspect of discourse processing is the identification of discourse constituents and the distinguishing of dependent and nondependent constituents. Given a dependent constituent, we know that this should be interpreted in direct relation to its superordinate constituent. As we shall see, these hierarchical relations between discourse constituents, in which some are subordinate to others, greatly aid conversants in identifying the relevant discourse context for any given utterance in a conversation.

The Basic Discourse Constituent: The Context Space

Though a conversation is a sequence of conversational moves, a participant's model of a conversation is not simply a listing of these sequential moves, and the structure of a discourse is not defined by this temporal sequence. Rather, a discourse is partitioned into a set of hierarchically related constituents, which are only partly defined by the conversational moves they contain. Discourse participants "package" pieces of discourse into these separate units and selectively bring these units in and out of the foreground of attention in the generation and interpretation of subsequent utterances. The fundamental unit of discourse processing—the constituent hierarchically related to other discourse constituents and brought in and out of focus in a discourse—we call a *context space*. The structure of a discourse can be specified by the identification of its context spaces and the relations between them. The discourse grammar derived from the context space analysis specifies some major context space types found in discourse, their relations, and the mechanisms by which discourse participants process these basic discourse constituents.

A major nondependent constituent in a discourse is what we refer to as an *issue* context space. Issue spaces act as "topic setters" and generally contain assertions that a given state of affairs is true or false, good or bad, possible or not possible, and so on. Such an assertion usually becomes a topic of discourse. Developing this topic consists of, for instance, supporting the assertion, challenging the assertion, discussing contingency factors of the assertion. Developments such as these create new context spaces that are subordinates of the issue context space. Proper interpretation of a subordinate necessitates identification of the issue space of which it is a subordinate. In this sense issue context spaces are the discourse analogues of sentential "head nouns" and "main verbs." They can stand alone, but their "modifiers" cannot. They are the *raison d'être* of a conversation at given points in time. They tell us what the topic of discourse is, explain why new utterances are being generated, and provide the context in light of which subparts of the discourse can be processed.

In figure 2.1 we have an overview of a context space configuration of the genetics-environment dialogue just presented. Notice, in particular, the nonlinear hierarchical organization of discourse units.

A context space is an abstract construct, defined not only by the utterances that constitute the conversational move fulfilled by the space but also by additional information concerning the other context space constituents to which it is related in the discourse. In determining which utterances belong together in a single context space, then, it is not sufficient to recognize the conversational move of the space alone; one must also recognize the part(s) of the preceding discourse in relation to which the move is developed.

As our example illustrates, the relation between a context space and preceding discourse is not limited to a linearly preceding utterance, nor does it extend to the entire preceding discourse. For example, M's claim that two children need not be treated identically in the same home (lines 43–45) serves as a challenge only to R's preceding statements of support (lines 23–25) and conclusion based on this support (line 26). Thus, though D did not challenge R's conclusion that for two children from the same home we cannot attribute any difference of behavior between them to the home, M directly challenges this conclusion. It should be clear that M's statements are not in challenge of D's immediately preceding statements, nor are they in further support of them; they are not directly related to D's statements at all. Yet they are easily understood because we grasp their relation to a preceding context space in the discussion—R's conclusion space of line 26, via attack on its support space of lines 23–25.

Notice also that a context space is not defined by the utterances of a speaker on a single conversational turn. D, for instance, performs three conversational moves (which belong to three distinct context spaces) in just part of his conversational turn (lines 32–36): stating an

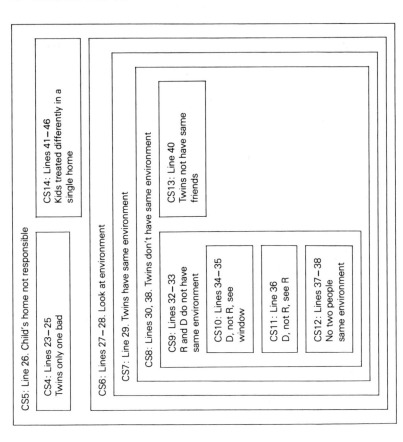

CS1: Lines 6—7
Aggressive nature of child not influenced by environment

CS2: Lines 1—5, 9, 11, 13—14
Documentary study, 10 years after kindergarten same behavior

CS3: Lines 15—16
Behavior learned in kindergarten

CS5: Line 26. Child's home not responsible

CS4: Lines 23—25
Twins only one bad

CS14: Lines 41—46
Kids treated differently in a single home

CS6: Lines 27—28. Look at environment

CS7: Line 29. Twins have same environment

CS8: Lines 30, 38. Twins don't have same environment

CS9: Lines 32—33
R and D do not have same environment

CS13: Line 40
Twins not have same friends

CS10: Lines 34—35
D, not R, see window

CS11: Line 36
D, not R, see R

CS12: Lines 37—38
No two people same environment

CS2 and CS3 are subconstituents of CS1 (Support and Challenge)

CS4, CS6, and CS14 are subconstituents of CS5 (Support, Challenge, and Challenge)

CS5 is a replacement claim for CS1

CS7 is a subconstituent of CS6 (Challenge)

CS8 is a subconstituent of CS7 (Challenge)

CS9 and CS13 are subconstituents of CS8 (Support and Support)

CS10, CS11, and CS12 are subconstituents of CS9 (Support, Support, Generalization)

Figure 2.1

analogy as a means of supporting an earlier claim and then with two examples supporting the claim of the analogy. In succeeding lines, still in the same turn, he makes four more moves: (1) stating the abstract principle under which the analogy and supports hold, (2) supporting this abstract claim, (3) resuming the initial subject of discussion (i.e., the initiating claim of the analogy), and (4) giving further supportive evidence of this initial claim.

The irrelevance of speaker turns to the identification of context spaces in a discourse can be illustrated another way. In the burn story excerpt of chapter 1 two different speakers' utterances perform the same conversational move and thus belong in the same context space: R's "Don't get too risqué here," and F's "Don't get too graphic." Thus speaker shifts do not, in this analysis, mark the boundary points of these fundamental discourse units.

Context space boundary points are also not marked by sentence boundaries. In the burn story excerpt all utterances relating to the specific events leading up to and including the burn (lines 6–12 and 24–27) belong in a single context space.

Finally, it is important to note that context space boundary points are not necessarily demarcated by shifts in reference situations. Two linearly following context spaces might refer to the same set of actors, the same location, and the same time period, but if the events reported illustrated different points, they would be partitioned into separate context spaces. In the burn story excerpt the portion of the story concerning the sleepers' intimacy, even though it is part of the same reference situation, belongs in a separate context space because it is not directly related to the explanation of how the burn occurred.

In our analysis of discourse and in the formal specification of the discourse grammar, context space boundary points are marked by the fulfillment of the conversational moves that initiate the creation of those spaces. As we shall see in chapter 3, each kind of possible conversational move is defined by specific semantic and/or logical criteria. Satisfaction of these criteria demark the completion of a conversational move and a context space boundary point.

Focused Processing

We have said that discourse utterances are generated and interpreted in the context of other discourse units, context spaces, and that conversants must be able at any point in a conversation to identify the relevant discourse context for any given utterance. How is it that participants determine what discourse context (what preceding context space) is currently relevant?

To begin to answer this question, let us return to the analogy between discourse interpretation and sentence interpretation. Given the utterance, "The boy with the telescope saw the girl on the hill," the prepositional phrase "with the telescope" clearly modifies "the boy." Given the utterance "the boy saw the girl on the hill with the telescope," however, it is not clear which noun the prepositional phrase modifies. Nevertheless, it is accepted that the phrase modifies only one of the nouns, either the boy or the girl, and not both of them.

Similarly in discourse thematic and relational development of a subordinate context space is in direct modification of only one other context space. Though at times it may be unclear which preceding space is being "modified," it is quite clear to all that only one of the spaces is meant to be modified.

The processing of discourse is thus highly focused. Depending on the discourse flow, different preceding context spaces are deemed the most *influential* at a given point in the discourse, and from the set of potential "combiners," the context space chosen is the one of most influential status. A context space's influential status distinguishes between the foreground versus background roles that it may play at different points in a discourse. Only a context space in a foreground role has a "direct" relation to the way that succeeding discourse utterances are generated and interpreted. For example, in the genetics-environment debate excerpt, R's initial support for her claim that a child's aggressive behavior is not influenced by his environment (lines 9, 11, 13) is invalidated by D's argument that the child learns his behavior in kindergarten (lines 15–16). R's citation of an alternative support in lines 23–25 reflects her concession to D's challenge. As a result of this concession the context space defined by R's initial support is at this point rendered a background role. No part of the succeeding discourse is directly related to this rejected support context space. As this example illustrates, and as we shall see in chapter 4, particular conversational moves have standard effects on the influential status of preceding context spaces. Knowing these standard effects is one of the ways that conversational participants identify the relevant discourse context for currently generated utterances. An important part of knowing how to communicate is knowing the conventional procedures by which to distinguish between those utterances that are yet influential to continued discussion and those that are not.

The focused processing of discourse is evident in the fact that not only do entire context spaces vary in influential status in the course of a conversation's development, but in addition different elements within a single space vary in influential status. Discerning the point of a speaker's utterances requires identification of those elements mentioned by the speaker that play a major role in what he or she is saying. For instance, if a speaker relates an episode that took place in a park between Dorothy and a poodle, in order to illustrate the claim that Dorothy is funny, the park in which the episode took place is not the element in focus for the speaker and is not part of the point being conveyed. An element's *focus level* is thus often predictable from the currently relevant discourse context and the type of conversational move being processed.

As we shall see in chapter 5, certain surface linguistic forms, such as pronominal reference, reflect and evidence these distinctions in different elements' focus levels. If a speaker's surface linguistic forms correspond to a listener's predictions of which elements are in focus, the conversation will flow smoothly, and the listener will feel that he or she correctly understands the speaker's statements. If, however, the speaker's surface linguistic forms conflict with the listener's prediction, the listener will be at a loss and need either to revise his or her discourse model and/or to request clarification. An important part of discourse processing then is the predictions listeners make about the probable surface forms in a speaker's utterances.

Discourse Expectations

Another important mechanism that aids listeners in their focused processing of discourse is reference to a set of "discourse expectations," which derive from the fact that the presence of one kind of discourse constituent is often predictive of constituents to follow.

In sentential processing, for example, we know that if a transitive verb is present, a noun phrase functioning as an object of this verb will follow. Similarly in discourse if a conversant's claim is challenged, we expect the following utterances to reflect either an abandonment of the claim in favor of a new one, a counterchallenge, or an offering of additional support. If discussion of a particular subject is interrupted by a digression, we expect the initial subject to be subsequently resumed and completed.

Thus, analogous to Grice's notion that some conversational moves are "unsuitable" at a given "stage" of the discourse, it is also the case that at particular stages of discourse, some conversational moves are "expected" and "most appropriate." Not only does a conversational move set up particular expectations of what type of move will follow, it also specifies the particular preceding context space in relation to which such a subsequent conversational move will be taken and often the speaker expected to take the move as well. For instance, it is the specific context space interrupted that will be resumed; it is the specific context space serving as a challenge that will be counter-challenged. As a conversation progresses, each discourse move thus constrains continuing options of conversational development and sets up expectations of the context relevant for interpretation of succeeding utterances. Discourse expectations are another clear example of the way that shared knowledge about discourse aids conversants in mutual understanding.

The extent to which our discourse expectations are governed by our understanding that utterances must be functional in a discourse is illustrated even at the very simple level of the selection of which elements to include as we develop various topics. Discourse generation and interpretation is clearly not entirely referent dependent. In the telling of an episode, for example, not all of the events that actually occurred are stated; the telling is limited to a specification of only those events needed to illustrate a particular point. Thus, though many events may "belong together" as they have occurred in the same time frame in the same location, they do not necessarily belong together in a given discourse context.

This understanding of the way that discourse function can govern the selection of utterances allows us to restate Grice's conversational maxim on quantity somewhat more precisely:

> *Quantity*   In the development of a context space, only specify those aspects of the referent being discussed that are needed for the accomplishment of the one specific conversational move served by this context space.

What particular descriptions of a subject enhance fulfillment of a particular conversational move, then, is determined by the discourse context in relation to which the move is being performed. Consider the following conversation taken from natural discourse:

F: 1. I'm starting to, you know, to get more insight
    2. about dreams. And, they're so revealing about
    3. where you're at. They really are.
    4. Like Susan and I spent an hour the other night
    5. just dissecting her dream.

C: 6. I know. I should write them down.

F: 7. And she wrote it down, and when I read it I
    8. saw new things into it. And, it was just so
    9. interesting. And it really reflected so much
   10. of where she's at in therapy and everything.

F's telling of the episode of dissecting Susan's dream is a subordinate context space in development of the issue context space of lines 2–3. Since the claim being supported is that dreams are revealing about people, unrelated events that took place during F and Susan's hour together—drinking a lot of coffee, discussing favorite films, or whatever—are excluded from this discourse. It is in terms of a currently relevant discourse context that speakers and listeners determine what belongs. Violations of our expectations of what belongs, given preceding context spaces and the context space that is at any point being developed, cause confusion and misunderstanding; fulfillment of those expectations allows conversation to proceed smoothly.

Thus far we have identified these major features of discourse:

1. A conversation is a sequence of conversational moves, each of which fulfills a particular function in the development of the discourse.
2. Utterances in discourse are generated and interpreted in light of their functional relation to preceding discourse units, called context spaces, each of which contains a single conversational move.
3. The smooth flow of discourse rests on identification of these functional relations between context spaces.
4. Context spaces may be independent discourse constituents or may be dependent subconstituents of other context spaces.
5. Interpreting a current utterance requires identifying the currently relevant discourse context—the particular context space—in light of which it is to be interpreted. The relevant discourse context for the generation and interpretation of any utterance is only a portion of preceding discourse and is not necessarily that portion that linearly precedes the utterance. Context spaces are hierarchically rather than linearly related. Thus in the course of conversation various preceding context spaces are brought in and out of the foreground, depending on their influence in the generation and interpretation of subsequent utterances.
6. Understanding the point of a speaker's utterances partially depends on distinguishing between the importance of the various items mentioned by a speaker.
7. The processing of discourse is thus focused processing. Each utterance is interpreted in light of the currently relevant discourse context to which it is related—the context space and its items that are most influential at that point in a discourse.

8. Among the mechanisms that facilitate focused processing are discourse expectations, which allow conversants to predict expected kinds of utterances (and the context to which they will relate) on the basis of utterances that have already been generated. Discourse expectations allow mutual knowledge of what type of conversational move is likely and to which particular section of preceding discourse it will be related.

The Formal Specification of Context Space Components

Let us turn now to a more formal characterization of the basic elements of the context space theory in order to define more precisely what we mean by a relevant discourse context and to prepare for an analysis of the specific types of conversational moves incorporated into our discourse grammar.

The context spaces that constitute discourse are formalized in the grammar as schematic structures with a fixed number of "slots" for holding various kinds of information. Some slots are common to all types of context spaces, and some are particular to specific types of spaces. For example, all context spaces have a *goal* slot, which specifies the conversational move to be fulfilled in developing a space, that is, the discourse function the context space fills (e.g., support, explanation). All context spaces have a *method* slot for specifying the method used to perform the conversational move (e.g., analogy, narrative). All context spaces have a *corelator* slot, which indicates the particular preceding part of the discourse (the relevant preceding context space) to which the space is related. Only some types of context spaces, though, have a *protagonist* slot (debative issue context spaces). A context space is thus characterized by its component slots and the particular values assigned to them. (The various types of context spaces identified in the current specification of the grammar, their component slots, and the potential values of various slots, are described in detail in chapter 4.)

That some context spaces fill as slot fillers for others reflects their hierarchical relationships. To reflect the distinction between dependent and independent spaces, independent spaces have as slot values their corresponding dependent context spaces. For instance, though issue context spaces can stand alone, they do form a constituent relationship with support context spaces for the claim contained in the issue space. All issue context spaces therefore have a slot that lists all the support context spaces developed in subordination to it.

Corresponding to the fact of focused processing in discourse, all the formalized relational rules in the context space grammar are written so that they relate utterances of a conversational move to (1) the context space under current development and (2) the one preceding context space in the discourse environment with the highest influential status. (During the development of a subordinate context space the preceding context space of which it is a part is considered also the space of most influential status, and it is in relation to just this one space that the subordinate space's utterances are generated and interpreted.) To identify the preceding context space of highest influential status, we use a slot, called a *status* slot, that is associated with all context spaces. A value of *controlling* in this slot denotes that the context space is the one of highest discourse influence; a value of *active* denotes that the context space is currently being developed.

We can now restate another of Grice's maxims for discourse in terms of our formal constructs. We have said that any utterance in a discourse is interpreted in light of its relevant discourse context. In our analysis a relevant discourse context is at any given point in time composed of two context spaces: the context space currently being developed (the active context space) and the preceding context space in direct relation to which the active context space is being developed (the controlling context space). Grice's "Relevance" maxim can thus be operationalized as follows:

> To be relevant means either to embellish the active context space by stating a succeeding utterance that continues the current conversational move or to shift to a different context space (new or old) via the development of a distinct conversational move, whose relationship to some preceding context space is clear. If all preceding topics have been fully developed (all criteria for the development of particular conversational moves satisfied), then the new move may begin an entirely new topic. If, on the other hand, there are uncompleted conversational moves in the discourse, the new move either will constitute a temporary interruption or will have to signal clearly to which portion of the preceding discourse it is related.

To understand how discourse participants use and fulfill this maxim, we must now turn to the specific description and analysis of those discourse developments we have called conversational moves.

Chapter 3
Conversational Moves

We have said that interpreting discourse requires a listener to understand the function that utterances serve in the development of discourse topics. These different functions constitute distinct types of conversational moves, and discourse development is a weave of these various moves. A conversation may include, for instance, the assertion of a claim, supports for the claim, challenges to the claim, explanations, illustrations, clarifications, concessions, and so on. Much of the implicit knowledge speakers and listeners share is knowledge of the particular components of various conversational moves—what kinds of utterances must be made in order to fulfill various discourse functions. This knowledge sets up many discourse expectations and also allows conversants to infer many implicit connections between discourse utterances. In accordance with their discourse functions, conversational moves have specific criteria for their development. Knowledge of these criteria enable listeners to delineate the boundaries of context space structures and to grasp the currently relevant discourse context in terms of which utterances are to be interpreted.

Formally conversational moves represent the various kinds of semantic and logical relations that can hold between utterances of a discourse.[1] The content-free specification of these semantic/logical relations is similar in kind to a formal logic system (see chapter 8). Our formal characterization of conversational moves specifies the components that explicitly or implicitly are required for the completion of particular moves. For instance, our formal analysis of all support conversational moves (moves maintaining a claim) entails inferring a standard set of elaborations underlying a speaker's statements of support. In the context space grammar all support context spaces have a set of slots to hold these standard, implicit components of the support move. This reflects the fact that in their processing of support conversational moves, speakers and listeners assume these components to be necessary and know them to be related to each other and to the goal of support in conventional ways. Only when the standard components of a support move have been presented (explicitly or implicitly) is the context space developed by that move completed.

Besides the specific expectations set up by the initiation of particular conversational moves, there is an additional mechanism that discourse participants use in the development and identification of context space structures. Speakers use specific surface linguistic signals—*clue words*—that usually accompany different types of conversational moves in a discourse.[2] These clue words signal that a context space boundary point has been reached; and simultaneously they specify the kind of shift (the kind of conversational move) about to take place.

To illustrate our analysis of the conversational moves common in discourse and some of the clue words associated with them, we shall look in some detail at the following types of moves:

Conversational Move	*Clue Word(s)*
Support	Because . . . ; Like . . . ; Like when . . .
Restatement and/or conclusion of point being supported	So . . .
Interruption	Incidentally . . . ; By the way . . .
Return to previously interrupted context space	Anyway . . . ; In any case . . .
Indirect challenge	Yes/Right but . . . ; Except, however, . . .
Direct challenge	(No) But . . .
Subargument concession	All right/Okay but . . .
Prior logical abstraction	But look/listen/you see . . .
Further development	Now . . .

Here conversational moves are described by category names. The discourse grammar incorporates many subtypes of these categories. Following our analysis, we shall proceed to discussion of the way such moves are integrated in extended discourse.

Because/Like/Like When: Support

The analysis of conversational moves that function to support a claim illustrates the importance of attending to the implicit components of conversational moves in understanding the functional relations between discourse elements. Consider a portion of D's argument in the genetics-environment debate of chapter 2:

> D: 32. . . . you and I are very close in this room right now
> 33. but we don't have the same environment.
> 34. *Because* I'm looking at you, I'm seeing that window
> 35. behind you. You're not seeing that window behind you.

Why is the statement of the fact of support (F), "I'm seeing that window behind you. You're not seeing that window behind you," a support of the preceding claim (C), "You and I are very close in this room right now, but we don't have the same environment." Something has been left unsaid; that something is the assumed principle (P), "*If* two people have the same environment, *then* these two people will see the same things." Without inferring some such principle, there is no way to understand how statement F supports statement C.

Also left unsaid, and requiring inference, are the connective links between C, F, and P. Some further process must be invoked to yield C from F and P. In fact two additional processes are necessary. One is instantiation, by which we mean that we can substitute an instance of some class for the class itself. The second is the application of some logic rule by which we can derive our claim—for instance, under the logic rule Modus-Ponens, if you are given A, and the assertion that A implies B, then you can conclude B; or under the logic rule Modus-Tollens, if you are given not B, and the assertion that A implies B, then you can conclude not A.

We have schemas of these kinds of logical relations that we use to process a support utterance. When such an utterance is made, we infer principle P and attempt to instantiate A and B with the utterance and the claim to be supported. Instantiation entails setting up bindings or mappings between objects mentioned in the utterance and the class descriptions contained in A and B.[3]

In our example, D supports his claim in line 33 that he and R do not have the same environment on lines 34–35. His principle of support is the unstated supposition that "if two people have the same environment, then they will see the same things." The "if . . ." part of the principle is the A portion of the Modus-Tollens schema, and the "then . . ." part of the principle is the B of the Modus-Tollens. D's claim in line 33 is then "Not A," by substituting himself and R for "two people," and his utterances of support in lines 34–35 is "Not

B," by substituting himself and R for "they" and window for "things." Under Modus-Tollens, then, D has proved his claim.

The components of D's support move can now be specified as follows:

C   (claim): It is not true that we have the same environment.
F   (fact of support): I am seeing the window behind you; you are not.
P   (principle of support): If two people have the same environment, then they will see the same things.
M   (mappings between C and P): We are two people, D and R. (mappings between F and P): "They" are us, D and R; "things" in this case is "the window behind you."
LR (logic rule): Modus-Tollens.

In our context space grammar all support context spaces are characterized by slots to hold these pieces of a support move. In addition the system characterizes other common forms of support, such as the citing of authorities. R's support utterances in lines 1–7 of this same excerpt, for instance, cite the source of her claim (a study), reasons for believing this source (excellent French TV documentary), and R's access to this source (seeing a presentation on TV). Support context spaces also have slots to hold such source, credential, and access components.

What is essential is that the context space system treats implicit components of a conversational move as much a part of the discourse as those that are verbally expressed. These components are necessary parts enabling a context space (i.e., its contained utterances) to fulfill a given discourse role. The clue word "Because" functions here to signal the listener not simply that the issue context space is complete and that a support move is to begin but also to expect utterances that reflect support components and that are related to each other and to the issue space in conventional ways. Finally, the listener knows that the support move will not be completed (or the support context space given a background role) until obligatory components of the support move have been provided.

Which components are obligatory and which are optional depends on the particular conversational move. In the case of the support move, elements of the support utterances must be able to fill either the authority slots of the context space; the F, P, and M slots of the context space; or slots specified for other methods of support (e.g., analogy, illustration).

In the context space grammar this kind of inferential elaboration applies to each conversational move. Here, however, we shall proceed simply to describe and illustrate various other types of moves and some of the clue words that serve as their signals.

So: Restatement and/or Conclusion of Point Being Supported

It often happens that after a claim (initially made in an issue context space) has been given support, the claim itself is restated. To signal the fact that the support move is complete, such restatements are usually introduced by the clue word "So." In the genetics-environment excerpt, for example, R begins resumption of her claim that the aggressive nature of the child is not influenced by his environment with the clue word "So": "So you couldn't blame it on the child's home" (line 26). The resumption occurs after R supports her claim by showing that two children sharing the same home environment manifested radically different social behaviors. Resumptions of this kind can either return us to an original issue space or, as in the present case, create a new issue space with a modified claim.

Incidentally/By the Way: Interruption

Often in the midst of the discussion of a specific topic of discourse, a conversant will shift to discussion of a related but tangential subject matter. Rather than waiting for the close of the initial topic, the conversant may signal its temporary suspension with such clue words as "Incidentally," "By the way," or "Oh, I forgot to tell you." Such clue words signal to a listener that discussion of a new topic is to ensue but imply as well that the current context space is only temporarily to be in the background and will be resumed later in the conversation.

Anyway/In Any Case: Return

Corresponding to the clue words for interruptions, clue words like "Anyway" and "In any case" indicate when a return to the interrupted context space is about to take place. Such a return, as we have said, would normally be expected.

The following excerpt, taken from a conversation between friends, exemplifies such context space digression and subsequent resumption.[4] Lines 1–9, context space C_1, represent the interrupted space; lines 10–29, context space C_2, the digression space; lines 30–31, the return to context space C_1.

A: 1. I remember what happened in January. I went home and I,
     2. um, was with my cousin. He's my age, I've mentioned him
     3. before. We were in his apartment and um we were talking.
     4. I just casually asked how my mother was doing, 'cause I
     5. hadn't, you know, I wasn't involved. I didn't know what
     6. was happening. And he goes, "Oh, I think she's depressed."
     7. This is before she changed—She had this whole fiasco with
     8. a job. She never liked her position in her job, which was
     9. a big part of her stupid problem, that she never changed it.
   10. *Oh, I didn't tell you,* when I was home a couple of—
   11. about two months ago, I was really angry 'cause I know how
   12. much she's suffered 'cause she hasn't had a career, or feelings
   13. of inferiority. And, here I'm doing it and she's trying to
   14. stop me. And so, you know, I get so angry, and she was sitting
   15. and talking how important it is to have a career and to be able
   16. to do what you're doing. And I was just sitting in the living
   17. room dying, really getting angry. But I didn't say anything
   18. which I thought was progress, that I didn't say anything.

B: 19. Is it?

A: 20. Oh, it was progress, 'cause I used to get into stupid arguments
   21. and fights with them.

B: 22. But isn't it hard work to keep all that in?

A: 23. But it was better. Because I would get into arguments and
   24. it wouldn't help. What would I do? Just scream or say, "How
   25. could you say you want"—I would have had an argument.

B: 26. There might be something between an argument and saying
      nothing.

A: 27. Yeah, but that wasn't

B: 28. Not to feel like you're bursting your gut.

A: 29. Yeah. That wasn't even that bad, that was just a thing.
   30. *But anyway,* I went home in January and he told me that she
   31. was upset.

Yes/Right But: Indirect Challenge

The clue words "Yes, but" or "Right, but" or "Except, however," are used by conversants in debate to signify that though the speaker (i.e., the antagonist) is not going to directly attack the argument put forward by the previous speaker (i.e., the protagonist), he or she is going to challenge that argument indirectly. Indirect challenges usually entail the specification of a claim which, if true, implies that the opponent's claim cannot be true.

In the genetics-environment debate, for example, R claimed that a child's aggressive behavior is not much influenced by the environment (lines 6–7). This claim is an indirect challenge of a claim previously made by D that, in general, an individual's aggressive behavior is not genetically determined. Though R's statement does not directly deny D's preceding claim, if one believes in the nature-nurture controversy, either genetics or the environment must be responsible for aggressive behavior. If R's claim is true, then D's preceding claim must be false.

In a later segment of this same excerpt, R once again uses these clue words as a means of indirectly attacking a challenge claim made by D that a child's aggressive behavior is caused by the environment: "Right, but the two brothers have the same environment" (line 29). This is not a direct denial of D's preceding statement, "It [aggressive behavior] has to do with the child's environment." But if R's statements are accepted, then she has invalidated D's preceding challenge to her (R's) position.

(No) But: Direct Challenge

Like "Yes, but," the clue words "No, but" or "But" alone often signal that the utterances about to be made should be viewed as a challenge of an opponent's preceding utterances. In this case, however, the challenge will be a direct rather than an indirect challenge: for example, a complete denial of the truth of the opponent's preceding claim, or the assertion that the opponent has overlooked a crucial factor that actually invalidates the claim.

All Right/Okay But: Subargument Concession

"All right, but" or "Okay, but" is used in the midst of argumentation of a conversant who, though accepting the validity of an opponent's preceding statements, chooses not to end the debate but to continue argumentation on another point at issue not yet conceded. This conversational move differs from the indirect challenge in that the latter's signal, "yes, but," does not entail any concession. In the indirect move, if the speaker's claims are accepted, the opponent's argument by default is dismissed. The "All right, but" move instead does entail acceptance by the speaker of the opponent's preceding argument. And in this case acceptance of the speaker's succeeding arguments will not invalidate the opponent's preceding one, since these arguments are not addressed to that point at all. Rather, the statements following "All right, but" are in relation to a preceding claim made by the opponent which led to the subargument that the speaker has just conceded. With "All right, but" then, the battle is conceded but not the war. These words therefore signal a close to the context spaces of a subargument and signal the beginning of a new one.

Support Challenges

We have delineated three methods of challenge available to a conversant in a debate and have exemplified these with illustrations in which a conversant challenges an opponent's preceding claim. However, challenge moves are not limited to an attack of a claim. They may be employed to challenge (either directly or indirectly) any one of a claim's supports. A challenge of a claim's supports of course constitutes a challenge to the claim itself.

There are many different methods by which a support of a claim may be challenged. One can respond to an opponent's support of a claim with an "emotive flat rejection"—a "So what?" type of response—implying that one cannot see the relevance of the purportedly supporting statements to the claim supposedly being supported. One can deny the truth of the purportedly factual statements given in support of a claim. One can challenge the truth of the principle on which the support is based. Or, one can claim that the domain specified in the support is inappropriately matched to the domain of the claim (e.g., if an opponent's support of a claim that adults should be made to pay for their crimes rests on showing that a child's aggressive behavior is not environmentally induced, one could challenge by arguing that it is illegitimate to compare environmental effects on children with those on adults). The context space grammar characterizes these different types of support challenges.

Consider, for instance, M's challenge to R's support of the claim that the environment does not shape a person's behavior; R's support was based on demonstrating that two twins living in the same home exhibited radically different social behaviors at an early age. To this M responds:

M: 41. And, I mean, they don't even—you know, to say that
    42. two kids come from the same family is really meaningless,
    43. because when you think of the difference in treatment
    44. that two kids can get in exactly the same family, it's
    45. incredible. You know, it's the difference between
    46. night and day.

We have seen that supportive statements depend on there being some generally accepted generic support principle as well as a possible set of mappings between the claim being stated, this principle, and the statements of support. Thus a challenge to either the validity of the principle or the mappings set up constitutes a challenge of the support itself. In this case M challenges the applicability of R's generic principle to the particular case at hand; formally speaking, she is challenging R's mapping of "two people sharing *the same environment*" onto "two twins living in *a same home.*" The challenge then does not directly deny the truth of the principle, nor the truth of the utterances, but rather challenges R's current attempt at the application of the principle.

But Look/Listen/You See: Prior Logical Abstraction

"But look," "But listen," or "But you see" is used to close a current context space and to shift the discourse into a context space whose topic is "logically prior" to that of the closed space.

Usually the preceding (closed) space is of an evaluative nature—that is, one in which the negative or positive aspects of a given state of affairs, S1, is discussed. In the new context space a state of affairs S2 is discussed, which is believed to be logically prior to S1 in that S2 provides the environment that enables S1 to occur in the first place. Shifting onto this logically prior topic of discourse closes all further discussion of the preceding context space. The following excerpt illustrates this type of conversational move:

J: 1. This happened last—in September of last year. Uh, a
     2. guy, another prisoner in death row, he was, uh, he was
     3. about to die of—he was to be executed within two days,
     4. okay? This is in Alabama, it's a Southern state. And,
     5. uh, he would refuse to eat or something like that. Well,
     6. I think it was a little longer, but, so they force-fed him
     7. until—up to his execution.

R: 8. Isn't that stupid?

M: 9. That's disgusting.

R: 10. That really makes sense though.

M: 11. But, you see, the whole idea of, of the death penalty is
    12. completely illogical. Because, you kill somebody for
    13. killing somebody, okay?

After M's last conversational move in the excerpt, discussion focuses on argumentation about the death penalty and leads to the subargument of who is to blame for the occurrence of crimes (i.e., society versus the individual, the environment versus genetics). The question of whether it was reasonable or unreasonable for the guards in the prison to force feed the about-to-be-executed prisoner is totally dropped from the discourse, and instead, the state of affairs creating this situation in the first place (i.e., there being such a thing as the death penalty) becomes the new topic of discourse. A logically prior shift signifies that continued discussion of the original state of affairs is deemed meaningless and that what one has to look at is the state of affairs enabling such situations to arise.

Now: Further Development

The clue word "Now" often signals that a new active context space is about to be developed that will contain elaborative comments on the topic and elements of the preceding active context space. Reflecting this, we often find the clue word "Now" accompanying a discourse utterance such as, "Now, it's a little bit more complicated or elaborate than that."

The following excerpt is taken from a conversation between a steam plant expert, M, and a layman, A. In this conversation M is explaining to A the workings of the steam plant.[5] M's explanation is highly structured and takes the form of a "breadth-first" presentation—that is, M explains the steam plant process by passing through the system a number of times, each pass through informing A of further complexities in its design. This excerpt occurs on M's second pass through the system, at a point where M is still at the stage of giving A only a rough outline of the steam plant process.

M: 1. The first thing you have coming out of the steam
2. generator, as it's pushing its steam along, is—you
3. have a main steam stop. Okay. And that's just an
4. emergency valve to shut off the steam, uh, so that you
5. can take this whole section, long section of piping, and
6. take all the uh steam out of it. Okay, so you
7. can isolate the valve. You want to isolate as close to the
8. steam generator as you can. And, that's all the valve is
9. there for. There is another valve, that's called the root
10. valve, down here. This is the root valve. And it's
11. just in front of the turbines, okay? And, there are a
12. couple of different turbines, I'm going just going to talk
13. about one of them now.

A: 14. All right.

M: 15. Okay. And there are also a couple of auxiliary loads too
16. that we won't talk about. Oh, I should mention on the turbine,

17. just before the main turbine here, there is also a throttle
18. valve. And I'm just going to indicate it with this little
19. thing here. That usually means a solenoid valve, all I
20. mean to indicate here is that it's a control valve. Okay.
21. It controls the amount of steam coming through to
22. the turbine.

A: 23. Okay.

M: 24. Okay? And that goes into the turbine.

A: 25. *Now*, is that normally set at open, or?

M: 26. It's initially shut and then it's opened up. Uh,
27. these are normally open, the root valve and the
28. main steam stop.

In most of his explanation M only mentions the component parts of a steam plant system and their respective functions; he does not explain how these parts perform their functions. A's question at line 25, however, raises the issue of how a particular valve works, moving to a deeper level of analysis than that made so far. The question thus begins a new move warranting the creation of a new subordinate context space.

Methods of Development: Analogy

We have in passing referred to the fact that various conversational moves may be accomplished through different methods. For instance, the support move may be accomplished through authority citation, the telling of a narrative, or the application of some logic rule.

A particularly versatile method of development characterized by the context space grammar is the offering of an analogy. An analogy may be used to support, to challenge, to assert implicitly a judgment, or, as in the following dialogue, to explain. G is explaining to J the workings of a particular accelerator; under current discussion is the cavity of the accelerator through which protons are sent and accelerated:

G: 1. It's just a pure electrostatic field, which, between
2. two points, and the proton accelerates through the
3. electrostatic potential.

J: 4. Okay.

G: 5. Same physical law as if you drop a ball. It accelerates
6. through a gravitational potential.

J: 7. Okay.

G: 8. And the only important point here is that the potential
     9. is maintained by this Cockcroft-Walton unit.

The analogy method, like other methods of development, has a number of specific inferential components, which are reflected in the context space grammar by its slots. In an analogy two domains are compared to each other. To process the analogy, one must be able to bind or map particulars of one domain to the other. In this excerpt, "electrostatic potential" is mapped to "gravitational potential," and "proton" is mapped to "ball." Most important, there must be a generalization to which events or propositions of the two domains can be mapped as well. In the excerpt the generalization is that "the moving body accelerates through a force field." The context space grammar identifies three slots to hold the implicit components necessary for the analogy development: a mapping slot, a generalization slot, and an ancillary relations slot. The importance of attending to implicit components of various methods of conversational developments is clearly illustrated by the discourse phenomenon of analogy rejection. Studying analogy rejection is actually quite enlightening: it puts into relief the fact that discourse function constrains what can be said when. Like Getner (1980) we recognize that the mappings of relations between two domains is the vital aspect of analogy. But we still need some criteria to determine which relations must be mapped. This criteria is derived from the discourse function the analogy is supposed to serve.

For example, in November 1978 after the mass suicide at Jonestown, some reports attempted to legitimatize the incident by comparing it to the mass suicide at Masada many centuries ago. Two conversants discussing the analogy rejected it (and thereby rejected legitimatization of the Jonestown incident) because, they claimed, the people of Masada were a "threatened people, about to be attacked by a foreign and murderous army," an attribute, they claimed, not true of the people at Jonestown.

Implicit in the conversants' rejection is the claim that despite the relation "People taking own lives" (to be referred to as R1) being true in the two domains, there are additional vital relations that are not constant between the domains. Specifically, the Jonestown incident is lacking the following relations found in the Masada incident: (1) an "attack" relation, R2, between a foreign group of people and the group of people taking their own lives, and (2) a "cause" relation, R3, such that R2 R3 R1.

Now it is precisely because of R2 R3 R1 that the Masada suicide is usually legitimatized. Since these relations are not true in Jonestown, it is impossible to map the legitimatization of the one onto the other: the discourse function of the analogy has failed, warranting its rejection in this discourse context.

The Succession of Conversational Moves

The following excerpt illustrates the way a succession of conversational moves play into each other in conversational development. The excerpt is taken from a taped conversation between two friends, M and N, in which M, a British citizen, is explaining to N, an American, the history of the current turmoil in Ireland. The conversational moves illustrated in the excerpt include assertion of a claim, challenge, clarification, support, concession, and further development.

M: 1. And, of course, what's made it worse this time is the
     2. British army moving in. And, moving in, in the first
     3. place, as a police force. It's almost a Vietnam,
     4. in a way.

N: 5. But, all within Northern Ireland?

M: 6. All within Northern Ireland. Moving in as a police force,
     7. being seen by everybody as a police force that was going
     8. to favor the Protestants.

N: 9. It'd rather be like Syria being in Lebanon, right?

M: 10. I don't know enough about it to know, maybe.

N: 11. There's—Where there's a foreign police force in one
    12. country. I mean, when you say it's like Vietnam, I
    13. can't take Vietnam. Vietnam is North Vietnam and South
    14. Vietnam.

M: 15. No, I meant war. You know, moving in and saying we're
    16. a police action and actually fighting a war when you got
    17. there.

N: 18. Oh, well, that's Syria, that's obviously Syria, right?
    19. Who are implicitly supporting—not supporting—'cause
    20. actually it's very similar in Lebanon, right? You have
    21. the Catholics and the Moslems. That's right, that's
    22. Lebanon.

M: 23. I suppose, yes.

N: 24. You have the Catholics and the Moslems, and then Syria's
    25. coming in and implicitly supporting the Moslems, because
    26. Syria itself is Moslem.
    27. Now, England is Protestant?

Like the burn conversation cited in chapter 1 and the genetics-environment debate of chapter 2, this is a dialogue that proceeds by twists and turns, and in which much is left unsaid. The identification of conversational moves and the analysis of context space structures, however, allows us to ferret out the implicit connections between utterances, to grasp the underlying functional relations between discourse components, and thus to understand the discourse as it proceeds.

Among the difficulties posed in the processing of this dialogue are the following: What is the meaning of N's question in line 5? Of course M is referring to Northern Ireland; Northern Ireland has been the sole subject of this conversation for the past half hour. Further why does N preface her question with "But?" N seems to be signaling an objection, but how do we know this and how do we understand the nature of the objection? In lines 13–14 N makes her objection more explicit: the Vietnam situation involved the North and South, whereas Ireland involved only the North. But why does this constitute an objection to M's claim? Finally, why, after the discussion of Syria and Lebanon, does N suddenly ask if England is Protestant—how does this fit into the conversation? And why does she preface her question with "Now?"

Notice that in lines 1–3 M claims that Britain's move into Ireland as a police force is a negative event. She then compares Britain's moving into Ireland to America's moving into Vietnam. Here she uses an analogy to convey her negative evaluation of the state of affairs, mapping the negative associations with America in the Vietnam situation onto Britain, which M claims is playing an analogous role in an analogous situation. N, however, challenges the analogy by challenging M's mappings. N argues that the Vietnam War involved both South and North Vietnam (i.e., two countries), whereas in M's situation we are only dealing with Northern Ireland so that the mapping is inaccurate. The rejection is not of course based simply on the one- versus two-country difference but on the relations that hold between Britain and Northern Ireland versus the relations that hold between America, North Vietnam, and South Vietnam. N does not disagree with M's negative evaluation claim but only with the analogy used to develop that claim. In particular, to accept the analogy, whose function is "negative evaluation," would entail agreeing with the supposition that America's involvement in Vietnam was negative.

Not willing to accept the negative evaluation of America as a given, N suggests a replacement analogy—let's blame the Arabs. N claims that here the relations between elements in the two respective domains *can* be appropriately mapped: the relations between Syria and Lebanon are the same as the relations between Britain and

Northern Ireland. Once M has conceded N's replacement analogy, it is possible to return to the initiating subject of the analogy, Britain's moving into Ireland. The "Now" prefacing N's return to the initiating issue signals also that the context space about to be developed stands in a further-development relation to a preceding context space; the further development consists of N's analyzing the (religious) motivations behind Britain's entrance into Northern Ireland, taken from the comparable religious motivations behind Syria's actions in the analogous domain.

Conversational move analysis can thus explain otherwise puzzling sequences of utterances; it explicates the discourse criteria for various surface linguistic features, and it provides a structural model of the discourse based on the functional roles of discourse elements. Participants in such conversations follow each other because of their shared knowledge of the conventions governing various kinds of discourse developments.

The identification of conventionalized conversational moves, their implicit components, and the relations between them defined by context space structures forms the basis for the elaboration of the context space discourse grammar. We are now prepared for a more formal characterization of the grammatical structures and mechanisms that facilitate the production and processing of conversational moves in discourse.

Chapter 4

The Discourse Grammar:

Context Space Constituents

A discourse grammar presupposes that a conversation can be decomposed into a limited set of constituents that combine with one another in regular ways. Just as sentence grammars describe the component elements of sentences—agents, predicates, modifiers— and their relations, the context space grammar describes the component elements of discourse—various types of context spaces—and the conventional relations between them. The grammar thus provides a structural description of discourse based on the functional relations between its parts.

The purpose of the discourse grammar explicated here, however, is not simply to provide a static description of discourse structure. Discourse generation and interpretation is after all an active, ongoing process. The context space system therefore has been designed to model this ongoing process. We have said that the various conversational moves taken by speakers can necessitate, facilitate, or preclude succeeding discourse developments and that conversational participants must be able to update their discourse models accordingly. In particular, the taking of specific moves changes the relevant discourse context in light of which utterances are to be interpreted at various points of conversational development. After explicating the ways these moves and the information associated with them are incorporated into context space structures, we shall describe the ways the relations between these structures are identified and updated as conversation proceeds.

Basic Components

A context space is essentially delimited by a specific set of utterances performing a conversational move. However, the analysis of a context space includes as well a specification of the roles its various elements play in the overall discourse structure. A context space is thus also defined by a marker reflecting the influential status of its utterances at any given point in the discourse, a pointer to the preceding discourse context space in relation to which the context space has been developed, and a specification of the type of relation the context space bears to a preceding relevant context space.

As we have noted, the categorizations of context space types and the component slots specified for different types mirror the different units and phenomena found in a discourse world. For example, corresponding to the fact that the presence of a certain type of discourse constituent is often dependent on the presence of some other independent constituent, distinct spaces have been defined for independent and dependent constituents, such that dependent constituent spaces fill slots of independent constituent spaces. Additionally, corresponding to the fact that the analysis of some types of conversational moves entails the explication of standardized implicit components, a context space containing the utterances serving such a move will have slots to contain such implicit components, and the grammar treats implicit components of a move as much a part of the discourse as those components that are verbally expressed.

All context spaces have the following slots, which are obligatorily filled (with possible values depending on the type of space) before the completion of a context space:

> TYPE: This slot specifies the context space's category name. (There are ten types of context spaces.)
>
> DERIVATION: This slot specifies whether the substantive claims within the context space were explicitly stated by the speaker or whether they were implicit and thus inferred by the grammar.
>
> GOAL: This slot identifies the function served—the conversational move performed—by the context space (e.g., support, clarification).
>
> CONTEXTUAL-FUNCTION: This slot is a structured slot consisting of the following two subcomponents:
>
>> Method: This slot contains the particular method used to perform the conversational move of the space (e.g., flat denial, Modus-Ponens, analogy).
>>
>> Corelator: This slot contains specific reference to the context space in relation to which the conversational move is being made.
>
> SPEAKERS: This slot contains a list of persons who have generated the utterances lying in the context space.
>
> STATUS: This slot contains specification of the foreground/background role of the context space at a given point in the discourse.

FOCUS: This slot specifies the influential status of individual elements within the context space. It is composed of four sub-slots, each of which contains constituents of the utterances contained in the space:

High: This slot notes the constituent in "high" focus.

Medium: This slot lists all constituents in "medium" focus.

Low: This slot lists all constituents in "low" focus.

Zero: This slot lists all constituents of "zero" focus.

Before describing the major types of context spaces and the particular additional slots specific to them, it will be useful to understand more precisely the information contained in the slots we have called "status" and "focus."

Status Assignments

Chapter 2's respecification of Grice's maxims states that a relevant discourse context is composed of two context spaces and that at any given point in conversation succeeding utterances are generated and interpreted in direct relation to these two context spaces. In addition, a context space may be in the background, but this is not synonymous with its having no influence on the continuing flow of the conversation. For example, it has been shown that unexpected digressions may occur in a discourse, suspending the instantiation of a particular discourse expectation or completion of a context space under discussion. Though the digression temporarily usurps the foreground role, and in the process relegates the interrupted context space to the background, the succeeding conversational development is still constrained and dependent on the now background context space. For instance, it would be inappropriate to begin a new issue context space after the digression context space has been completed. To use Grice's terms, such a conversational move would be "unsuitable at this stage of the discourse." Instead, what is demanded is that one return to, and resume discussion of, the interrupted background context space.

Mirroring the different roles that a context space may play, all context spaces have an associated status slot. The value of this slot denotes the changing influential status of the utterances contained in the context space. The influential status of a context space is used to (1) determine whether or not this context space will be accessed in our focused processing of succeeding discourse utterances, (2) reflect other levels of influence that this context space may have on succeeding discourse development, and (3) determine the type of referring expressions to elements of the utterances contained in this context space that would be both unambiguous and sufficiently informative. The following seven types of conversational influence have been distinguished:

Active   The context space in which current utterances are being placed. There can be only one active context space at a given point in the conversation.

Controlling   The context space in direct relation to the active context space being developed. There can be only one controlling context space at a given point in the conversation.

Precontrol   A previously controlling context space whose controlling status is temporarily usurped by (1) the creation of a subordinate space to the subordinate space that it was controlling or (2) a digression—the controlling context space does not control development of the digressive space. When, however, the digression is completed and the original active space is reactivated, then this precontrol space is reassigned a controlling status to control further continuation of the interrupted, active space.

Open   A previously active context space that was interrupted before completion of its corresponding conversational move.

Generating   A context space in indirect relation to which an active context space is being developed. For example, this often occurs in debates where argumentation of a given claim leads to some subargumentation, the outcome of which can affect the outcome of previous debate about the initiating claim. A context space containing an initiating claim of some subargument has a generating status value while the subargument is in progress.

Closed   A context space whose discussion is believed completed for the present time (i.e., it is reasonable to believe that its point has been reached).

Superseded   A context space whose discussion is concluded by its being replaced by a new context space whose claim is either a "finer restatement" or a "further generalization." This too most often occurs in debates where an opponent's challenge can lead one to give up on the scope of the claim but not on the claim in its entirety.

Of these seven the two most prominent are the controlling and active context spaces, since at any given point in a conversation, utterances are generated and interpreted only in direct relation to the utterances contained in these two context spaces. Later in this chapter we shall discuss some of the grammar's updating characterizations for when conversational moves are performed. These actions change the status assignments of preceding context spaces and often cause the construction of new spaces. Such updating enables adequate reflection of the effects of a given conversational move on a current discourse context.

Focus Levels

We have mentioned that the focus level slot is used to specify the influential status of individual elements within a context space and that a particular element's focus level governs one's choice of surface form to refer to that entity. Corresponding to the different means we have to reference elements, we have different possible focus level assignments: a pronominal reference reflects a high focus level; reference by name, a medium focus level; reference by description, a low focus level; and implicit reference, a zero focus level. In chapter 5 we shall examine some specific rules of correspondence between an element's focus level and the conversational flow. In general, the discourse role played by the conversational move governs an element's initial focus level assignment, and then the conversational moves, through their effects on the status of the space in which the reference element is contained, governs the element's updated reassignments.

As an illustration of a context space, consider the essential specification for context space C2 in the following conversation:

A: 1. I think if you're going to marry someone in the Hindu
    2. tradition, you have to—Well, you—They say you give
    3. money to the family, to the girl, but in essence, you
    4. actually buy her.
B: 5. It's the same in the Western tradition. You know,
    6. you see these greasy fat millionaires going around with
    7. film stars, right? They've essentially bought them by
    8. their status [money?].

Context Space C2: Lines 5–8

TYPE: Issue
DERIVATION: Explicit
GOAL: Generalization
CONTEXTUAL-FUNCTION:
    Method: Analogy
    Corelator: C1 (the current controlling context space)
SPEAKERS: B

STATUS: Active
FOCUS: It [buying and selling of women]—high focus; Western
tradition—medium focus

Types of Context Spaces

There are basically two major types of context spaces composing a
discourse world: issue and nonissue spaces. Issue spaces, we have
said, are the "topic setters" of discourse, the independent constituents in light of which all subordinate context spaces are generated
and interpreted.

Issue Context Spaces
All issue spaces have three additional slots:

CLAIM: This is a structured slot composed of two parts:
State of affairs: This slot specifies the proposition of the
utterances in the context space.
"Type" predicate: This slot specifies the modality of the
proposition (true, not true; good, bad; etc.).
TOPIC: This slot specifies the topic being set by the issue space
(generally a generic formulation of the state of affairs specified in
the space).
SUPPORT-CS: This slot contains a list of all the context spaces
developed in support of the claim of the issue space.

In an issue context space the truth, necessity, goodness, or appropriateness of a particular state of affairs is discussed. Mirroring these
different types of assertions about a state of affairs, there are three
types of issue spaces defined in the grammar: epistemic, evaluative,
and deontic.

In an epistemic issue context space the truth or necessity of a state
of affairs is discussed. The type of predicate associated with the claim
is an epistemic predicate, the values of which are "true," "not true,"
"necessary," or "not necessary."

In an evaluative issue context space the goodness of a state of affairs is discussed. The type of predicate associated with the claim is
an evaluative predicate, the possible values of which are pairs consisting of a particular evaluative adjective and a corresponding positive or negative valence. For example, "crazy, negative" is a possible
value for this slot. If a speaker negatively evaluates a state of affairs under discussion, the discourse system usually infers that the
speaker is advocating a change in the state of affairs. In this case the

grammar provides an "advocated-inference" slot to note this inferred advocating of a change.

In a deontic issue context space a speaker questions the appropriateness or fairness of a state of affairs. The type of predicate associated with the claim is a deontic predicate, the possible values of which are "why should" or "why shouldn't" x be the case.

These three types of context spaces are not subcategories of issue spaces but exist at the same (highest) level of categorization. Any one of these three types, however, can be further subdivided into *debative* or *nondebative* issue spaces. Nondebative issue spaces are ordinary issue context spaces. Debative issue spaces have the following four additional slot definitions:

> PROTAGONISTS: This slot replaces the usual "speakers" slot associated with a context space, and it contains a list of conversants advocating the contents of the claim slot.
>
> ANTAGONISTS: This slot contains a list of conversants attacking the assertion advocated by the protagonists.
>
> COUNTERCLAIMS: This slot contains a list of context spaces developed in challenge to the claim of the protagonists.
>
> COUNTERSUPPORTS: This slot contains a list of context spaces developed in challenge of the supports of the claim under attack.

In addition to the specific slots defining particular types of issue spaces, spaces developed by certain methods may require additional slots to reflect the components of those methods. For instance, the grammar's explication of any conversational move using an analogy as its method of development entails inferring implicit components of an analogy (e.g., mappings between the two domains under discussion); thus any issue context space developed by analogy will have the following additional slots:

> ABSTRACT: This slot contains the generic proposition, P, of which the initiating and analogous claims are instances, and also a listing of all generic propositions relevant to the purpose of the analogy (explicitly stated or implicit ones that are causally related to stated propositions).
>
> RELATIONS: This slot contains a list of the relations used in the propositions of the abstract slot.
>
> MAPPINGS: This slot contains a list of mappings between constituents of P onto the constituents of the propositions in the analogous and initiating context spaces.

Nonissue Context Spaces
The second category of context spaces encompasses comment, narrative, and two types of support context spaces.

Comment and Narrative Context Spaces   In our context space partitioning of the following excerpt, J's utterances (lines 1–7) would form a narrative space, and both R and M's utterances serve as comments on this narrative:

J: 1. This happened last—in September of last year. Uh, a
     2. guy, another prisoner in death row, he was, uh, he was
     3. about to die of—he was to be executed within two days,
     4. okay? This is in Alabama, it's a Southern state. And,
     5. uh, he would refuse to eat or something like that. Well,
     6. I think it was a little longer, but, so they force-fed
     7. him until—up to his execution.

R: 8. Isn't that stupid?

M: 9. That's disgusting.

The distinction between comment and issue context spaces reflects the fact that a comment space is not a topic setter and does not necessarily introduce a proposition to be evaluated. If a speaker's comment does become the next issue of discussion, then the comment is put into the claim slot of a new issue space. If the comment does not become a matter of discussion, it is appended to an "old comments" list in a currently active context space. A comment context space is a temporary subconstituent of another kind of space that is currently active.

The following additional slots are specific to narrative spaces:

ORIENTATION SECTION: The opening of a narrative usually consists of an introduction to the participants in the narrative and the time and place at which the episode occurred. Corresponding to this the orientation slot of a narrative space is composed of the following subslots:

Actors: This slot contains a list of lists, where each list is composed of two parts: an actor identifier and a list of predications specified about this actor.

Time: This slot specifies the time of the episode and any particulars stated about this time period (e.g., "It was a ghastly period in world history.")

Location: This slot specifies the location of the episode and any predications given this location (e.g., "It's a Southern state.")

o-EVENTS: A list of events that occurred in the episode. The events are usually ordered in linear time and causality.

H-EVENTS: A list of contrastive events that could have, but did not, occur in the episode.

Support Context Spaces   There are two major types of support context spaces: narrative-support and nonnarrative-support spaces. The former consists of the telling of a story in which one event, led up to by preceding told events, is an instance of the claim being supported. The latter consists of the uttering of a particular state of affairs which, using some generic principle of support and some formal rule of inference, leads one to conclude the claim being supported.

Both forms of support can be accompanied by naming some authority for the information cited, or an authority citation may be the sole support for a claim and constitute a support conversational move in itself.

All support context spaces have the following special slots:

SUPPORT-FACT: This slot contains some propositional representation of a "narrative support" event that is an instance of the claim being supported, or for nonnarrative supports it contains a propositional representation of the state-of-affairs that implies (by reliance on some generic principle and rule of inference) the validity of the claim being supported.

MAPPINGS: For nonnarrative-support context spaces this slot will be filled by the mappings of elements of the generic principle of support onto the support statements and the mappings of the elements of the principle onto the claim being supported. For narrative-support context spaces it will be filled by the mappings of the elements of the claim being supported and its instance of support.

AUTHORITY: This is a structured slot consisting of the following four parts:

Source: This slot specifies the person or group cited as an authority.

Method: This slot specifies the origin of the authority's information.

Credentials: This slot specifies the authority's credentials.

Access: This slot specifies the speaker's access to the authority's information (e.g., "I saw it on TV").

An analysis of substantive nonnarrative support utterances entails the explication of many implicit components. As illustrated previously, such support moves rely on some principle of support and mappings between this principle, the stated fact of support, and the claim being supported.[1] Reflecting this, context spaces containing utterances filling a nonnarrative support discourse role have the following additional slot definitions:

SUPPORT-STATEMENT: This slot is a propositional representation of the actual utterances stated in support. The slot's value will usually be identical to either the slot value of support fact or principle-of-support.

PRINCIPLE-OF-SUPPORT: This slot contains the generic principle underlying the support and is subdivided into "If" and "Then" parts.

In exemplification of a complete context space specification for a portion of discourse, consider the specification of this excerpt from the genetics-environment debate of chapter 2, which contains an issue context space and a support context space related to it:

R: 1. Except, however, John and I just saw this two hour
      2. TV show
M: 3. Uh hum,
R: 4. where they showed—it was an excellent French TV
      5. documentary—and they showed that, in fact,
      6. the aggressive nature of the child is not really
      7. that much influenced by his environment.
M: 8. How did they show that?
R: 9. They showed that by filming kids in kindergarten,
M: 10. Uh hum,
R: 11. showing his behavior among other children,
M: 12. And then
R: 13. and showed him ten years later acting the same way,

Context Space C1

TYPE: Epistemic debative issue
DERIVATION: Explicit
GOAL: Challenge
CONTEXTUAL-FUNCTION:
      Method: Exclusive-or (either A or B)
      Corelator: [precedes excerpt]
PROTAGONISTS: R
ANTAGONISTS: Empty [filled later in the discourse]
STATUS: Controlling

FOCUS: Aggressive nature of the child—high focus;
environment—low focus
CLAIM:
   State of affairs: The aggressive nature of the child is influenced by his environment
   Type predicate: Not true
TOPIC: The influence of the environment on a child's behavior
SUPPORT-CS: C2
COUNTERCLAIMS: Empty [not later filled]
COUNTERSUPPORTS: Empty [later filled]

Context Space C2

TYPE: Nonnarrative support
DERIVATION: Explicit
GOAL: Support
CONTEXTUAL-FUNCTION:
   Method: Modus-Tollens
   Corelator: C1
SPEAKERS: R
STATUS: Active
FOCUS^2:   Child/kids—high focus;
his behavior—medium focus;
TV show/documentary—low focus;
kindergarten/other children—low focus
SUPPORT-FACT: A child's social interactive behavior ten years after kindergarten was identical to his social interactive behavior in kindergarten.
AUTHORITY:
   Source: Study
   Method: Investigative filming of kids over time
   Credentials: Excellent French TV documentary
   Access: R and J watched on TV
SUPPORT-STATEMENT: A child's interactive behavior ten years after kindergarten was identical to his social interactive behavior in kindergarten.
PRINCIPLE-OF-SUPPORT:
   IfPart: One's behavior is influenced by one's environment.
   ThenPart: One's behavior will change over time.
MAPPINGS:
   IfMappings: ((child, one)(aggressive nature, behavior))
   ThenMappings: ((child, one)(ten-year duration period from kindergarten, over time))

In addition to the context space types we have so far described, other discourse phenomena—such as descriptions, small talk, question and answer pairs—may ultimately be incorporated into context space structures for the purposes of discourse analysis. The limited set of context space types thus far characterized by and incorporated into the grammar, however, has been found to be adequate for describing a wide range of discourse forms.

Updating the Discourse Model

The context space system provides not only a static structural description of a discourse but also a way to model its active development. In chapters 6 and 7 we describe a computer program that specifies some of the actions required to generate the context space structures used in discourse processing and to identify their changing relations. Before describing the details of this processor, however, we can turn to a more precise description of the mechanisms described in the grammar which are used to assign and update the slot values of context space constructs.

We have indicated that in a discourse, various context space structures have differing influential status at different points. Further, as noted in our discussion of Grice's maxims, taking one option of discourse development—a particular conversational move—can preclude the later taking of previously available options and facilitate the taking of others. Our discourse grammar thus must characterize how the taking of particular options constrains later conversational development.

The primary means of reflecting such effects is in the values of the status slots of the context spaces. We can now provide an explicit description of what updatings accompany particular conversational moves. In each discussion we shall pay particular attention to the way the grammar characterizes reassignment of the status slot of the context space which is active immediately before the conversational move is taken.[3]

The Support Move

A support conversational move can either close a preceding context space or put it in a controlling status. If the preceding active context space, is a support context space, then the move closes this preceding support context space; if the preceding active context space is an issue context space, then the move puts this issue context space in a controlling status. These differences reflect the different discourse environments available for a support conversational move.[4]

In the following excerpt (cited earlier), F's brief narrative illustrates a support move:

F: 1. I'm starting to, you know, to get more insight
    2. about dreams. And, they're so revealing about
    3. where you're at. They really are.
    4. Like Susan and I spent an hour the other night
    5. just dissecting her dream.
C: 6. I know. I should write them down.
F: 7. And she wrote it down, and when I read it I
    8. saw new things into it. And, it was just so
    9. interesting. And it really reflected so much
   10. of where she's at in therapy and everything.

F begins by developing an issue context space in which the claim is that dreams are very revealing and that she has recently acquired insight into them. She then signals her shift onto a support context space for this preceding issue space with the clue word "like" and begins the narrative that describes her being able to dissect a girl-friend's dream.

The discourse effect of F's switching from a generic claim to a support of that claim is the reassignment of the status value of the context space containing the generic claim about dreams from active to controlling. This reflects that the forthcoming utterances are said in subordination to this preceding context space and is interpreted in relation to it.

In the genetics-environment debate of chapter 2, after D challenges R's support context space of R's preceding claim that a child's aggressive nature is not influenced by his environment (where the support was based on the fact that one child's behavior did not change from kindergarten to ten years later), R's succeeding conversational move is to accept D's challenge and to offer an alternative support for her initial claim. Before stating this alternative support, R signals that her succeeding utterances should be seen as fulfilling such a discourse role by saying the explicit shift words "Now another thing," "Oh, and it was twins," "The important thing was." Corresponding to the discourse effects of providing alternative support for a claim, a closed status is assigned to the initial support context space, and the replacement support statements are put into a new active support context space. The issue context space, which contains the initial claim being supported, remains in a controlling status.

The Restatement Move

As noted earlier, a restatement of the claim of an issue context space occurs after supportive evidence is given to the claim. Thus, right before such a conclusion statement, the issue context space being resumed is in a controlling status, and the preceding active context space is the last support context space developed for this issue context space. The restatement reinstantiates this controlling context space as the active context space and closes the previously active support context space.

In the genetics-environment debate, for example, R's utterance, "So you couldn't blame it on the child's home," follows her preceding support context space containing her statement of support that two children sharing the same home environment manifested radically different social behaviors. The clue word "So" signals (1) the close of this preceding support context space and (2) the reinstantiation of the issue context space that it supports as active.

The Interruption Move

Suspending discussion of a context space before completion results in an assignment of open to the status slot of the interrupted context space. A context space's status slot having such a value reflects that it is expected that the speaker will return and complete discussion of this interrupted context space after the digression has been completed.

The Return Move

The return move occurs in the context of a preceding interruption move. It is signaled by such clue words as "But anyway," "In any case," and the like, which signal the close of the digression context space and the reinstantiation of the open context space as active in the discourse context.

The Indirect Challenge Move

Since the purpose of the set of utterances constituting an indirect challenge is in direct conflict with the purpose of the set of utterances contained in the preceding active context space (i.e., the context space containing the claims about to be challenged), it is clear that the challenge utterances must be placed in a different context space. The invocation of this move therefore results in the creation of a new active context space in which these succeeding discourse utterances are placed. The status of the preceding active context space is reassigned a value of controlling, denoting that the claims about to be put forward are being said in direct relation (here argumentation) to the claims contained in this preceding active context space.

The Direct Challenge Move

The updating of the discourse environment here is identical with that performed in the indirect challenge case. The preceding active context space which is about to be challenged is put in a controlling status, and a new active context space is created to contain the challenge about to be given.

The Subargument Concession Move

Though the subargument concession and indirect challenge moves both have similar clue word signals, "All right, but" and "Yes, but," respectively, they are substantially different in argument form and result in different restructurings of the discourse context.

Thus, whereas a "Yes, but" move causes the current active context space, containing the opponent's preceding argument, to be put in a controlling status (reflecting the fact that the argument about to be put forward is still in some way a challenge of this preceding argument), the "All right, but" case causes this active context space to be assigned a closed status value. The closing of this context space reflects that having been accepted, the claims contained within it are no longer open to attack.

In place of this context space, a preceding issue context space, currently in a generating status, is reassigned as the controlling context space of the discourse environment. This reflects that the challenge about to be put forward, which will form the new active context space, is being developed in argumentation of, and hence subordination to, this preceding context space. A full discussion of this type of conversational move is presented in chapter 7.

The Prior Logical Abstraction Move

This move results in the dropping of one topic of discourse for another. Thus the preceding active context space is closed, and a new active context space is developed in which to place the succeeding utterances dealing with the new topic of discussion. We have seen illustration of this earlier when discussion of the force-feeding of a prisoner is dropped for discussion of the death penalty per se.

The Further-Development Move

Since a further-development move entails finer discussion of an element of a superordinate space, the superordinate space is given a controlling status assignment during discussion of the subordinate elaborative space.

Various conversational moves thus have standardized effects in the creation of new context spaces and the modification of the influential status of previous ones. It is in part their knowledge of these standardized effects that allows conversants to share compatible models of the current relevant discourse context as conversation proceeds.

We have thus far shown how the constituent components of discourse are identified and segmented into context space units, how their relations are established and inferred through the assigning of values to standard slots for holding values possible to different context space types, and how the relevant discourse context for a current utterance is established and, in the course of conversational development, continuously updated by the reassigning of status slot values. In the chapters to follow, we shall describe our discourse grammar and processor in more detail and illustrate its simulation of the active process of discourse generation and interpretation.

First, we will develop our theory of discourse further by looking at and analyzing some surface linguistic phenomena found in natural discourse.

Chapter 5
Surface Linguistic Phenomena

An adequate theory of discourse must be able not only to account for the selection and ordering of major discourse constituents but also to be predictive of surface linguistic phenomena that depend on structural aspects of discourse. An important feature of the context space analysis is its provision of a way to understand reference choice in ordinary conversation as governed by structure-dependent rules.

In the context space grammar, rules of reference are formulated using the conventionalized effects of a conversational move on the status of a relevant discourse context. It is the relevant discourse context at a given point in a conversation that governs whether a pronominal, nonpronominal, or "close" or "far" deictic-referring expression is warranted.

Theories of reference that are not based on an analysis of conversational speech lack predictive power because they ignore the integral relation between reference choice and a discourse structure. The choice of syntactic category for a reference (e.g., pronoun, deictic, name, description) is strongly governed by the thematic flow of a discourse. We will show, for example, that the many cases of nonpronominalization found in discourse are not simply the result of an option to pronominalize not being taken. According to our theory, and supported by the data, the option is nonexistent. Discourse analysis reveals that pronominalization and deictic choice is constrained quite differently than previously thought.

Our methodological approach to reference has been always to use data from naturally occurring conversation, since reference is intricately bound with our subconscious processing mechanisms for discourse. In general, then, investigation of when and where pronominalization is appropriate, in the absence of studying extended spontaneously generated discourse, is a hopeless endeavor. Utterances in violation of our discourse reference rules are not visibly "ungrammatical" like the starred sentences of sentential linguistics. One therefore cannot construct counterexamples and get a popular consensus that indeed the countercases are ungrammatical. Superficially the cases are quite grammatical. In fact, in many of the cases where a pronominal form is prohibited by the discourse rules, a speaker's use of a pronominal in any case probably would not cause listeners undue difficulty in correctly retrieving the referent intended (though Goodman 1984, in analyzing task-oriented dialogues, has been able to show that a number of referent miscommunications are a direct result of a speaker violating these discourse reference rules). On the other hand, their implicit understanding of the discourse structure, which they need in order to model adequately the discourse flow, would be confused. Choice of reference mode is an important means by which conversants signal to each other their private models of the current relevant discourse context in terms of which succeeding utterances are to be interpreted.

Another reason for the data gathering approach is that it enables us to see what people actually do in everyday conversations. In analyzing what they do, it becomes clear that their performance is not simply a degradation of some hypothetical competence model. There are too many patterns and standardized cases of nonpronominalization and deictic reference choice. The data says something about human cognitive processing, and it reflects an alternate set of rules under which people must be operating. The data cannot be ignored with a simple "But the speaker could have"; if in an ample corpus of relevant data speakers do not do the "could have," then something else must be going on.

A speaker's choice of referring expression involves much more than choosing an expression that will enable a listener identification of the referent involved. There are three equally important aspects to maxim-abiding reference: the listener must be able to determine the referent of the referring expression, this identification process should come "easily," and the listener must be able to integrate discussion of a given referent into the overall structure being developed in the discourse.

The Idea of Focus in Recent Theories of Reference

A major aspect of a conversant's discourse model is identification of those elements currently in the focus of attention. Focus plays a basic role in the context space grammar; not only are context spaces assigned varying foreground-background roles, but all individual entities referenced in a context space are assigned differential focus rankings—high, medium, low, zero focus. This corresponds to Kantor's notion of "activatedness" which is a continuum rather than an all or nothing phenomenon (Kantor 1977). These rankings are determined by the role of the entity with respect to its context space, and the role of this space in the rest of the conversation. Tracking the focus assignments of an entity during the development of discourse is fundamental to our discourse reference system. Specifically, intersentential pronominalization is reserved only for those entities in high focus.

A number of researchers have recognized the connection between focus and pronominalization.[1] Grimes (1978) has pointed out that in many languages other than English, speakers use different modes of reference to convey the different roles of elements in a discourse. He shows, for example, that in the Bacairi language of Brazil some pronouns are mainly used for a discourse element that is important to the overall global thematic topic of the discourse. Other pronominal forms are used for elements that are only important vis-à-vis a small section of a local discourse topic. In this same language deictic reference is also governed by the thematic structure of the discourse. For example, if a minor character of a story is a boy who is close by and a major character of the story is a woman who is physically far away, after initial introduction of these characters, a close deictic referring expression will be used for the woman, while a far deictic will be used for the boy.[2]

Chafe (1975, 1976) has used the notions of "foregrounding" and "consciousness" to elucidate constraints on pronominalization in discourse. Chafe claims, for example, that the terms "new" and "old" information are better thought of as "conscious" versus "nonconscious" information. "Given (or old) information is that knowledge which the speaker assumes to be in the consciousness of the addressee at the time of the utterance. So-called new information is what the speaker assumes he is introducing into the addressee's consciousness by what he says." Pronominalization "can be applied only to items that convey given information" (1976).

Kuno (1975, 1977) has also stressed pragmatic constraints on discourse pronominalization. The constraints he identifies are based on the constructs of "empathy" and "topic." "Empathy" is based on a speaker's psychological identification with a character under discussion. Kuno's topic rules, however, are discourse-context directed. For example, he presents the following example of topic (non)pronominalization:

17. I have three children: John, Jane, and Mary. John is not terribly bright, but among John, Jane, and Mary, he is the brightest.

18.   I have three children: Jane, John, and Mary. Jane is clearly
       the brightest.
  *Between John and Mary, he is the brighter.

Explaining why 17 is acceptable while 18 is not, Kuno states that
"While the first part of 17 establishes John as the discourse topic, that
of 18 does not" (1977).

Karmiloff-Smith (1979), studying the developmental aspects of discourse, had children spontaneously generate narratives from a set of
pictures. Her experiments conclusively show that a major aspect of
child language development is children's acquisition of sensitivity
to "intralinguistic cohesion." Karmiloff-Smith has evidenced that a
major aspect of this developmental growth is children learning to
limit their use of a pronominal form to refer to only the main character in a story—that is, "for the thematic subject of the narrative
which the child is now treating as a whole."

Chafe's notion of consciousness and Grimes's, Kuno's, and Karmiloff-Smith's notion of "thematic subject" stress the importance of
focus of attention in reference choice. For example, in the process of
comprehending a story, it is the story's central character (i.e., the
thematic subject) whose actions, motivations, and desires we usually
follow, and it is this character of the story, then, who is in our focus
of attention and may be referred to pronominally.[3]

Though some recognition has been given to the importance of
focus of attention for reference phenomena, many theorists do not
regard this as a discourse-dependent mechanism. Furthermore most
discussions of focus are limited to reference phenomena within a
single paragraph (or, more precisely, in our terms a single context
space). Our thesis stresses the strong interrelationship between reference choice and the structural *flow* of discourse: the dynamic shifts
in the current relevant discourse context over time. Many of the phenomena we shall observe occur coextensively with various types of
context space shifts.

At the level of discourse analysis the works of Linde, Grosz, and
Sidner are somewhat closer to the effort undertaken here. Both Linde
(1974) and Grosz (1977) studied task-oriented dialogues. In Linde's
work subjects were asked to describe their apartment layouts; in
Grosz's work they were asked to interact with an expert in the
building of a water pump. Both Linde and Grosz analyze the resulting discourses in terms of a partition of the utterances into related,
but distinct, discourse units. The relation between units in both
systems is "subpart," and the resulting dialogues were partitioned
into a tree of units and subunits. In Linde's system each room de-

scription is put into a separate unit; in Grosz's system each subtask of a task is put into a distinct unit. Linde's analysis demonstrated that in referencing an object from some other unit, speakers use the deictic "that" rather than the pronominal "it." Grosz demonstrated that in popping back to a controlling unit of some subunit, one can continue pronominalization to entities of the popped-back unit despite possible discussion of syntactic or semantic potential contenders for the pronominal reference in the subdiscussion.

The approaches of Linde and Grosz then strongly support the type of reference analysis being given here. The context space theory shares the notion of partitioning a discourse and interrelating discourse reference and discourse unitization. In our model, however, (1) partitioning does not correspond to some intrinsic partitioning of a particular domain of discussion, (2) a larger variety of suspension statuses and associated reference phenomena are delineated, (3) a large set of possible relationships between discourse units is specified, (4) elements within a given unit are differentiated along a focus level continuum, and this continuum differentiates between possible reference choices to elements within a same unit of discourse, and (5) nonpronominalization, rather than pronominalization, is the focal point of analysis.

An extensive work on the use of pronominalization for focused discourse elements in conversation is Sidner's (1979). As a conversation proceeds, Sidner's system keeps track of the various discourse elements that have been in focus during the course of interaction, and in the main, pronominalization is reserved for these high focused discourse elements. Sidner's focus rules, however, are mainly based on syntactic and semantic criteria; the context space's rules depend on discourse criteria as well. Additionally, given no syntactic or semantic ambiguity, Sidner's system allows for immediate repronominalization of old focus elements, whereas in the context space approach, as we shall see, old focus elements can only be repronominalized under certain strict discourse constraints. Finally, in Sidner's system high focus can be established by pronominal reference, whereas in the context space system high focus must be independently established.

The Context Space Theory of Reference

The concepts underlying the context space grammar are totally independent of reference; the rules of reference are dependent on the discourse structure that the grammar provides. This corresponds to the approaches taken by Kantor (1977) and Klappholz and Lockman

(1977; Lockman 1978). The grammar's rules for reference choice depend on (1) the current and preceding foreground-background status assignments to the context space in which the referent lies, (2) outstanding discourse expectations for the future discourse role of the referent's context space, (3) the referent's focus level within the context space, (4) the other potential referents in the current relevant discourse context, and (5) the discourse role being played by the utterance in which this referent is contained. These criteria are interwoven. For example, the status value of a context space often reflects what, if any, expectations have been created for the context space's future role in the discourse. Moreover the discourse role played by an utterance is derived from the conversational move it performs. This in turn dictates context space updating of status assignments. In the discussion that follows we shall explicate and exemplify further the operation of the grammar's reference choice rules.

Status Value of the Referent's Context Space
As delineated in chapter 4, there are seven possible status assignments a context space may have at any given point in the conversation:

1. Closed
2. Superseded
3. Generating
4. Open
5. Precontrol
6. Controlling
7. Active

For most purposes status values of closed and superseded are equivalent. They both signify that their respective context spaces play no role in the current discourse development and that there is no expectation that they will do so in the near future.

A generating context space, on the other hand, though not directly related to current discourse development, is indirectly related to it: (1) the resolution of the current discussion usually affects one's opinion of the claims or events described in this generating context space, and (2) it is expected that at some future point in time there may be a resumption of this generating context space.

An open context space similarly plays an indirect role in the current discourse development. This value reflects the discourse expectation that there will be immediate return to a discussion of the subject of this interrupted context space and that new topics of discourse will not be established prior to resumption.

Correspondingly a precontrol context space plays an indirect (but important) role in discourse development. Its role is comparable to that of an open context space in the strength of the expectation of resumption. Though, as noted earlier, there is usually some expectation of returning to a generating space (especially from subargumentation), in essence such returns are optional. Not returning to an open or precontrol context space, however, involves violation of maxim-abiding rules of discourse.

The controlling context space also plays a major role in the current discourse development because succeeding discourse utterances are generated and interpreted directly in terms of the utterances contained in the controlling context space. Reflecting this important role, all but one of the discourse grammar relational rules responsible for generating substantive discourse utterances describe high level thematic relationships between the utterances contained in the controlling context space and the context space currently being developed.

The active context space is in the foreground of discourse development, as it is in this space that utterances currently being generated are placed.

These status assignment distinctions are of great relevance to a conversant's choice of referring expression. For example, one rule of discourse reference is that pronouns can only be used to refer to discourse elements in high focus in the *foreground* of conversation. Tracking the active and controlling spaces delimits this foreground part of the conversation.

Olson (1970) notes that "words designate, signal, or specify an intended referent relative to the set of alternatives from which it must be differentiated." Olson made this generalization in relation to the physical surroundings of a given object to be referenced, but the same principle applies to discourse reference. We require criteria for delimiting the surrounding discourse objects that need to be differentiated from the one being referred to. This delimitation is provided by the context space's mechanisms for knowing where context space partitions lie. Thus, given that pronominalization can only be used for elements in the foreground of discussion, before using a pronominal form, one must simply ensure that there are no other high focus elements in the active and controlling context spaces that may be contending for this pronominal.[4]

The grammar's reference rules are quite simple:

R1. Only elements in high focus in a currently active or controlling context space may be referenced pronominally.

R2. Only elements in a currently active or controlling context space may be referenced by a close deictic referring expression.

R3. Full definite descriptions are needed to reference elements in a closed context space.

R4. Only far deictic or full descriptive referring expressions can be used to refer to elements of a generating context space.

Thus, to determine an appropriate reference form, the context space processor must track (1) the status assignments of preceding spaces and (2) the focus levels of entities within these spaces. In the next sections I present procedures for doing this.

Focus Level Assignments

In natural language we observe four major ways of referring to an object under discussion: pronominally, by name, by description, by implicit reference. The context space theory posits four possible levels of focus for a given entity corresponding to these four modes of reference:[5]

Mode	*Focus level*	*Example*
Pronominal	High	Your having called him up.
Name	Medium	Your having called Mark up.
Description	Low	Your having called your son up.
Implicit	Zero	Your having called.

At first glance it may seem surprising that the grammar associates a zero focus assignment with an entity referenced elliptically, since up until this point there seems to be a constant inverse relationship between the amount of description given in a reference and the referent's assigned focus level. The noncorrespondence here, however, only serves to emphasize the grammar's distinction between an element's "focus-interest level" and its "givenness." Clearly to reference maxim-abidingly something elliptically necessitates that the element be "known" and in "consciousness." However, this does not necessitate the element's being of importance to current discussion. If it were important, it would have been mentioned.

Further, in discussion continuing after an elliptical reference, one finds that when referencing this elliptical item, conversants do so by name or description, not by pronominalization. If the elliptically referenced element were brought into high focus by mere virtue of such a reference, then a conversant would immediately pronominalize her or his next reference to this element. That conversants do not do so supports the zero focus assignment to such elements.[6]

The discourse processor based on our grammar uses these correspondences to decide the appropriate reference choice for an entity under discussion. For pronominalization in particular, a speaker must establish independently the element's high focus level before using a pronominal form. An individual cannot simply cause an entity to be in high focus by referring pronominally to the entity. For example, if based on the discourse structure, element X is in high focus, then a speaker cannot use simply a pronoun to shift the focus onto an element Y, even where the pronominal reference to Y does not cause any semantic confusion between X and Y. Doing so would violate the discourse constraints and would cause confusion to the listener working within these same constraints. On the other hand, a speaker is free to choose between a descriptive term and name for some entity on first reference. This choice itself can reflect a differentiation in focus level assignment that need not be set up by other means.

Focus Level Assignments during Activation

When a context space is created, it is always assigned an active status assignment. As utterances get filled into this space, we associate initial focus level assignments to all semantic entities being talked about. In addition, during the time that a space is remaining active, some focus reassignments are possible. Rules F1–F13 cover both contingencies:

F1.   The entity referred to by the grammatical subject of an utterance is assigned a high focus level assignment.

F2.   The subject of a there-insertion clause is assigned a high focus level assignment.

F3.   The subject of a pseudocleft, cleft, or topicalized clause is assigned a high focus assignment.

F4.   All other entities accompanying the subject in the event or situation being described are as a unit put into high focus. However, members of this unit are subjected to special treatment. They are kept in the unit only as long as each succeeding utterance involves their participation. Thus this unit can be reduced or eliminated by each succeeding utterance.

F5.   A nonsubject referenced by name is assigned a medium focus level assignment.

F6. A nonsubject referenced by description (e.g., "her boy-friend") is assigned a low focus level assignment.

F7. Time and locative constituents are usually initially as-signed a low focus level assignment, unless otherwise war-ranted by a rule.

F8. Initial focus level assignments to entities in a digression context space, which were previously mentioned in the context space that this space interrupted, are carried over from the interrupted space.

F9. Initial focus level assignments to entities in a support or a challenge context space, which were previously mentioned in the issue context space being supported or challenged, are those that the entities had in the initiating space.

F10. Entities of an analogous context space are assigned the same focus level assignments as their correspondents in the initiating space of the analogy.

F11. An entity referenced by name after previous references by description is reassigned a high focus assignment.

F12. If an entity's high focus level assignment is usurped by an-other entity (i.e., by the other entity warranting a high focus level assignment due to one of the rules noted previ-ously), then the old high focus constituent is reassigned to a medium focus level.

F13. A constituent removed from high focus, by F12, must have its high focus status explicitly reinstantiated by one of the focus level rules.

In such a single rule system, we find different sorts of infor-mational criteria governing focus establishment. Rules F1–F3 are syntactically based, rule F4 is semantically based, rules F5–F7 are lexically based, and rules F8–F13 are discourse contextually based. This synthesis of information reflects some of the integrating features of language underlying our rule systems. (Rules F1–F4 correspond to Sidner's work on focus.)

Examples and Analysis during Activation

The following excerpts from spontaneous discourse illustrate the ef-ficacy of identifying rules R1–R4 and F1–F13 in modeling and pre-dicting certain contextually dependent surface linguistic referring expressions:

M: 1. And, so steam goes into the turbine. And, it goes in as
    2. very high pressure steam, comes out as very low pressure

3. steam, okay? And it goes into a thing called the condenser.
4. The condenser's job is to convert the steam into water,
5. okay? And, it's actually at a vacuum.

Notice that in line 4 M unpronominalizes his earlier pronominal references to the steam and that he references the condenser by name. Why does he do this? Certainly either the steam or the condenser, if not both, could have been referenced pronominally without any resulting semantic ambiguities.

The context space reference rules provide a formal system by which to describe M's behavior. By syntactic criteria we know that the steam is in high focus in lines 1–3 (it is the subject of all these utterances). From a semantic perspective we know this as well because the steam is the agent of the events described. The overall structural organization of the dialogue also supports the high focus assignment. M's organization is to give a piece by piece description of the parts of the steam plant in the order through which the steam passes: the steam generator, the turbine, and the condenser. In lines 1–3 M's focus is on the steam as he is tracing its path through the system.[7] Entrance of the steam into the condenser, however, ends this trace and the associated focus on the steam (see Reichman 1979, 1984).

In line 4 M turns his attention to the next part of the system, the condenser. M's internal semantic representation of his utterances in lines 4–5 probably has the condenser in high salience, as the utterance is about the condenser. However, though the condenser was just referenced in the earlier utterance, it is not yet available for pronominal reference: in terms of the discourse structure it has yet to be established in high focus. Making it the subject of the utterance establishes the high focus. Only after this establishment can the condenser be referenced pronominally—hence the nonpronominalization.

Similarly reference to the steam in line 4 cannot be via a pronominal. This results from dual effects of positioning the condenser as subject: not only is the condenser established in high focus (F1), but the preceding high focus status of the steam is removed (F12). The steam's high focus position has been usurped, and pronominalization is blocked (R1).

As a second illustration of the focus rules, consider the following piece of discourse taken from a conversation between friends. S, the speaker, has just recently broken up with her by friend, Albert, and on preceding turns of the talk she has described aspects of the breakup in full detail. At this point in the conversation, however, S turns the discussion away from the breakup to a discussion of her own general state of mind (resulting from her emotional makeup, the recent breakup, and other breakups in her life).

S: 1. I put everything, my feeling, in a total intellectual
2. basis. I said that—It's funny 'cause, by the way,
3. when I was thinking about Albert, I was thinking about
4. how I would think about Albert, years from now. You
5. know, look back upon it and what context Albert would
6. fit in my life.
7. And my gut phrase was, and I said, "And I decided that
8. history will really be kind to Albert."

Here again are instances of nonpronominalization that cannot be explained by ordinary measures of recency and potential semantic ambiguity—S's repetitive nonpronominalizations of Albert. In contrast to this section of talk, in preceding sections when S was describing the events of the breakup, she consistently used the pronominal "he" to refer to Albert. For an explanation of this striking contrast, we must refer to our focus level and reference rules.

The context space analysis of this dialogue is as follows: In line 1, S begins an issue context space wherein she brings up a generic proposition for discussion. In line 2, S is about to support her stated proposition by citing some event in the past. This shift in conversational move (from asserting to supporting), signalled by a shift from generic present to past tense, would cause the generic space to be reassigned in a controlling status and would cause the creation of a new active context space to hold the expected supporting event. However, S immediately interrupts her support move, indicated by a shift back to present tense and the clue words "By the way," and she digresses. The support space must be put on hold—assigned an open status assignment—and another new active space in which to hold the digressive utterances would be created.[8]

Notice that Albert is not mentioned in lines 1–2. Throughout the utterances in lines 3–7, Albert does not appear as the subject of an utterance or of a there-insertion, and he is not mentioned in a pseudocleft, cleft, or topicalized clause. Nor is Albert mentioned as an agent or experiencer of an event. Therefore, according to the grammar's focus-level assignment rules, Albert is not in high focus; he is not considered a thematic subject of discourse (as discussed before, it is rather S and her own emotional state), hence the predicted nonpronominalizations to Albert in all these utterances.

The next three excerpts demonstrate the effects of a shift in focus within the development of an active context space. They exemplify rules F12 and F13: once an entity A's high focus status is usurped by another entity B, A must have its high focus status reestablished before it again becomes available for a pronominalized reference (even if immediate repronominalization would not introduce any semantic or syntactic ambiguity).

Let us look first at an excerpt first presented, as a puzzle, in chapter 1:

P: 1. What happened, her boyfriend from Holland ["her" refers
    2. to a woman named Tammy]—they just left today as a
    3. matter of fact, but we've been spending the past couple
    4. of days together, no just evenings at home—and somehow
    5. they got into this discussion about Americans. And they
    6. were still doing it. And this—his name is Tom—and
    7. he said something, "Oh yeah, Americans are so open. The
    8. minute they meet you they tell you their whole life
    9. history." And I was getting very upset because despite
    10. everyone saying that—and even her own—Tammy's own
    11. saying, "Oh, who said that was right?" or "I wouldn't
    12. tell anyone what to do," they were sitting and
    13. categorizing people.

We can now understand the reference choices in the excerpt as follows: on line 1 Tom, Tammy's boyfriend, is in low focus. This low focus status is reflected in the speaker's use of Tammy as the ground by which to describe Tom (Kuno 1975). In line 6, P seems about to cite an event whose agent of action is Tammy's boyfriend. According to the grammar's rules, this would put Tom in high focus. However, the casual descriptor "this guy" reflects low focus. The utterance, if completed, would then have conveyed conflicting cues about Tom's discourse status: is he or is he not to be the current thematic subject? By specifying the boyfriend's name, the speaker subtly indicates that Tom is about to play a more important role in the discourse. Having established this, the speaker can then cite him as agent of some action not involving Tammy without sending conflicting messages about the current focus of discussion.

In the discourse grammar only one entity or a set of entities involved as a unit in some event may be in high focus at a time. Reserving pronominalization for a single high focus element or for the entities mentioned together in a preceding event, then, explains P's self-correction in line 10. In line 6 Tom has usurped Tammy's high focus role in the discourse. Tammy is not a part of the event in which Tom is main actor. She is therefore not part of a unit with Tom which would have allowed for her pronominalization (cf. F4). Thus P's initial repronominalization to Tammy violates the focus pronominalization constraint, hence the self-correction.

As a second example of focus level usurpation and accompanying nonpronominalization, consider the following naturally occurring dialogue:

G: 1. So I said, "Let me tell you about my chess game." And
2. he goes, "You don't do what I want you to do, so I'm
3. not interested in anything you do" ["he" refers to G's
4. father]. And so I said, "Oh," and we just hung up the
5. phone, you know. And then my mother called me back and
6. I didn't tell her I was angry. I didn't say anything,
7. but I guess she knew. She said, "Why'd you hang up?"
8. And I said, "I thought we had said our good nights."
9. Because sometimes she gets involved, and then she
10. becomes the victim, right? And I didn't want to have
11. that happen.

B: 12. This was between the two of you.

G: 13. Between me and my father, and I didn't want her to get
14. involved.

G initially focuses on her father and a disagreement that they had. Then in line 5 she switches her focus and discusses her mother's role in the interchange. As G's mother is subject and agent of the event being described, generation of this utterance results in G's mother replacing G's father in the high focus slot of the context space (F1, F12).[9] B's statement, however, indicates that she has not gone along with G's switch in focus and that she is continuing to focus on G's father and G's argument with him. This is strongly reflected in B's speech by her use of "this" to refer to the argument and her use of a pronominal reference, embedded in the plural personal pronoun "you," to refer to G's father.

Of current interest is G's response to B's statement. There is no apparent reason for G's explication of B's phrase, "between the two of you." The referents were clear to both B and G, as reflected by their nonquestioning intonation patterns for the respective phrases and G's continued talk without pause for a response from B. Why then the explication? Why the nonpronominal reference to her father?[10] The answers lie in the fact that G, unlike B, has shifted her focus of attention. Her father is then not available in her own discourse model for continued pronominalization. Her response strongly signals this shift to B, as does her continued pronominalization to her mother in line 13.

As the third example of focus level shifts, consider the following excerpt from M's descriptive explanation of the steam plant to A:

M: 1. And the condenser converts the low pressure steam now
    2. into water, okay?

A: 3. It uses sea water to do that?

M: 4. It uses sea water to do that. It has a pump in the sea
    5. water line, okay? It takes, um, water—And there are
    6. valves isolating it from the outside and it pumps the
    7. stuff around and pushes it over the side.

A: 8. Now, the sea water does not mix with the steam, is that
    9. correct?

M: 10. No, it does not.
   11. Do you want to talk about the internal workings of
   12. the condenser?

A: 13. Whatever you think is important. I just wanted to be
   14. clear on that.

M: 15. Okay. Essentially what it—the condenser—has, is . . .

Since the condenser is repeatedly referred to pronominally, why does M suddenly self-correct to the nominal form in line 15? Note that in lines 11–12 M suspends description of the plant system and questions A about subsequent thematic development of the discourse. The grammar has a separate path to generate such transitional utterances in which conversants question, describe, or predict continued development of the discourse. Transitional utterances are metastatements in that the conversation itself becomes an object of discussion within its own development. Metadiscussion results in a temporary suspension or reassignment of focus level assignments. Reassignment is appropriate here since agreement that the next topic be the internal workings of the condenser is not yet finalized. Therefore at the time of M's utterance in line 15 the condenser is no longer in high focus. Realizing this, M self-corrects his premature pronominal reference.

Focus Level Reassignment in Suspensions and the Consequences in Resumptions

Conversants often suspend discussion of a topic only to return to it later. In the grammar such resumption is reflected by reactivation of the context space containing the last discussion of the topic before the suspension. The grammar provides rules that delineate our maxim-abiding reference options, given a resumption of a suspended context space.

The context space grammar's action characterizations for suspending a context space include a number of bookkeeping tasks to update the discourse model. One such task is to reassign focus level assignments where appropriate. In general, there is a direct relation between the type of suspension involved—its import on the subsequent flow of discussion—and the nature of focus level reassignments. For each possible suspension status—precontrol, controlling, open, generating, closed, superseded—the grammar has focus level reassignment rules.

SH1. *Controlling—No Change to Focus Assignments* Putting an active context space into a controlling or precontrol status does not change its foreground status in the discourse context. As a result no focus reassignments are needed.

SH2. *Open—No Change to Focus Assignments* Interrupting and temporarily suspending completion of an active context space puts it into an open status. Figuratively this results in a "freeze storage" of the context space until it is resumed. Thus any current focus level assignments to its constituent elements are held constant, and the point of exposition remembered.

SH3. *Generating—High Focus Reassigned to Medium* Reassignment of an active or controlling context space to a generating status, on the other hand, entails suspending the space in a somewhat completed state, with only some slight possibility of its being returned to. In this case its high focus element is reassigned a medium focus assignment.

SH4. *Closed and Superseded—All Elements Reassigned to Zero Focus* Reassignment of an active, precontrol, controlling, or generating context space to a closed status entails suspension of the space in a completed state. Similarly reassignment to superseded signals the close of any further development of this space. In these cases the suspensions are total. There is no particular reason to expect resumption. Reflecting this, such shifts result in a removal of all elements from focus, which is reflected in their reassignment to a zero focus level.

We can use these rules of focus level reassignment that accompany a change in status assignment to predict the reference forms speakers will choose in different discourse situations. For example, we would expect that on reentrance to an open context space, we would have immediate continued pronominalization to an entity pronominalized before the digression. Similarly we would expect not to have such immediate pronominalization on reentrance to a closed context space. Such predictions are borne out in naturally occurring discourses.

Returning to an Open Context Space
Returning to an open context space is like going back in time to the exact discourse situation that we had before the interruption occurred. Therefore, before continuing development of the open context space, all context spaces established in the interim are closed (and using SH4, all of their constituent entities' focus level values are assigned to zero), and the status of preceding context spaces is set back to where it was before the interruption occurred. At the point of resumption, then, the only high focus elements in the current discourse context are those introduced prior to the point of digression (SH2, SH4). Immediate repronominalization on reentry to an interrupted (open) space is illustrated in the following dialogue, which we cited earlier in our discussion of the Return conversational move of chapter 3:

A: 1. I remember what happened in January. I went home and I,
    2. um, was with my cousin. He's my age, I've mentioned him
    3. before. We were in his apartment and um we were talking.
    4. I just casually asked how my mother was doing, 'cause I
    5. hadn't, you know, I wasn't involved. I didn't know what
    6. was happening. And he goes, "Oh, I think she's depressed."
    7. This is before she changed—She had this whole fiasco with
    8. a job. She never liked her position in her job, which was
    9. a big part of her stupid problem, that she never changed it.
    10. Oh, I didn't tell you, when I was home a couple of—
    11. about two months ago, I was really angry 'cause I know how
    12. much she's suffered 'cause she hasn't had a career, or feelings
    13. of inferiority. And, here I'm doing it and she's trying to
    14. stop me. And so, you know, I get so angry, and she was sitting
    15. and talking how important it is to have a career and to be able
    16. to do what you're doing. And I was just sitting in the living
    17. room dying, really getting angry. But I didn't say anything
    18. which I thought was progress, that I didn't say anything.
B: 19. Is it?
A: 20. Oh, it was progress, 'cause I used to get into stupid arguments
    21. and fights with them.
B: 22. But isn't it hard work to keep all that in?
A: 23. But it was better. Because I would get into arguments and
    24. it wouldn't help. What would I do? Just scream or say, "How
    25. could you say you want"—I would have had an argument.

B: 26. There might be something between an argument and saying
     nothing.
A: 27. Yeah, but that wasn't
B: 28. Not to feel like you're bursting your gut.
A: 29. Yeah. That wasn't even that bad, that was just a thing.
     30. But anyway, I went home in January, and he told me that she
     31. was upset.

Lines 1–9:   Context space C1, the interrupted space.

Lines 10–29: Context space C2, the digression space.

Lines 30–31: Context space C1, the return.

Notice A's use of the clue words, "But, anyway," to signal her
return to the interrupted context space and her subsequent immediate repronominalization to her cousin in line 30 of the excerpt.
This pronominal reference refers to a discourse entity who was last
mentioned in line 6. Its occurrence supports the claim that pronominalization is not governed by recency but by the discourse structure
and the appropriate updating of the relevant discourse context.

Returning to a Closed Context Space
As noted earlier, when a context space is suspended in a complete
state, it is assigned a closed status, and all contained entities are assigned zero focus levels. Using the discourse reference system, we
should find no immediate repronominalization on resumption of
such a space. The next dialogue shows this prediction being borne
out in natural discourse:

B: We could briefly discuss something, my mother—you see, I
    don't really want to because I don't really want to sit
    and talk about her here. You know, in a way I'm talking
    poorly of her, I guess.

    [*approximately thirty minutes of talk*]

B: I think in a way that's what she does to me, and I don't
    like it. So, I try not to do to her. ["she" refers to B's mother]

A: But, you said you have some feelings about bringing up this
    whole topic of what goes on between you and your mother.
    You said because it was negative?

Since there are no intervening elements competing for a "she"
pronominal, and B's mother was just referenced pronominally in B's
last utterance, we must ask ourselves why A felt the need to refer to
B's mother nonpronominally in her immediately following utterance.

An explanation can be found in thematic structural constraints operative in discourse pronominalization.

A's conversational move in the excerpt shifts the topic of discussion from how B interacts with her mother and returns it to B's earlier discussion of how she doesn't want to talk about her mother with A. The move, signaled by the clue word "But," is a respecification. Characterizations for this move include closing the currently active context space and all spaces developed in the interim from the specification of the context space being returned to. Closing a context space not only zeroes out all of its focus level assignments, it causes removal of the context space from one's reference frame for subsequent discourse engagement, so it is ignored in subsequent reference resolution. Hence the appearance of A's mother in this linearly preceding space is basically tangential to subsequent reference resolution.

The respecification move entails reactivation of a previously closed context space (i.e., one other than the one just closed). Since the context space rereferenced was in a closed status before this reactivation, by the time of A's reference, B's mother, an entity of this space, still has its zeroed-out focus level assignment, hence A's nonpronominalization to her.

Returning to a Controlling Context Space
The grammar's characterization of status reassignment for a suspended context space is governed by more than just the completion status of the space being suspended. Reassignment also depends on the relation between the to-be-suspended context space and the next space to be activated. In particular, the status reassignment depends on the type of conversational move being made. For example, an assertion followed by a support move results in the assertion space being reassigned to controlling. On the other hand, if followed by a return to some previously interrupted space, the assertion space is reassigned to closed.

The following excerpts exemplify the effects on status and focus level assignments of using an analogy in a discourse to make a conversational move. The excerpts illustrate how the context space system's functional analysis of discourse utterances allows it to determine the influential role of preceding context spaces on the subsequent discourse development. In turn the analysis is then able to predict speakers' reference form choices in the move to be performed.

We have said that the analogy method can be used in fulfillment of a number of different discourse roles, including explanation and support. Both of these moves result in the creation of subordinate spaces, leaving their respective counterparts in a controlling status. This is appropriate, since analogies entail only a local shift of topic and concepts under discussion; at a more global level the topic is not changed during analogy development.[11] In general, then, after discussion of an analogy (including supports of and challenges to it) we have immediate resumption of the initiating context space. Mirroring this, characterizations for a move performed by analogy include creation of the discourse expectation that the context space containing the initiating claim will be resumed after the analogy is completed.[12]

The analyses accompanying the excerpts indicate how the context space grammar accounts for the types of referring expressions speakers use on resumption of the initiating space of an analogy. It is also shown how these discourse occurrences support the claim that reference expression is dependent on (1) the current and preceding status assignments of the context spaces involved, (2) the focus level assignments of their contained entities, and (3) any discourse expectations associated with these context spaces. In the excerpt that follows, presented first in chapter 1, the analogy is used by an expert, G, to explain the workings of a proton accelerator to a layman, J:

G: 1. It's just a pure electrostatic field, which, between
     2. two points, and the proton accelerates through the
     3. electrostatic potential.

J: 4. Okay.

G: 5. Same physical law as if you drop a ball. It accelerates
     6. through a gravitational potential.

J: 7. Okay.

G: 8. And the only important point here is that the potential
     9. is maintained by this Cockcroft-Walton unit.

Lines 1–3: Context space C1, the initiating space.

Lines 5–6: Context space C2, the analogous space.

Lines 8–9: Context space C1, the resumption.

As noted in chapter 1, this excerpt contains surprising deictic references. On resumption of context space C1, the close deictic "here" is used to refer to C1, though in terms of linear order, context space C2, the explanation by analogy space, is the closer space. Also notice that G uses a close definite reference, "the potential," to refer to one of C1's elements (last mentioned in line 3) and that this occurs despite that in the interim, in line 6, G had referred to a "gravitational potential."[13]

Characterizations for an explanation include setting up the discourse expectation that after the explanation there will be a resumption of the main topic of discussion, and a reassignment of controlling to the status of the space to be explained. The expected resumption occurs in line 8. The resumption corresponds to executing the discourse expectation created when the explanation was begun. Updating actions associated with this discourse move serve (1) to close the subordinate explanation space and (2) to reinstantiate the initiating space of the explanation as active.

Since the grammar's rules for discourse pronominalization, type of deictic, and definite reference are determined by a context space's current status and focus level assignments, the close deictic reference to the initiating space and nonmodified reference to one of its elements (i.e., to "electrostatic potential") do not cause any semantic ambiguity. Such close deictic referring expressions could not be referring to elements of the closed analogous context space. Such references are appropriate for elements in the initiating space, since their focus level assignments were not changed at the time of controlling status reassignment.

As a further example of the effects of using analogy on discourse reference, consider the following excerpt from the genetics-environment debate of chapter 2:

R: 26. So, you couldn't blame it on the child's home.
D: 27. It has nothing to do with the child's home.
    28. It has to do with the child's environment.
R: 29. Right, but the two brothers have the same environment.
D: 30. They do not have the same environment.
R: 31. Why not?
D: 32. Because you and I are very close in this room right now,
    33. but we don't have the same environment.
    34. Because I'm looking at you, I'm seeing that window
    35. behind you. You're not seeing that window behind you.
    36. You are not looking at you. I am doing it.
    37. Two people can't be in exactly the same place at the
    38. same time, otherwise, they'd occupy the same space.
    39. They do not have the same environment.
    40. They don't have the same friends.
M: 41. And, I mean, they don't even—you know, to say that
    42. two kids come from the same family is really meaningless,
    43. because when you think of the difference in treatment

44. that two kids can get in exactly the same family, it's
45. incredible. You know, It's the difference between
46. night and day.

The first reference warranting analysis is D's immediate repronominalization ("they") of the "two brothers" in line 39, even though
they were last mentioned in line 30 and in the interim the pronominal "they" had been used to refer to "two people." In line 39 "they"
must refer to the two children of the study and not the hypothetical
two people discussed in lines 37–38, since the modality of this utterance is not hypothetical. Why then is the utterance maxim abiding? Why does it not cause a semantic ambiguity?

An answer requires an analysis of the excerpt in terms of the conversational moves performed and recognition of the effects of these
moves on the discourse context. In supporting his claim in line 30 (in
response to R's challenge in line 31), D begins by comparing the situation of the brothers to himself and R sitting in the room where they
are having their conversation—that is, he sets up an analogous claim
to the one just challenged. He supports this analogous claim in lines
34–36. Recall that performing a support move leaves the assertion
space to be supported in the foreground of conversation—the assertion space is assigned a controlling status. Since the initial support
is by analogy, there is still the expectation that D will later return to
the specific subject of the two twins, leaving discussion of himself
and R.

Line 37 begins the return to the initiating space of the analogy. The
return is via specification of the abstract principle validating the
point of the analogy—no two people, not D and R nor the two twins,
can ever be said to share the same environment. The effects of this
move are (1) to close the analogy support space and its supports
and (2) to begin a new active issue context space to hold the
generalization.

After generation of the abstract principle, the original assertion
space can be resumed, or some subordination to the new issue space
may follow. If the latter option is chosen, the discourse expectation
that the original assertion space will be resumed remains current.

After line 38 of the excerpt, where a support space for the abstract
claim is developed, the discourse expectation of resuming the initiating space of the support analogy is met. Therefore the abstract
principle space and its support space are closed, and the initiating
space of the analogy is reassigned an active status.

By the time the substantive remarks of line 39 are generated, the
initiating space is once again active, and all intervening spaces have

been closed. Since during intervening discussion the initiating space was always in a controlling or precontrol status, its focus assignments are the same as they were before the analogy. Therefore immediate pronominalization is viable.

Now, what about M's pronominalization to "the two brothers" in line 41 of the excerpt? D just referenced them pronominally. In terms of linear order and potentiality of semantic ambiguity there seems to be no reason for this nonpronominalization.

There are a number of different factors that may have led to M's initial pronominalization and later self-correction. One of these factors has to do with the fact that M's remarks are not a continuation of the context space developed by D on his preceding turn. M's move entails a return to an earlier point in the conversation. As discussed earlier, M is challenging R's earlier argument that since the two kids have the same home and exhibited radically different behavior, one could not blame a child's home for aggressive behavior. D accepted this argument, counterchallenging that there was still the environment outside the home to deal with. M, on the other hand, refused even to concede this point to R. In lines 41–46 she argues that differential treatment is quite possible in a home. Since R's preceding support argument about the home (lines 26 and previously), which M is now challenging, has already been given a closed status assignment by D's nonchallenge of it, M's reference to one of its constituents (two twins) must necessarily be nonpronominal, thus her self-correction.[14]

We have shown that the context space theory's structural analysis of discourse yields a single, coherent, and specifiable explanation for otherwise unexplainable instances of nonpronominalization and deictic reference choice in discourse. Nonpronominalization in discourse turns out not to be simply a matter of a speaker's not choosing an option to pronominalize; rather, it is a behavior required in specific contexts by conventionalized discourse rules.

Any system attempting to model conversants' reference forms in spontaneous discourse must be able to track the ongoing segmentation of a discourse into constituent context spaces brought in and out of the foreground of discussion. In addition this system must be able to differentiate between the different focus level assignments of elements within these spaces. The system must be capable of determining (1) initial focus level assignments, (2) shifts in focus level assignment during activation of a context space, and (3) shifts in focus level assignment due to suspension of a context space. The context space system described here has the characterizations needed to do such tracking of conversational moves and their associated effects.

Reference is thus a feature of conversation based on a set of discourse-specific constraints. These rules and the surface linguistic forms they generate provide us with a rich and subtle mechanism by which conversants can identify and track a coconversant's changing model of the underlying discourse structure.

Let's now look in some detail at the context space grammar and see how its characterizations support tracking the changing relevant discourse context as a conversation progresses.

Chapter 6

The Grammar: An Abstract Process Module

The context space theory does not simply provide a means of analyzing discourse constituents and structures as if a conversation were a static, finished product. Rather, the theory includes an abstract process module of the dynamic, ongoing process of discourse development. The module, a data-processing program, has been designed to act as a generator/interpreter of maxim-abiding, well-formed discourse. Its organizational design, data structures, and control structures have been selected to enable modeling of the many context-sensitive features of natural dialogues. In order to achieve this goal, the module must be capable of performing the following tasks:

1. Recognize and manipulate the formal structures constituting a discourse.
2. Reflect a conversation's structure and current status in terms of these constructs.
3. Represent the dynamic aspects of conversational speech (the way the taking of a single conversational move affects a current relevant discourse context and directs and constrains succeeding discourse development).

The Augmented Transition Network Paradigm

The context space grammar has been patterned after Augmented Transition Network (ATN) grammars (Woods 1970). In ATN systems grammar rules are represented by a network of "states" and "arcs," where states reflect the linguistic units developed or identified thus far and arcs reflect possible moves or transitions through the system. Consider the following simple network for a sentence grammar shown in figure 6.1 (Woods 1970).[1]

The network specifies the constituents and processes by which an English sentence can be generated or interpreted:

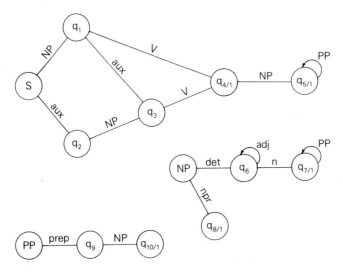

Figure 6.1   A sample transition network: S is the start state; q_4, q_5, q_7, q_8, and q_{10} are final states.

NP = noun phrase,
aux = auxiliary,
v   = verb,
det = determiner,
npr = noun,
PP = prepositional phrase,
adj = adjective,
S   = the start state
q_4, q_5, q_7, q_8, and q_{10} = final states.

In the figure notations are added along the arcs to show specific tests that must be met before a given transition may be taken to reach another state. For example, to go from the start state S to state q_1, we must successfully parse a noun phrase (NP). Notice that corresponding to the NP test on the arc between these two states, we have a separate NP state in the grammar that recognizes noun phrases (and specifies their possible subconstituents). The NP test along the arc creates what we call a "push" to the NP state. Meeting the NP test requires that we start at the NP state and transit the arcs in this part of the grammar, so that we end up in state q_7 or state q_8, either of which will "pop" us back to state q_1. At this point we have the subject of our sentence and can proceed through the other tests along succeeding arcs to determine the presence of other elements (e.g., a

verb) required for a sentence. Notice too that the network provides
for the fact that we have options in sentence development; for instance, auxiliaries, prepositional phrases, adjectives may or may not
occur before we reach a final state, that is, before we have generated
or parsed a complete sentence. Also "loops" in the diagram reflect
the fact that any number of the represented constituents may appear.

In addition to states and arcs ATNs have another important feature
called "registers." Not all tests along the arcs in a network require a
push to another state represented in the grammar. For transiting
some arcs, the only requirement is the testing of a register. A register
can contain information that must be available for a particular test
before a transition can be made along a path. Registers are thus used
as a means of passing values between the states of the ATN and as a
means of controlling transitions along its path. On any arc between
two states of the grammar, any number of register tests may be required to determine whether the current environment warrants or
requires such a transition. Say we wanted the network in figure 6.1
to be able to accept such sentences as "John was believed to be a
crook." We would have to begin by changing the network to allow q_4
to accept a past participle verb if the verb in the "Verb" register (i.e.,
the one put there as an action of the successful traversal of the arc
between states q_1 and q_4) is a "be" verb.

In sentence grammars the basic unit of analysis is the word, and
complete traversal of a sentence ATN such as the one in the figure
entails the production or interpretation of a single English sentence.
In the discourse grammar the unit of analysis is a context space, and
this may contain a set of utterances, a single utterance, or a portion of
one. Traversal of the discourse ATN entails the production or parsing
of a single conversational move. Arc tests specify the developmental
options available at any point in a discourse—what moves are viable
in the given discourse context. A complete discourse is facilitated by
many cycles through the different network paths.

All conversational moves have an associated set of tests and actions. The tests correspond to the requisite discourse environment
for the move to be appropriate. Actions correspond to the effects of
the conversational move on the discourse structure. A major effect is
to update the foreground-background status slot of preceding context
spaces. This standardization and correlation of effects and moves
enables the context space system to track the changing relevant discourse context as a conversation proceeds.

The specification of an ATN analysis for a particular sentence or
discourse is referred to as a "trace." A usual sentence ATN produces
a trace of an utterance's parse through the system, and the final out-

put indicates the utterance's underlying sentence structure. In sentence grammar traces frequently reflect surface syntactic forms (e.g., noun or verb phrase), and output structures represent an utterance's deep structure in terms of more thematic relations (e.g., subject/agent-predicate-object). In discourse grammar there are few such surface and deep structure distinctions. This stems from the fact that in discourse there is not much formal "surface structure;" the only useful description that can be produced by a discourse grammar is an underlying functional one. The traces of discourse we shall present annotate the network paths traversed in the generation or simulation of a conversation, and the outputs correspond to a deep structure representation of the discourse in terms of its context space constituents. (As we have seen the goal and contextual function slots of the context spaces designate their relations to other discourse context spaces and the status slot provides a running history of a space's varying conversational status at given points in the discourse.)

Thus in discourse grammar possible paths and states are all written in terms of functional discourse relations. For example, an issue context space is an independent constituent of the discourse grammar. Just as a noun phrase may serve different functional roles in a sentence (e.g., subject or object), an issue context space may serve the different functional roles of setting up a new topic of discourse, challenging a previously made claim, being an analogy to a previously made claim, and so on. For each functional role that an issue context space can serve, different paths leading to the creation of a new issue context space occur in the grammar. By the time the set of utterances constituting this space has been generated, its functionality has already been decided. This functionality is an integral part of the definition of the context space itself.

In addition to the fact that in discourse grammar both the trace and the final output reflect deep rather than surface structure, there is another important difference between the discourse and sentence ATNs. As we have discussed, taking a conversational move often places certain expectations and constraints on possible following conversational moves. Therefore, unlike in sentence grammars, on each entrance to the start state of the discourse network, we must have access to a history of previous passes through the network. In the ATN, register assignments set on preceding passes through the system, which indicate the current discourse state, are available on each new pass through it. This provides a system capable of handling extended discourse in which utterances of succeeding conversational moves are semantically and organizationally related to those of preceding moves.

Because of this distinction between discourse and sentence ATNs, we do not push for subconstituent building resulting from distinct conversational moves. Consequently we are prevented from falling into the quandary encountered by Bruce (1975) in his design of a natural language management system for setting up travel budgets. There the traditional ATN push approach was inadequate and noninsightful on two accounts: (1) traditional pushes would result in a system where not all pushes were accompanied by a following pop, and (2) preceding conversational development often places certain "priority ordered demands" on a coconversant. Usual ATN configurations leave no room for such dynamic changing aspects governing subconstituent development. To accommodate these features of discourse, Bruce suggested that "correct" discourse modeling requires a "demand model" in place of (or in addition to) a traditional ATN grammar. Our avoidance of pushing for successive moves and the availability in subsequent cycles of the Expectation and other register contents set on preceding moves solve the problem.

A final difference between sentence and discourse ATNs is that whereas sentence grammar generally takes transitions on the basis of a few fixed word categories, discourse grammar is much more sensitive to the logical relationships among successive utterances in the discourse than to their individual "kinds." Thus in our system transition tests really correspond to calls on other sophisticated subsystems of a full computerized natural language system. Such subsystems of course do not currently exist, though they are the center of much current research effort.

The following list briefly summarizes our module's use of ATN states, arcs, registers, and actions:

1. States represent the places where we test to see if the current discourse environment facilitates a given thematic development and where we push to subprocesses that must take place before the current conversational move can be continued or completed. Being in a given state roughly characterizes the decisions and actions performed thus far on a single conversational move.

2. Arcs represent the conversational moves available in a discourse or the component actions of such moves. Just as in sentence ATN's we have arcs for the successive constituents of a phrase, the discourse ATN provides arcs for the constituent utterances and decisions made in a discourse.

3. Registers are used for two purposes: they represent the basic elements (slots) of a "deep structure" analysis of conversa-

tional material, much as the registers used in a sentence ATN represent the basic constituents into which an utterance is broken down, and they are used to track dynamic aspects of the discourse (e.g., its focus) and to constrain the traversal of paths through the ATN at various points in the discourse. (The register contents often denote specifics of the preceding discourse environment and thus influence the appropriateness of subsequent conversational moves.)

4. Actions on arcs fall into two categories: they set registers and construct and update context space constructs, and they generate the clue words associated with a given conversational move and the substantive utterances filling its mode of development.

Register testing on arcs captures the context-sensitive relationships that govern utterances in a discourse. The register testing is comparable to that in sentence ATN's, where, for example, before accepting a past participle verb we first ensure that we have processed a "be" verb. In discourse grammar register testing plays a much more central role because at the discourse level we have less useful surface category information. In general, the discourse ATN's traversal tests are more complex than those found in sentence ATN's and usually entail testing of logical relationships between the utterances being generated and those of context spaces in a current relevant discourse context. The grammar's registers point to such currently relevant context spaces. (A description of these registers is provided later in this chapter.)

The "deep structure" constructed by the ATN processor includes (1) the discourse unit under discussion; (2) the preceding unit currently most influential in the discourse; (3) a list of current conversational expectations (e.g., interrupting a discourse unit before completion results in the expectation that the unit will be resumed after the digression); (4) any active domain constraints on the discourse context (e.g., in a debate, once a speaker concedes an argument as invalid, neither speaker can reuse this flawed argument in challenge to an opponent's claim); (5) a history of previously cited context space; (6) the relation of each of these context spaces to preceding discourse context spaces; and (7) the status and internal focus level assignments of all these spaces. We refer to this deep structure as a "discourse model." The discourse model therefore reflects a conversation's structured partitioning and development: all context spaces have links to their related preceding spaces and specification of the relation involved. We assume that just as our processor is building such a model of the discourse during its discourse processing, conversants in actual engagement build such models as well. Moreover we recognize that in discourse each participant may build a discourse model that is in conflict with that of a coconversant. The grammar as written does not directly address conflicts; it assumes that each participant follows the preceding speaker's conversational move, updating her or his discourse model appropriately. In this way the context space processor is able to simulate the conversation from the perspective of each speaker, building one discourse model as it goes along. To model conflicts, the grammar could be amended so that it provides for separate discourse models for each participant. The processor then would only update a given participant's discourse model retrospectively based on the participant's response to a previous speaker's conversational move. Alternatively, this grammar could be used as a constituent of a higher level module that could handle the fact that the grammar had two or more distinct parsings simultaneously. In any case the structural analysis captured by the grammar can already be used as a way to understand such conflicts (i.e., major elements of conflicts are participants having different status assignments for context spaces, different context space structuring of utterances, etc.).

Alternate Representations of the Discourse Grammar

ATN Representation

Figure 6.2 presents some of the grammar of the discourse module in an ATN representation.[2] Notice that on most arcs between states, there are tests that must be met before the corresponding state transition can be taken. In appendix 6A (at the end of this chapter) an explanation and specification of some of these tests are given.

States of the ATN are indicated in the diagram by circles. From any state in an ATN grammar one can either "push" or "go" to another state. If one pushes to another state, then on completion of that state, control is returned to the point immediately following the push action. If, on the other hand, a go is performed from one state to another, on completion of the second state, control is either passed on with another go or is returned to the point in the grammar where the last push occurred. In figure 6.2 a push action is represented on the arc; the state in the circle at the end of the arc is where control passes on return from the push.

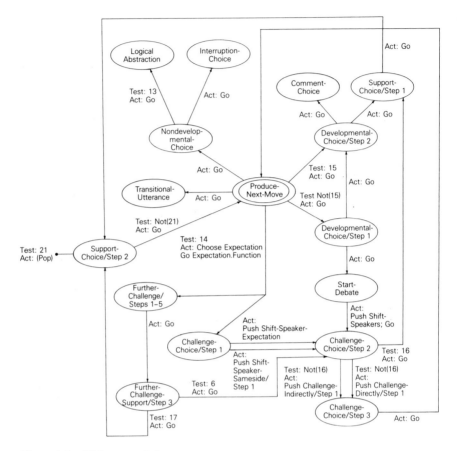

Figure 6.2   ATN representation

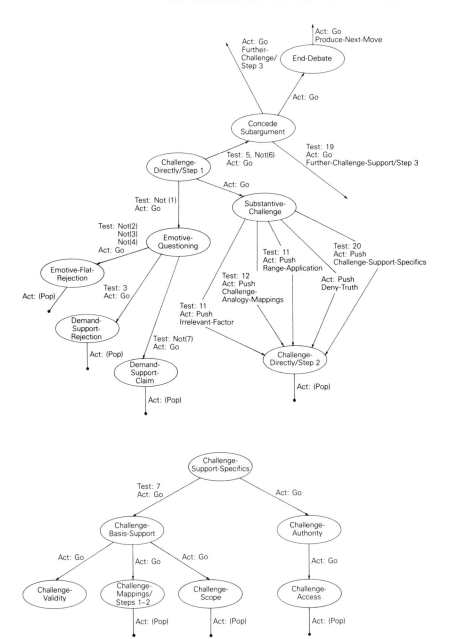

Figure 6.2, cont.

Program Representation

A small sample of the grammar is presented in a computerlike program in appendix 6B. It includes all actions associated with a given state transition, specified in terms of function or routine definitions. (There is a one-to-one correspondence between the states of the grammar and its functions.) The functions are written in a predicate calculuslike language. The language is composed of a number of primitive predicates (some procedural in nature, others logical or semantic) such as PUSH, GO, FOR SOME, NOT, NE (not equal), DENY, TRUE, INSTANCE, ENTAIL, AND INFER. All the rules of the grammar use these types of predicates, dummy variables (e.g., "I"), and the context space structures and registers of the system. Infix notation is used for multiargument predicates, with spaces delimiting the elements (e.g., Expectation APPEND Expectation-List), and should be read like English sentences; prefix notation is used for single-argument predicates (e.g., NOT(X)); the selection of a slot of a construct is indicated by "name of construct.name of slot" (e.g., Expectation.Context); and indexes are notated by { }'s (e.g., CCS. Counterclaims{I}).

There is a one-to-one correspondence between the ATN representation and the program. For example, the "Go X" and "Push X" statements in appendix 6B correspond to state transitions in figure 6.2 (i.e., "X" will appear as a state in the figure). Equivalently, all "Step" statements in appendix 6B represent some state of figure 6.2. For example, "Step 2" in the "Developmental-Choice" routine of appendix 6B corresponds to the "Developmental-Choice/Step 2" state of figure 6.2.

Step statements have been used in the grammar as a means of indicating automatic passing of control between the different parts of a routine. In other words, unless otherwise directed, after completion of Step I, control is automatically passed to Step I+1 of the routine. Routines have been broken down into steps as a means of conceptually distinguishing between different types of actions and showing the place of return after a push.

Discourse Modeling

The discourse system is written as a generator of conversations involving two or more speakers. To demonstrate and explain this system, we trace through paths in the ATN that would yield generation of a given piece of dialogue. At each point of simulation we have the computer taking the role of the current speaker, so, for example, if in a dialogue A and B speak, the computer will first play the role of A and then the role of B. The actions that the computer takes are supposed to correspond to the actions taken by A and B when they generated their utterances. For each conversational move being simulated, then, we have the computer finding a path through its ATN that, first, yields a category of conversational move, second, the conversant who will perform the move (i.e., a choice of next speaker— the last speaker may continue to hold the floor), and third, the paths to traverse for substantive utterance generation.

The discourse system can also be used in the interpretive process. Its major features of expectations, cues, and segmentation are common to both processes. With minor transformations it can be made a parser. For example, all calls on the grammar routines responsible for generation of substantive discourse, called the "Express" function, could be transformed into calls onto a corresponding routine responsible for the interpretation of discourse (e.g., "Interpret"). Then, where in the Express function it is stated that a pronominal form can be used for a set of specific entities, within the Interpret function it would be noted that pronominal references should be resolved in terms of this same of identified entities. Analogously, where a first action along the network path of a conversational move is saying some specific clue word, in the interpretive version of the grammar the first test along the taking of such an interpretive path would be the existence of such a clue word.

Updating the Discourse Model: The Registers

Discourse model updating is a major requirement of conversational engagement because the relevant discourse context to which succeeding utterances are generated and interpreted continually changes and because preceding conversational development can constrain and set up predictions for subsequent development. Each traversal through the grammar cycle represents the taking of a single conversational move, and since standardized effects are associated with all moves, the grammar, along its path for a given conversational move, has updating actions corresponding to such effects. On subsequent traversal these effects can be accessed, and this enables correct processing of the different dependencies between preceding and succeeding discourse utterances.

We assume that as a conversation progresses, each conversant builds a model of the dialogue. This model captures the underlying structure of the communication which includes the context space structure built so far, the current topic of discourse, the elements in focus within this topic, and the like. Our discourse system is written so that a computer can be a conversational participant. Intrinsic to the system, then, is having the computer build itself a model of the ongoing exchange. This model is created and updated by actions along the ATN paths. Major updating actions are (1) updating the status values of preceding context spaces, as illustrated in chapter 4, and (2) setting and updating discourse registers. We can now look in some detail at the various registers used by the system to record the effects of conversational moves on the discourse model.

We have said that ATNs use registers for passing values between states and blocking inappropriate arc transitions. On any arc between two states, any number of register tests may be made to determine whether the current context warrants or requires such a transition.

In the context space grammar extensive use is made of registers for transition testing. The grammar uses the same rules of generation over and over again, which it can do because its rules are written in terms of registers that are updated before each application of a rule. Context space and register values are set by conversational moves (i.e., by preceding passes through the system). Hence testing these constructs on subsequent cycles through the network can forestall conversational development that is inappropriate in light of the preceding development. Later we present pieces of discourse that show how transition of an arc (in performance of a conversational move) in violation of register tests leads to the production of uncooperative and often gibberish discourse. For the moment, however, without reference to any particular pieces of discourse, let us briefly review the major discourse registers used in the system.[3]

The Expectation Register
Taking a conversational move often sets predictions on the type of moves to follow—such as when a conversant's claim is challenged—it is usually expected that the challenged conversant will counter-challenge. A conversant's demand on another to support a claim is usually followed (in cooperative discourse) by the questioned conversant giving the requested support. Other examples of expected behavior include expected resumption of the initial subject of an interrupted context space; expected resumption of the subject that initiated an analogy; expected further challenging of an opponent's preceding claim in a debate. All such discourse expectations result from the taking of a particular type of conversational move. Along the grammar's path for each such move, then, the discourse processor appropriately sets up these discourse expectations. For example, along the grammar's path for a challenge move, the processor

sets up the discourse expectation that the challenged conversant will counterchallenge. In addition to setting up the expectation of a particular move to follow, a conversational move also sets up the expectation of who will perform this move and it cites the context space to which the move applies. The register used to create such discourse expectations is called the Expectation register, and it is defined in terms of four constituent parts:

1. *Function*   A state in the grammar which corresponds to a conversational move category.
2. *Speaker*   The conversational participant expected to carry out this discourse move.
3. *Context*   The context space that will most likely be active or controlling during the processing of this conversational move.
4. *Associated constraints*   The constraints that have to be met when this expectation is fulfilled, if any (e.g., in debate, not using a point already conceded).

The Expectation-List Register

Though a preceding conversational move often predicts a subsequent move, the prediction is not necessarily limited to one move, nor will the predicted move necessarily take place immediately (or even at all). For example, a challenge conversational move sets up both the predictions that the challenged conversant will respond with a counterchallenge and that the challenger will give further challenges beyond his or her initial challenge. After the antagonist's challenge move, either of these two predicted moves are feasible. Alternatively, a digression could take place, forestalling the challenged conversant's immediate response to the challenge.

Due to this range of possibilities, we must somewhere keep track of discourse expectations and delete them from record when they are no longer viable (e.g., ending a debate would result in the removal of all Challenge and Further-Challenge move predictions). The discourse register in which the grammar keeps a running history of discourse expectations that can be taken up at later points in time is called the Expectation-List register; this list sets up in sequential order all viable expectations in the current discourse context.

On each successive return to the start state, the grammar provides the option of choosing an outstanding discourse expectation. Choosing an expectation results in this expectation being deleted from the list of outstanding expectations (noted in the Expectation-List register) and put into the Expectation register. Control is then passed to the grammar state noted in the expectation (i.e., Expectation.Function), wherein further discourse model updating, as predicted by the information contained in the expectation, is performed (i.e., likely reassignment of next speaker to Expectation.Speaker, readjustments to the statuses of preceding context spaces, in particular resetting Expectation.Context to active or controlling). Specific examples and details of the processing of such expectations are presented in chapter 7.

The CCS Register
The CCS register points to the active context space in the current discourse environment, which is the context space under current (or last) discussion.

The Head-CCS Register
The Head-CCS points to the controlling context space in the current discourse environment (i.e., to the context space in direct relation to which the active context is being, or was, developed). Most of the grammar's rules of substantive utterance generation use the Head-CCS register. Thus, as long as the Head-CCS is appropriately updated by the time a rule is processed, the rule is applicable in any number of places in a given discourse.

The Discourse-Mode Register
The grammar at present distinguishes between two discourse modes: the discussion mode and the debate mode. The distinction is made because certain moves are more appropriate in one mode rather than in the other.

The Type-Further-Challenge Register
The Type-Further-Challenge register may take on one of three values: Challenge, Support, and Nil. A Nil value designates that the challenge being given is an initial challenge against a preceding context space; a non-nil value indicates that the challenge is a further challenge. Corresponding to the two options available for further challenge, the register can have one of two possible non-nil values: Support, where the challenge will take the form of giving replacement support for an earlier flawed supportive argument, or Challenge, where the challenge will be a new counterclaim or countersupport.

The Speaker Register
The Speaker register denotes the conversant whose conversational move is currently being processed.

The Participant-List Register
The Participant-List register contains the names of all the conversants of the discussion except the one currently holding the floor (i.e., except for the conversant named in the Speaker register). It is updated each time a new speaker is chosen.

The Sides Register
The Sides register contains lists of the participants on each side of an argument during a debate. The Sides register is continually updated and allows for participants to change sides and play, among other roles, the devil's advocate.

The Future-Defender Register
In the midst of a debate, before reassigning the Speaker register to an antagonist, we record the name of the conversant about to be challenged in the Future-Defender register. The processor can then set up the discourse expectation that this challenged conversant will respond with a counterchallenge.

The Domain-Constraints Register
This register contains all the points already conceded by conversants within an argument, to ensure that these "flawed" points are not re-used.

The * Register
The * register contains the value just returned from a pushed to routine.

The Analogous-Space Register
When the validity of an analogy is contested, this register contains the identifier of the analogous context space.

The Re-Enter Register
This register is used in reassignment of the status of a controlling context space. If it is set, the space is reassigned a precontrol status, else it is reassigned a generating status.

Flow Description for Discourse Processing

Organizational, Constructive, and Productive Routines
There are three major modes of processing performed in discourse generation: (1) finer and finer categorization of the type of message

to be generated, (2) updating our discourse mental models in preparation for generation of such remarks, and (3) actual production. Correspondingly, the grammar's states (via their associated actions on arcs) are of three types: (1) organizational, wherein tests and decisions are performed in finer categorization of the forthcoming conversational move category, (2) constructive, wherein the updating actions associated with a given move, which include register assignments and the creating and updating of context spaces, are performed, and (3) productive, wherein actions produce the message to be generated (or recognize it in recognition mode).

Organizational routines are high level, traffic directing. Constructive and productive routines can be considered low level, or the terminal stations to which traffic is directed: they can only be reached via transition of an organizational state. Organizational states first push to constructive states and only subsequently push to productive ones. In this manner any necessary updating of the discourse model is performed befor∂ a productive state is reached. This is needed because, as described, all productive actions are written in terms of a current relevant discourse context. This context usually must be updated before message formalization.

For example, a speaker's further argumentation after concession of a flawed subargument (as signaled by the speaker's clue words, "All right, but") usually entails a rechallenge of an opponent's preceding claim which led to the subargument just conceded. Before subsequent generation, then, the processor must update the relevant discourse context to have it reestablished to the context space being "popped" back to that contains the claim to be rechallenged. Pushing to a constructive state and then to the productive state wherein the message to be generated is formalized enables such context updating.[4]

Discourse Expectations

We have said that effective modeling of maxim-abiding discourse rests on recognizing that preceding thematic development usually constrains and sets up predictions for subsequent development, and that the grammar records all such predictions in its Expectation-List register. On each subsequent cycle through the transition network the processor usually begins in the grammar's start state (which is called "Produce-Next-Move"), whose five possible transitions correspond to the grammar's highest level characterization of different categories of conversational moves. One category is performing a predicted conversational move. The processor can determine (if desired) whether there are any outstanding discourse expectations by checking the Expectation-List register which contains the discourse expectations that have not yet been fulfilled or canceled due to intervening conversational moves. If there are such outstanding expectations, the processor can either choose to fulfill one of them, choice A, or it can choose to ignore the outstanding expectations by choosing another category of move, choices B–E.

When viewed as a generator, the processor's choice of one discourse expectation over others is totally random—that is, in its current stage of development there is no routine to call at this point to choose one expectation over another based on some criteria of recency, severity of expectation, and the like. In addition the processor's choosing or not choosing to follow a discourse expectation is entirely optional. Criteria of prominence and optionality will be added to the grammar at a later point in its development.[5] When viewed as a parser or simulator of existing dialogues, choices of course are dictated by the flow of discourse being analyzed.

When a discourse expectation is chosen, the expectation is taken out of the Expectation-List register and put into the Expectation register, and control is passed to the state predicted in the discourse expectation (i.e., the state specified in Expectation.Function). Currently the grammar provides discourse expectations for resuming an interrupted context space, returning to the initiating subject of an analogy (when mandated), further challenging an opponent's claim or support in a debate, and counterchallenging an opponent's challenge.

Discourse expectations carry along with them a lot of information: they cite a conversational move, the speaker expected to execute this conversational move, the conversational context in which this move is to be performed, and a list of associated constraints that the move will have to fulfill. Discourse expectations are one of the major means of tracking the effect of preceding discourse utterances on a conversation's ensuing flow.

Any routine reachable through a discourse expectation is inaccessible by other means. This is because the routines accessed through an expectation are all initial paths of conversational moves and would therefore only be accessible by some other choice in the Produce-Next-Move state or by an initial choice in the Developmental-Choice/Step 1 or Nondevelopmental-Choice/Step 1 states. If states accessible by a discourse expectation were also specified as explicit choices at these arc transitions, then the processor would be simultaneously choosing and rejecting a course of conversational development under identical conditions. Simultaneous acceptance and rejection does not seem a correct model of human performance.

When to Choose Next Speaker

Contrary to a common conception of a discourse grammar, this grammar does not characterize the beginning of a new conversational move with a choice of the next speaker. The grammar's organizational schema has been constructed in terms of those aspects of the preceding conversation felt to be most constraining on succeeding conversational moves. These aspects, in general, do not usually hinge on speaker shifts. For example, in discussion mode, independent of which conversant first introduced a particular issue (i.e., claim) into the discussion, it is equally likely for all conversants to agree with and support this issue. As a result first paths in the grammar have to do with deciding what type of conversational move can, and will be, executed rather than focusing on who will perform this move.

One goal in writing our grammar was to illustrate the steps involved in generating a piece of discourse. Thus we can take existing dialogues and hand simulate a trace through the grammar of its generation. To accommodate speaker shifts, therefore, we have a path in the grammar where speaker assignment is made. Since there are some conversational moves where it is felt that a particular conversant is more likely than another to be the executor, we could not choose a speaker at random without introducing complications into the grammar's design. For example, in debate mode a speaker will usually counterchallenge an opponent's claim rather than his or her own claim or a claim by a member of the same side. The grammar's state responsible for counterchallenges, currently only accessed via execution of a discourse expectation, is the Challenge-Choice/Step 1 state. Let's say that in its start state the processor begins by selecting person A as next speaker, and A is known to be on the same side of the argument as the last speaker, person B. For such a case the processor would somehow have to restrict its next transition so that it did not view going to the Challenge-Choice/Step 1 state (which would result in A's challenging B's statements) as a likely (or frequent) path to be followed.

Rather than complicating the grammar's design by having to direct the flow of control (i.e., possible transitions) in terms of those expectations that it has for a particular speaker, we delay immediate speaker selection and use the discourse expectation register as a means of facilitating such traffic dependencies. For example, whenever speaker C's claim is challenged by speaker D, the grammar specifies the construction of the discourse expectation that C will respond with a counterchallenge to D's challenge. By forestalling the choice of next speaker and beginning instead with the choice of a conversational move (e.g., executing a discourse expectation), the processor can then determine the most likely executor of this conversational move (i.e., by having the accessed routine use the expected speaker information contained in the discourse expectation).

This design choice of not beginning a conversational move with next speaker selection seems to be a good psychological model of actual discourse production. If we consider the point at which the processor chooses a next speaker as that point in time when a conversant actually decides to speak, then it seems most probable that by the time a conversant has made this decision, he or she has at least performed enough initial processing to have an idea in mind of what he or she will say. In other words, one would expect that conversants first consider their reaction to a previous speaker's statements (in the context of the discourse flow in general) and then, based on that reaction, decide whether or not they will perform a conversational move and if so what form it will take (e.g., getting back to a previously interrupted subject, agreeing with and therefore supporting the preceding speaker's statements, or not agreeing with and therefore challenging the preceding speaker's statements). It seems less likely that without any prior processing, conversants just decide that it is their turn to speak and "speak they will." The type of processing specified in the grammar before selection of a next speaker is precisely deciding on such high level conversational move decisions.[6]

Violation of Tests

For a transition to be appropriate in an ATN, tests along the transition arcs must be met. We shall now examine pieces of generated discourse that necessitate violation of some transition test. However, they seem incoherent, strange, and unresponsive to a preceding conversant's conversational move.

Let us consider a portion of the grammar characterizing direct challenges (Challenge-Directly/Step 1, see figure 6.2 and appendixes 6A and 6B). For each test along a transition arc, we present a short piece of dialogue in violation of the test.[7] All utterances (except those prefaced with a * or otherwise noted) are taken directly either from the genetics-environment debate excerpt presented earlier or sections of discourse preceding or succeeding this excerpt, which occurred in a natural conversation between friends. Test numbers used within the descriptions correspond to the numbering system used in figure 6.2 and appendix 6A. The '*' is used to indicate the unacceptability of the move taken.

Emotive-Flat Rejection

A response like "So what," "Big deal," or "That means nothing" constitutes an emotive-rejecting challenge. Used appropriately, it can be quite an effective form of attack and undermining of one's opponent, since a major point in argumentation is that your opponent recognize the impact of your statements on his or her preceding claim (Challenge-Directly/Step 1, choice A/1).

At times, however, this form of attack is inappropriate and, if used, would be either totally incoherent or, at best, could only be taken sarcastically. An example of dialogue in violation of a test is presented for each transition test accompanying this choice:

TEST 1. *Expecting Support of an Unsubstantiated Flat Rejection*

R: 1. Son of Sam killed a woman, right? By keeping him in
    2. jail—I know this is disgusting, but still—by keeping
    3. him in jail alive, that woman whose daughter was killed
    4. by this guy, she's paying her taxes to have this man
    5. fed. Why should she?

M: 6. Well, that doesn't impress me at all.

R: 7. Why not?

M: * So what?

M's move in line 6 is an Emotive-Flat-Rejection challenge. R's counterchallenge demands that M replace her unsubstantiated dismissal with a substantive challenge. Responding to such a demand with a "So what" is incoherent: assertions, not demands, warrant emotive flat rejection.

TEST 2. *After Denial of Truth*

D: 28. It has to do with the child's environment.

R: 29. Right, but the two brothers have the same environment.

D: 30. They do not have the same environment.

R: * So what.

A "So what" response, while undermining of an opponent's position, gives implicit acceptance to its truth. Given that the opponent's position directly denies one's own assertion, giving such implicit acceptance is self-contradictory. In addition an opponent's denial of the truth of one's claim is always undermining and relevant to one's position in an argument. Therefore countering such a challenge with a flat emotive response, at best, reflects some skewed reasoning process.

TEST 3. *After a Flat Rejection*

R: 1. Son of Sam killed a woman, right? By keeping him in
   2. jail—I know this is disgusting, but still—by keeping
   3. him in jail alive, that woman whose daughter was killed
   4. by this guy, she's paying her taxes to have this man
   5. fed. Why should she?

M: 6. Well, that doesn't impress me at all.

R: * So what.

To respond to an emotive or irrelevance rejection with an emotive flat rejection is at best sarcastic because in a debate it is clearly relevant if your opponent does not recognize the importance of your argument.

TEST 4. *After Apply Expansion*

R: 26. So you couldn't blame it on the child's home.

D: 27. It has nothing to do with the child's home.
   28. It has to do with the child's environment.

R: 29. Right, but the two brothers have the same environment.

D: * So what?

D's challenge in lines 27–28 is the extended form of an Irrelevance-Rejection challenge. In this form of challenge one first dismisses the scope of an opponent's claim (claiming that it is irrelevant to the subject of discussion), and then one specifies what one considers to be the actual scope of relevance. Having just claimed that the scope at issue is X, and an opponent argues that his or her claim supports such a scope, one cannot then dismiss the opponent's claim as irrelevant: the opponent has just addressed the issue that you yourself have claimed is relevant.

Demand Support Rejection
The appropriate context for a demand for support or a rejection is an opponent's preceding emotive rejection of one's claim. It entails one's generating a "why" question which is interpreted as a demand that the antagonist replace her or his preceding unsubstantiated dismissal with a substantive challenge (choice B).

As this form of challenge does not entail citation of any substantive assertion, its generation does not result in a shift in context space or reestablishment of a relevant discourse context.[8] Rather, it results in creating the discourse expectation that the addressed speaker will, on his or her next turn, provide such a substantive challenge (i.e., the Associated-Constraints slot of the counterchallenge expectation for the Future-Defender is set to Supply-Support-Rejection).

Given a preceding emotive flat rejection or the short form of an irrelevance rejection (i.e., CCS.Comment.Contextual-Function.Method = "Flat-Rejection"), this form of challenge is appropriate. Given an intervening demand for support of a flat rejection, it is not. The grammar therefore has two transition tests along this arc: (1) ensure that the antagonist has previously given an unsubstantiated dismissal of the protagonist's claim (by checking the method of the comment slot of CCS), and (2) ensure that there has been no intervening demand support (by checking the Expectation register). The following excerpt illustrates a violation of this second test.

TEST 1. *Expecting Support of an Unsubstantiated Flat Rejection*

R: 1. Son of Sam killed a woman, right? By keeping him in
    2. jail—I know this is disgusting, but still—by keeping
    3. him in jail alive, that woman whose daughter was killed
    4. by this guy, she's paying her taxes to have this man
    5. fed. Why should she?

M: 6. Well, that doesn't impress me at all.

R: 7. Why not?

M: * Why?

In line 6 M emotively flatly rejects the importance of R's argument. In line 7 R demands support for this emotive flat rejection. M's subsequent "why" response is highly irregular since a major aspect of the set of acknowledged rules governing informal debate is that conversants can demand opponents to support their claims and that opponents in turn answer such requests. To ask an opponent why he or she wants you to support your earlier stated position is a violation of this rule.

Argument Concession

Subargument concession can either entail total concession with an ending of all debate or only partial concession followed by one's "fixing" of a subargument. As noted earlier, the latter form of this move usually entails some discourse popping and a recursive transition to the challenge state of the grammar, wherein the speaker generates some replacement subargument by rechallenging (from another vantage point) an opponent's context space that has led to the lost subargument (choice D).

There are two constraints along this path: there must be something to concede at this point, and this must be an initial challenge of an opponent's argument. The excerpt that follows (not taken from actual discourse) illustrates a violation of the first of these constraints:

TEST 5. *After a Nonchallenge*

> SP1: It's a beautiful day today.
> SP2: Yeah, isn't it?
> SP1: * All right, but, X.

TEST 6. *Not a Further Challenge*

Further challenges come about from one of two reasons: preceding concession of a subargument, or a team member (or the same speaker) giving further argumentation against a prior claim that has led to current subargumentation (i.e., popping back to the context space that caused this yet nonconceded subargument and further attacking). Neither situation warrants subargument concession.

Case 1: Previous Concession
Previous concession means that we have reached this state on a recursive call to it after having popped the discourse environment and having already generated the clue words "All right, but." Clearly, if we've just come from this state with no intervening argumentation, a second transition of it is not warranted (i.e., we would inappropriately allow for double generation of the clue words "All right, but" and a popping of the discourse context).

Case 2: Joining Forces
The joining forces situation always entails a succession of argumentation by one side of the debate and corresponding discourse popping. It is facilitated by executing a Further-Challenge expectation, transition to the Further-Challenge/Step 1 state, wherein the processor pops its discourse model, and subsequent transition to the Challenge-Choice/Step 2 state. Subargument concession, which involves generation of the clue words "All right, but," always entails concession of an immediately previous argument, not one popped back to. The moves therefore are inconsistent with one another. In addition the immediately previous argument in this context is necessarily one of the current speaker's side, and one does not usually concede arguments to team members.

Modeling Discourse Engagement

The discourse module presented here illustrates how the context space ATN can be used in the generation and interpretation process of discourse engagement. In particular, we have briefly illustrated how the grammar's data structures and tracking characterizations of the effects of preceding conversational moves enable it to constrain inappropriate conversational development, predict and execute most likely forms of subsequent development, and formalize messages to be generated in fulfillment of a given type of discourse function. The effects characterized by the grammar include, among other things, an explication of the implicit components of conversational moves. It is in terms of such explicated components that the grammar is able to formalize the connection between subsequent and preceding discourse utterances.

Appendix 6A: Some Transition Tests

1. Expecting Support of an Unsubstantiated Flat Rejection

Discourse expectation predicts that the antagonist will actually engage into the validity of the protagonist's position. This expectation results from a protagonist's demand that the antagonist back up his or her preceding emotive flat rejection or irrelevance rejection of the protagonist's earlier argument.

Expectation.Associated-Constraints = "Supply-Support-Rejection"

2. After Denial of Truth

The speaker is counterchallenging an opponent's preceding challenge of the truth of the current speaker's preceding claim.

For Some I, CCS.Contextual-Function.Method{I}
    = "Deny-Truth"

3. After Unsubstantiated Flat Rejection

Current speaker is counterchallenging a "So what" or "The X which you speak of has nothing to do with anything" type of challenge.

CCS.Comment.Contextual-Function.Method = "Flat-Rejection"

4. After Apply-Expansion

The speaker is counterchallenging an opponent's claim that her or his argument does support the scope of relevance claimed by the speaker.

For Some I, CCS.Contextual-Function.Method{I}
    = "Apply-Expansion"

5. After a Preceding Challenge

The speaker is responding to a previous challenge, i.e., is counterchallenging.

CCS.Goal = "Challenge"
Or (CCS.Goal = "Fix-Claim"
    And For Some I,

CCS.Contextual-Function.Corelator{I}.Goal
   = "Challenge")
Or (CCS.Goal = "Support"
   And (HEAD-CCS.Goal = "Challenge"
   Or
   (HEAD-CCS.Goal = "Fix-Claim"
   And For Some I,
   HEAD-CCS.Contextual-Function.Corelator{I}.Goal
     = "Challenge"))))

6. Further-Challenge

This is a second challenge to an opponent's claim, where this second challenge may have been immediately preceded by clue words like "All right, but," i.e., a subargument concession.

Type-Further-Challenge = "Challenge"

Appendix 6B: Program Representation

Produce-Next-Move

Choose(A: If Not(Expectation-List = Nil)
        Then Expectation <- Choosed(Expectation-List)
        Go Expectation.Function

    B: If Discourse-Mode NE "Debate"
      Then Go Developmental-Choice/Step 1

    C: If Discourse-Mode = "Debate"
      Then Go Developmental-Choice/Step 2

    D: Go Nondevelopmental-Choice

    E. Go Transitional-Utterance)

Developmental-Choice/Step 1:

Choose(A: Go Start-Debate/Step 1
    B: Go Step 2)

Step 2:

Choose(A: Go Further-Development-Choice
    B: Go Support-Choice/Step 1
    C: Go Generalization-Choice
    D: Go Negative/Positive-Evaluative-Choice
    E: Go Explain-Choice
    F: Go Question-Choice
    G: Go Comment Choice)

Challenge-Directly/Step 1:

Choose(A: If Not(Expectation.Associated-Constraints
              = "Supply-Support-Rejection")
          AND
          Not(For Some I, CCS.Contextual-Function.Method{I}
              = "Deny-Truth")
          AND
          Not(CCS.Comment.Contextual-Function.Method
              = "Flat-Rejection")
          AND
          Not(For Some I, CCS.Contextual-Function.Method{I}
              = "Apply-Expansion")
          Then Choose(1: Go Emotive-Flat-Rejection
                      2: Push Irrelevance-Rejection
                          If * EQ Nil THEN (POP))

       B: If Not(Expectation.Associated-Constraints
              = "Supply-Support-Rejection")
          AND
          CCS.Comment.Contextual-Function.Method
              = "Flat-Rejection"
          Then Go Demand-Support-Rejection

       C: If Not(Expectation.Associated-Constraints
              = "Supply-Support-Rejection")
          AND
          Not(CCS.Comment.Contextual-Function.Method
              = "Flat-Rejection")
          AND
          (CCS.Goal NE "Support"
          Or
          CCS.Support-Fact =Nil
          Or
          CCS.SupportCS = Nil
          Or
          CCS.SupportCS.Support-Fact = Nil)
          Then Go Demand-Support-Claim

       D: If Type-Further-Challenge EQ Nil
          AND
          (CCS.Goal = "Challenge"
          Or
          (CCS.Goal = "Fix-Claim"
          And

For Some I,
CCS.Contextual-Function.Corelator{I}.Goal
    = "Challenge")
Or
(CCS.Goal = "Support"
And
(HEAD-CCS.Goal = "Challenge"
Or
(HEAD-CCS.Goal = "Fix-Claim"
And
For Some I,
HEAD-CCS.Contextual-Function.Corelator{I}.Goal
    = "Challenge"))))
Then Go Concede-Subargument
    .
    .
    .

Chapter 7
Context Space Suspensions and Resumptions

We began our analysis of spontaneous discourse with the observation that a major feature of such discourse is topic suspension and resumption. This feature initially presented a puzzle: how do conversants follow each other through these kinds of topic shifts? We have presented a mechanism that accomplishes this task. Fundamental to the mechanism is the view that discourse utterances are hierarchically structured into a set of formally related context spaces and that, as a conversation progresses, one updates the influential status of these spaces to reflect shifts in the currently relevant discourse context. Using this schematization, our context space processor is able to support the conversational phenomenon of a "discourse pop": the resumption of a preceding section of discourse—a return to a context space—not under current discussion.

Some context space resumptions can be predicted by a grammar; other resumptions seem less predictable. In the latter class we must include such conversational moves as returning to a closed context space. When a context space is closed, current discourse is not generated or interpreted in terms of it, and we have no specific reason to think it will be returned to. To resume a closed context space, in fact a speaker usually prefaces his or her resumption with some explicit indication like "Getting back to what I told you about X, I should also really tell you Y." In contrast, for more predictable resumptions usually no such explicit shifting mechanisms are used; rather, a speaker will simply say something like "But anyway, Y." To accommodate "unexpected" returns, the grammar includes a "transitional-utterance" state. The more expected types of resumption are facilitated by the grammar's specification of discourse expectations for them.

The Abstract Process Module

In the following discussion, we shall describe and illustrate in some detail the grammar's characterization of one type of expected resumption: the resumption of a context space that has generated some subargument. Our description of the characterization will detail each ATN state that has to be traversed in this type of resumption. The description will include the tests and actions performed in the transitions through these states.

We have chosen to describe this particular aspect of the system because a major function of the discourse module is to track the changing relevant discourse context as a conversation progresses. A subargument discourse pop often involves a large amount of context reidentification. It should therefore give the reader a better feel for the mechanics of our system.

As stated in the introduction, in a fully computerized system our module would be only one of a number of other language modules. Our module's main tasks are first to track the changing discourse context and then to specify a set of high level semantic and/or logical constraints that a surface form has to meet in order to fill a certain discourse role at a given point in the conversation. These constraints should be seen as system calls onto other hypothesized modules of a language system. We have not implemented our system, and no actual function calls are made. In the description then we will simply try to point out when and where such calls would be made.

Similarly, we have written the system as a one-person show—everyone builds the same discourse model, and we assume that speakers and listeners perform analogous updating actions. Therefore to stimulate, for example, generation of a particular piece of existing dialogue, the module plays the role of that conversational speaker choosing him or herself as speaker and making the same choices that that person would have made at that point in the dialogue. Again the system is not implemented, and really no choices are being made. We are only describing the choices, relative to the grammar, that would have been made had the discourse actually been generated.

Resumption after a Subargument

During argumentation all context spaces not under current discussion that are a part of the debate and have not yet been conceded have a generating status. Depending on the flow of debate, a speaker may wish to return to one of these preceding spaces. When such a return occurs, resumption is not limited to literal continuation of the context space being returned to, as it is so limited in resumption of an open (interrupted) context space. Rather, as noted in our discussion of the Concede-Subargument conversational move in chapter

6, such a return may entail giving an additional counterclaim to the claim of the subargument generator context space, or it may entail giving further support to a previously stated counterclaim. Returning from a subargument can be prompted by a conversant's acceptance of defeat in the subargument, or it may occur by a team member's joining in attack of the claim of the context space that generated the subargument. M's conversational move in the genetics-environment excerpt illustrates this latter form of resumption:

R: 23. Oh, it was twins. The important thing was that
    24. there were two children from the same environment,
    25. whereas only one of the brothers acted that way.
    26. So, you couldn't blame it on the child's home.

D: 27. It has nothing to do with the child's home.
    28. It has to do with the child's environment.

R: 29. Right, but the two brothers have the same environment.

D: 30. They do not have the same environment.

R: 31. Why not?

D: 32. Because you and I are very close in this room right now,
    33. but we don't have the same environment.
    34. Because I'm looking at you, I'm seeing that window
    35. behind you. You're not seeing that window behind you.
    36. You are not looking at you. I am doing it.
    37. Two people can't be in exactly the same place at the
    38. same time, otherwise, they'd occupy the same space.
    39. They do not have the same environment.
    40. They don't have the same friends.

M: 41. And, I mean, they don't even—you know, to say that
    42. two kids come from the same family is really meaningless,
    43. because when you think of the difference in treatment
    44. that two kids can get in exactly the same family, it's
    45. incredible. You know, it's the difference between
    46. night and day.

Context space C6: Lines 23–25, supporting context space of C7.
Context space C7: Line 26, generator of subargumentation.
Context spaces C8–C16: Subargumentation context spaces.
Context space C17: Lines 41–46, further challenge of C7 via attack on C6.

Corresponding to our two forms of subargument termination (i.e., case 1: preceding concession of subargument; case 2: joining forces with a team member), we have different discourse environments preceding the resumptions. Simulation of the different cases are realized by different updating procedures as described shortly.

Conceding a Subargument

After acceptance of an opponent's challenge, a conversant can either end all further debate (i.e., total concession), or he or she can continue the debate by beginning a new subargument. For example, two forms available for the new subargument are a replacement claim for a claim just conceded and, if what was conceded as flawed was support of a claim, the claim can be salvaged by offering some replacement support of it. This latter type of resumption is illustrated in the fabricated dialogue given next:

A: 1. I resent that portion of our species that is not female.
B: 2. Why?
A: 3. Because, they're such bastards.
B: 4. They are not.
A: 5. All right, but you must admit that they're emotionally
    6. underdeveloped.

Lines 1–5 can be partitioned into the following discourse structure:

C1: Line 1, initial claim.
C2: Line 3, support of claim in C1.
C3: Line 4, challenge of C1 via attack on C2.
C4: Line 5, acceptance of C3 and alternative support of C1.

B's challenge of A's support for her attitude toward men is accepted by A. After the acceptance, A can either give up on her initial claim, or she can provide alternative support for it. A chooses the latter option and in line 5 begins a new support context space in which she gives a replacement support for her earlier support context space, C2. The following actions in the grammar would enable the context space processor to simulate generation of this predictable conversational move:

1. Any time a conversant's position is challenged, the processor sets up an expectation that this conversant will respond to the challenge with a counterchallenge.
2. Choosing a counterchallenge expectation results in a transition to the challenge organizational state, wherein a finer characterization of the form of challenge to be generated is decided.
3. Subargument concession is one possible subcategorization of a counterchallenge move.
4. In subargument concession a speaker first concedes the challenge by generating clue words like "All right"/"Okay" and

then may indicate further argumentation with generation of the clue word "But."

5. One mode of further argumentation is to cite replacement support for a flawed previous support.

Conceding a subargument but continuing debate necessarily entails "popping back" to one of the context spaces that generated the subargument. Once an argument is conceded as flawed, the context space in which it is contained is no longer directly influential on the succeeding discourse. Additionally the context space containing the opponent's accepted challenge is also of no further relevance to the discourse: the protagonist of the challenge has no need to support it further, and the antagonist has relinquished the option of counterchallenging it. Instead, a currently nonactive context space, of which the argument conceded is a subargument, becomes directly relevant to continuing discussion. This necessitates updating the discourse model to reflect reestablishment of a relevant discourse context. Specifically we want to preclude utterances being interpreted in direct relation to the preceding accepted challenge or flawed argument context spaces.

Discourse register contents and context space status value assignments are used to identify a relevant discourse context. Therefore reestablishment of a relevant discourse context corresponds to updating these discourse constructs. In the case of subargument popping this entails (1) reassigning to controlling the status value of the resumed generating context space, (2) reassigning the Head-CCS register to point to this resumed space, (3) closing the conceded challenge and flawed context spaces, (4) removing any outstanding discourse expectations involving these spaces, (5) creating a new active context space to hold the forthcoming replacement argument, (6) reassigning the CCS register to point to this new space, and (7) updating the Domain-Constraints register so that the same "mistakes" are not made again.

These actions are all internal to the context space module. In the case of the fabricated excerpt, by line 5, CCS would be pointing to B's challenge context space, C3, and Head-CCS would be pointing to A's support context space just challenged, C2. By A's acceptance of B's challenge, we know that A's succeeding statements will not be related to either of these two context spaces. In fact as her new context space, C4, contains replacement support statements for C1, the Head-CCS register should be pointing to C1 by the time the substantive remarks of C4 are generated (and CCS obviously should be pointing to C4). In addition the status assignments of both context spaces C2 and C3 should be reassigned to closed, and the discourse expectation that A will further challenge B's challenge should be deleted from the Expectation-List register. These last two actions reflect that context spaces C2 and C3 play no further role in the succeeding discourse (unless they are explicitly reentered). Also we need to add onto the Domain-Constraints register the accepted proposition that nonfemale humans are not bastards.

Thus, when a speaker simultaneously concedes a subargument and indicates continued argumentation (i.e., by the generation of such clue words as "All right"/"Okay," "But"), the processor immediately closes the current active context space containing the opponent's accepted challenge. In addition, if the just closed context space is a support space, then the context space that it supports, being pointed to by the Head-CCS register, is closed at this point as well.[1] This reflects that one's acceptance of an opponent's support statements entails acceptance of the claim being supported as well.

We also will want to close the conceding conversant's flawed context space and reinstantiate as controlling the context space being resumed. However, the processor must perform some further analysis of this flawed space to identify the context space to which it is most likely being returned. In particular, it has different likelihoods as to which preceding space will be reinstantiated based on whether the flawed space is a support or an issue context space.

A's acceptance that not all men are bastards illustrates a conversant's acceptance of a challenge to a support context space. After such concession a conversant has one of two options: salvage the claim meant to be supported by offering alternative support for it, or concede the invalidity of the claim as well. The first alternative corresponds to that chosen by A. The processor's actions for such a situation are quite simple:

1. The rejected support space is reinstantiated as the active context space with CCS pointing to it.
2. Head-CCS is set to point to the rejected space's controlling context space (i.e., the context space containing the claim this space was to support).
3. The Type-Further-Challenge register is set to Support.
4. Transition is made to the Further-Challenge-Support/Step 3 state of the grammar, which will characterize some aspects of the forthcoming replacement support.

The Further-Challenge-Support/Step 3 organizational state is reached when (1) multiple supports are given in succession to a single preceding issue space, (2) an immediately preceding flawed support context space is replaced, or (3) a subargument replacement occurs after some extensive discourse popping has been performed. For the first two cases a "carry-over" of some components of the immediately preceding support space is facilitated (e.g., reliance on a same authority for the subsequent support). After setting registers to denote any such carry-over, actions are executed to close the last support space given and to reinstantiate the issue space which will be further supported as the active context space in the discourse model. Control then passes to the Support-Choice/Step 2 state, which expects such a configuration. This state will create a new support context space and will begin to subcategorize the forthcoming replacement support move.

Sometimes, however, a conversant is forced to concede as flawed not only a particular support of a claim but a claim in its entirety (or the speaker may just feel the claim not worth further defending). Let's call the space in which such a claim lies debative-issue space C3.[2] Now, given that a conversant concedes as invalid the claim of a debative-issue context space and yet continues to debate (as reflected by the conversant's use of the clue word "But" after the concession), this issue space, C3, must have been developed in challenge to an opponent's preceding debative-issue context space. The flawed issue space, C3, fills the counterclaims or countersupports slot of this preceding debative-issue context space, which we shall call C2.

As the current speaker has just accepted that his or her own argument in C3, against the opponent's argument in C2, is invalid, the speaker can now either offer an alternative argument against C2 (i.e., not yet concede the validity of C2) or, if C2 was developed in challenge of a preceding debative-issue context space, C1 (developed by the speaker or a team member), the speaker can instead yield on C2 as well and pop back even higher in the debate structure to "fix-up" his or her side's earlier argument in C1. At this point the conversant can pop as high up in the debate structure as he or she wishes, giving either alternative support (if appropriate) for one of his or her own preceding claims that is currently in jeopardy (as he or she has lost a subargument generating from it) or a new counterclaim or countersupport.[3]

The context space processor handles any of these options (i.e., the current speaker's next move of offering some replacement counterclaim or countersupport for a previously given counterclaim or countersupport, or offering alternative support for one of these preceding claims) with a single mechanism: it uses a yet unfulfilled discourse expectation that the conceding conversant (or team member) will further challenge a context space against which he or she or a team member earlier argued. (At the grammar's highest level of abstraction it treats replacement supports as further challenges.) At this point then the processor simply chooses such a discourse expectation from its Expectation-List register, and it passes control to Expectation.Function which is the Further-Challenge state in the discourse grammar.[4]

First steps of this routine of subargument fixing include an analysis of the context space to be further challenged, in order to establish whether a replacement support for one of its counterclaims or countersupports is warranted or whether the only option available at this point is a replacement counterclaim or countersupport.[5] If both options are available, a separate module is responsible for choosing which one to pursue. Based on its choice, the routine sets the Type-Further-Challenge register either to support or challenge and updates the discourse model to reflect the closing of all intervening subargumentation.

The Further-Challenge state is able to reestablish the space being popped back to as the forthcoming relevant discourse context by traversing the corelator links of spaces from the current active space to the one pointed to in the discourse expectation being processed. This discourse model traversal, however, does not include traversing the links of closed context spaces. This reflects the fact that closed context spaces (and those to which they point) are deemed irrelevant to all current discourse processing.

By the time the Concede-Subargument routine is ready to pass control to Further-Challenge, CCS points to a closed context space, the space containing the opponent's accepted challenge. Before passing control and initiating the traversal, the processor must therefore first reassign CCS to a nonclosed context space: it chooses the context space containing the speaker's conceded flawed claim.[6]

This description illustrates some of the mechanisms and workings of our system to support resumptions of suspended discourse contexts. Features enabling context reidentification include (1) partitioning a discourse into a hierarchy of distinct but related and linked context spaces, (2) keeping track of the effects of preceding moves in a discourse model, which includes discourse expectation construction, and (3) preparing for generation of forthcoming utterances by noting the discourse effects of the forthcoming move via sensitivity to clue word signals and different subcategory possibilities for the move.

The tests and actions characterized in the grammar for a speaker can analogously be used by a listener—the grammar can function in the interpretive mode as well. In both generation and interpretation of discourse we set up expectations of conversational move categories most likely to follow preceding conversational development, and we use our knowledge of clue words and of the standardized effects of conversational moves to update our discourse models in preparation for the interpretation of subsequent moves. For example, a conversant who has just challenged an opponent's support of a claim is quite prepared for the opponent to reply to this challenge with a counterchallenge or a concession; of these which will occur is usually differentially signaled by the clue words prefacing the opponent's response ("But" and "All right, but," respectively).

At this point let's turn to the situation where resumption in the argument structure occurs due to a team member's joining forces with a speaker currently engaging in debate against an opponent. Since in this case we have no preceding concession, we will clearly have very different aspects of the discourse model to consider, analyze, and update.

Joining Forces

Sometimes a return from subargumentation occurs by further challenging a context space that generated the subargument without an intervening attack by an opponent or a concession by the current speaker. This usually happens when a team member chimes in with an additional challenge to the initial claim which has been generating current subargumentation. To illustrate the options available, and the mechanisms used, to process this form of conversational development, we shall look in detail at the context space processor's simulation of M's conversational move in the genetics-environment excerpt. Portions of the grammar accessed in the modeling of this piece of discourse are included in appendix 7A, and a trace of the simulation appears in appendix 7B (see figure 6.2 as well).

M's utterances in the debate do not directly further support D's preceding claim ("The two brothers do not have the same environment"), nor do they further support D's support utterance ("They don't have the same friends"). Rather, M's utterances serve as a direct further challenge to R's claim that a child's home is not to blame for a child's aggressive behavior. M's challenge, as described in chapter 3, is an attack on R's support for her claim; formally speaking, the challenge attacks R's mapping of "two twins living at home" onto "two people sharing a same environment."

To simulate this challenge move, the relevant discourse context by the point of generation should consist of a new challenge context space into which M's challenging remarks can be placed and R's support context space (C6) containing these mappings. Currently, however, the relevant discourse context is composed of D's debative-issue context space containing his preceding claim (C10) and its support context space (C16). Thus some discourse model updating is necessary. We begin by first describing all states accessed in simulation of M's conversational move.

States Accessed in the Simulation

1. *Produce-Next-Move*   The Produce-Next-Move state is the ATN start state where the paths of most conversational moves begin. Conceptually, the new conversational move can be related to the preceding discourse in one of five ways, as captured by choices A–E of this state:

> a. *Expectation*   Execute a move predicted and/or required by preceding conversational development (e.g., answer a question, return to an interrupted context space, resume discussion of the initiating subject of an analogy).
> b. *Developmental1*   Have the move be a developmental continuation of the preceding discourse but one not necessarily expected or mandatory (e.g., argue against, support, comment on, question, further develop, restate).
> c. *Developmental2*   Same as Developmental1 with exclusion of starting a debate.
> d. *Nondevelopmental*   Have the move be a nondevelopmental continuation of the preceding discourse (e.g., restart the discussion of a closed context space, abstract onto a topic logically prior to the one currently being discussed, attempt to interject something tangentially related to the current topic of discourse).
> e. *Transitional*   Generate a metastatement that will explicitly state the connection between the next conversational move and what went on before (e.g., "Speaking of discrimination, I wanted to tell you this story.").

2. *Further-Challenge/Step 1*   The Further-Challenge/Step 1 state can only be reached via execution of a further challenge discourse expectation in the environment of an ongoing debate, and it is where a next speaker is chosen. Associated with the discourse expectation that leads us to this state is the name of the conversant whose further challenge is expected—namely the conversational participant who earlier challenged the context space about to be further challenged. The processor uses this expected speaker information in one of two ways:

a. Push to the Shift-Speaker-Expectation state, where the expected speaker is selected as next speaker (maybe current speaker);

b. Push to the Shift-Speaker-Sameside state, where a conversant already known to be on the same side of the argument as the expected speaker is selected as next speaker (maybe current speaker); a previously uncommitted speaker is selected as next speaker (This conversant is appended onto the expected speaker's side of the debate, i.e., updating of the Sides register.); a conversant from the other side switches sides and is selected as next speaker. (This change in a conversant's position is recorded in the Sides register.)

In simulating a piece of dialogue, we have the processor choose as next speaker the speaker cited in the dialogue. We then perform the updating actions associated with this choice.

3. *Further-Challenge/Step 2*   Here there is the single action of allowing for generation of the clue words that usually accompany a further-challenge move (e.g., "And," "And furthermore").

4. *Further-Challenge/Step 3*   As noted earlier, this state is responsible for discourse resumptions incurred by further challenges and subargument concessions. Actions performed in this state result in a reestablishment of the relevant discourse context for subsequent processing.[7] As described, context reestablishment in these cases entails closing all intervening subargumentation context spaces and deleting all outstanding discourse expectations involving these spaces. This state's first action is to push to a constructive state of the grammar where such updating is performed.

5. *Find-and-Delete-Expectations-Irrelevant-Contexts/Step 1*   This state recursively calls on itself on each pass: adding the next intervening subargument context space onto an intervening subarguments list, deleting from the Expectation-List any outstanding expectations involving this space, and retrieving the next intervening subargument to be closed by following the corelator links of the context space just added to the list. This traversal begins with the active context space and ends when the only spaces retrieved for readjustment are (a) context spaces already closed, (b) context spaces already on the intervening subarguments list, or (c) the context space named in Expectation.Context.

6. *Further-Challenge/Step 4*   The expected response to a further challenge is the same as to an initial one—the party being attacked will counterchallenge. The first action associated with this state then is to assign a protagonist of the about to be attacked context space the

Future-Defender role (one of Expectation.Context.Protagonists). Second, finer characterization of the form of challenge to be generated begins. As noted earlier, two subcategorizations are possible: (a) further support of a preceding counterclaim or countersupport, or (b) a new counterclaim or countersupport specification.

The further-support option of a further challenge is somewhat complex. It is only viable if current subargumentation stems from one's support of a preceding counterclaim or countersupport. If, instead, the subargumentation stems from a preceding nonsupported counterclaim or countersupport, one simply cannot return to this preceding claim and suddenly support it. This is because support moves warrant a clear identifiable claim to be supported. Since intervening subargumentation stems from a previously unsupported claim, it is clear that providing support for the claim is not at issue or expected. To begin to support such a claim, one must first explicitly reestablish the claim as the relevant discourse context, thereby setting up a context wherein support is warranted and expected. On the other hand, if current subargumentation does stem from support of a counterargument, then of course support of this preceding claim is at issue and is of direct relevance to current subargumentation. In this case then the resumption can entail an immediate citation of a replacement or a further support for this preceding argument.

Correspondingly the processor's actions along this choice path are subject to certain criteria of acceptability, which are listed alongside the actions to be performed. The following actions are performed where a further support is appropriate and chosen:

a. Head-CCS is set to one of the counterclaims or countersupports of the space resumed, which has been involved in the current subargumentation (i.e., it is a space noted on the intervening subarguments list).
b. This chosen context space is assigned a controlling status.
c. CCS is set to a preceding support of the chosen counterclaim or countersupport space.
d. Type-Further-Challenge is set to Support.
e. These two spaces are deleted from the intervening subarguments list.

The second option—giving a new counterclaim or countersupport—is much simpler: CCS is reset to the issue context space about to be further challenged (i.e., Expectation.Context); Type-Further-Challenge is set to challenge, and all spaces noted on the intervening subarguments list are closed.

In a discourse context where tests for both a further support and a new counterclaim or countersupport are met, a choice has to be made. There are a number of different aspects to such choice points. First, we could have the processor itself choose all possible choices in parallel. It would then construct hypothetical spaces in which all the different lines of development were being pursued simultaneously. Along the way many further tests have to be met. After all possibilities have been explored to conclusion, a separate module would choose to generate one of the choices that met all tests to conclusion. Alternatively, one could envision a system where processing is done serially and the first choice to succeed is chosen. Further tests along these choice points usually involve being able to infer or retrieve something from memory. What actually gets generated of course will depend on what the speaker knows. Similarly in interpretation mode the processor might have to explore a number of viable choice paths.

Now, from the perspective of hand simulating an existing dialogue, we simply say that the processor chooses path X because that is the choice taken in the dialogue we are simulating.

7. *Further-Challenge/Step 5*   Having established which context spaces of the intervening subargument are to be terminated by the resumption, the processor now closes these spaces to reflect that they are irrelevant to further argumentation (i.e., their status slots are set to closed, and their focus level assignments are set to zero). In addition, where we have had preceding concession, all claims of the opposition noted in these spaces are appended onto the Domain-Constraints register to reflect their implicit acceptance by the current speaker's side.

8. *Further-Challenge-Support/Step 3*   The Further-Challenge-Support/Step 3 state of the grammar is accessed for either a further challenge or a further support. Depending on preceding assignment to the Type-Further-Challenge register, control is either passed to a support or to a challenge organizational state.

9. *Challenge-Choice/Step 2*   There are three major subcategorizations of a challenge conversational move:

> a. *Direct challenge form*   A conversant emotively undermines an opponent's claim, demands that the opponent support a claim or unsubstantiated dismissal challenge, or makes an assertion that directly opposes the opponent's.
>
> b. *Indirect challenge form*   A conversant does not verbalize explicit disagreement with an opponent's claim but rather cites a claim, which if true implies that the opponent's claim is either not true, irrelevant, or only one skewed version of the truth.

c. *Support form*   A conversant responds to an opponent's demand that he or she support a claim. As this move occurs in response to an opponent's challenge (of the demand support category), it is treated as a counterchallenge much as are other responses to an opponent in a debate.

A conversant is always free to choose a direct or indirect form of challenge except in the case where he or she is expected to respond to an opponent's preceding demand for support. In that case the grammar, following maxim-abiding discourse development, limits subsequent transition to the support state.

Here, too, given that tests are met for either an indirect or direct challenge, we need to call some higher level module to do the final choosing. Again, in simulating an existing dialogue, we choose what the speaker has chosen.

In the Challenge-Choice/Step 2 state then we get our first subcategorization of the challenge conversational move. Actions associated with this move are to append the current speaker onto the antagonist list of the current active context space (the space about to be challenged) and to create the discourse expectation that the current speaker may, at a later point in time, further challenge this space.

These actions however are not performed under the following conditions:

a. The current speaker is challenging an opponent's preceding flat dismissal of his or her argument in the active space (i.e., CCS.Comment.Contextual-Function.Method = "Flat-Rejection"). One only has two means of countering a flat dismissal: accept the dismissal and concede the subargument or demand the opponent to replace the unsubstantive challenge with a substantive one. There is no room here for further-challenges.

b. The current speaker is responding to an opponent's demand that an earlier claim be supported (i.e., Expectation.Associated-Constraints = "Supply-Support-Claim"). In this case, the challenge is really just supporting one's own claim in the active space. Setting up a further-challenge of this context space by its protagonist is inappropriate.

c. The current speaker is responding to an opponent's demand that a substantive challenge be made against CCS in place of an earlier unsubstantive challenge (i.e., Expectation.Associated-Constraints = "Supply-Support-Rejection"). In this case, the further-challenge expectation set up when the conversant first challenged CCS with the flat dismissal is still on the Expectation-List register; the challenge currently being processed is the counterchallenge expectation to the support demand. A new further challenge is not needed.

10. *Challenge-Directly/Step 1*   There are many ways of directly attacking an opponent's argument. Within a given discourse context, however, only some of these types of attack are appropriate. Corresponding to each possible form of attack, a distinct arc transition emanates from this state. The transition tests on the arcs capture the context-sensitive features of these different developmental options. There are three main conceptual subcategorizations of this move:

a. *Emotive/questioning challenges*   Keep the burden of proof on the opposition; it undermines an opponent's position, but it does not cite any evidence or specific claims against it—for example, a "So What" challenge (choices A, B, and C).
b. *Subargument concession*   Concedes a flaw in one's argument, followed by either ending all debate (i.e., total concession) or a fixing of the flawed argument (choice D).
c. *Substantive challenges*   Attack the validity of the opponent's argument, usually by citing some contrary claim and/or evidence against it—for example, denying the truth of the opponent's claim or support fact (choice E).

Choosing any one of these direct challenge forms, and their many forms of subcategorization, is constrained by preceding conversational development. For example, given no preceding challenge, a subargument concession is inappropriate.

If the substantive challenge form (choice E) is chosen, there is first the choice of generating the clue words "No, but." In a counterchallenge of an opponent's argument which was based on a state of affairs that did not occur, the clue words "Well, of course," or "But, of course," are allowed as well. An opponent claims a state of affairs A did not occur (a Modus-Tollens form of challenge) when the other opponent's claim, if true, would have included the event A. Claiming A does not occur then argues against the initial position. To counter such an argument, a defender of the original position must illustrate that this nonoccurrence of A does not violate predictions of the initial argument and that, on the contrary, its nonoccurence is quite consistent and expected by the initial position (i.e., the "unexpected" event is not unexpected at all)—hence the use of "Well, of course," or the like, in such counterargumentation. In a further challenge no clue words are allowed since at an earlier state clue words like "And" or "Furthermore" would have already been generated.

This design choice of clue word generation before full subcategorization of the conversational move correctly models some prosodics found in conversational speech (i.e., a person's use of a clue word, pause, and later substantive speaking). The later choosing of one of the subchoices of choice E, and the initial processing done along each of these paths, can give us some insight into what type of processing a conversant might be performing during this pause period between uttering a clue word and later substantive remarks.

In general, a conversant can challenge an opponent's claim (i.e., issue context space) or an opponent's support of a claim (i.e., support context space). The first action along the substantive challenge form is to decide whether to attack an opponent's claim or support of a claim. We briefly summarize the two cases where updating actions have to be performed:

a. Current active space is an issue context space. If we choose to challenge a preceding support of an active issue space, we must reassign the active issue space to generating, reassign its high focus element to a medium focus, and reactivate the last support context space of this issue space.

b. Current active space is a support context space. If we choose to challenge an issue context space, and one of its support spaces is currently active, we must close this active support space, reassigning its focus level assignments to zero, and reactivate the issue space to be challenged which is currently pointed to by Head-CCS.

Choosing a substantive challenge is choosing a general subcategory of the challenge move. This subcategory is then further subcategorized in the ATN. Each further subcategory has additional tests and updating actions. For example, the Challenge-Support-Specifics subcategory (choice E/A) is only appropriate as a counterchallenge to specifics of an opponent's preceding support space; the Range-Application subcategory (choice E/C) is only appropriate as a counterchallenge to a preceding New-Factor type of challenge; and the Challenge-Analogy-Mappings subcategory (choice E/F) is only appropriate against a preceding analogy. Again, once tests are met, the remaining possibilities must be decided by some other module.

At this point further updating is performed for all subchoices of choice E: a new active issue context space is created for the substantive challenging remarks about to be generated. The following slots of this new active space are filled: (a) goal: "challenge"; (b) status: "active"; (c) corelator: CCS (the current active context space). Next, the current active space (the one about to be challenged) is reassigned a controlling status, Head-CCS is set to point to it, and CCS is set to the new challenge space just created. After this discourse model updating, control is passed to the state specified along the transition chosen—one of the subchoices of choice E.

11. *Challenge-Support-Specifics*   The grammar distinguishes between two main subcategories of challenging some support context space: (a) challenging an authority of support; (b) challenging the substantive utterances of support. Given no authority, only the substantive support utterances can be challenged; given no substantive support, only the authority can be challenged. Given neither, we could not have entered this state. Again, where both options are available, some other module decides what to choose.

12. *Challenge-Basis-Support*   This state is responsible for challenging the underlying principle of support used in the construction of a preceding support argument. The main three types of challenge (as captured by choices A–C in this state) are (a) challenge of the applicability of the principle to the case at hand, (b) challenge of the scope of the principle in general, and (c) total denial of the truth of the principle. Associated with each possibility is a different arc emanating from this state. Which path is chosen again will be decided by some other module or by a hand simulation of an existing dialogue.

13. *Challenge-Mappings/Step 1*   The argumentation generated in this state is one that challenges the applicability of the support context space's underlying principle of support to the particular case at hand. It does this by illustrating that the mappings used for instantiation of the current situation to the generic one is inappropriate and untrue.

As for all the states where substantive utterance generation occurs, here we cite the abstract characterization that must be met for the utterances to serve the current conversational move. All such states first specify the "Express" function, which should be seen as a function call to some syntactic module which, given a proposition A, can transform this proposition into natural language. Second, to formulate the proposition A, we usually access and manipulate information in the discourse model and in an underlying knowledge base. The manipulations are semantic and logical in nature and again correspond to calls on some other modules in a fully computerized natural language system. For example, in the Challenge-Mappings/Step 1 state, other modules are expected (a) to be able to retrieve pieces of knowledge from some data base, (b) to determine whether one piece of knowledge is a presupposition of another, (c) to determine whether one piece of knowledge implies another, and (d) to determine whether one thing is a denial of another.

14. *Challenge-Mappings/Step 2*   At this point the processor appends onto the active space the substantive remarks just made. It then returns control to its caller, Challenge-Directly/Step 1, the re-emerging state for all forms of direct substantive challenges, and control proceeds to Step 2.

15. *Challenge-Directly/Step 2*   Here the processor appends the challenge space just completed onto the challenged issue space's counterclaim or countersupport slot. Control is then returned to Challenge-Choice/Step 3, the remerging state for all forms of challenges.

16. *Challenge-Choice/Step 3*   Having generated the challenge in whatever form the processor now constructs and appends onto the Expectation-List register the expectation that the conversant earlier assigned the Future-Defender role will counterchallenge the challenge just given. The Type-Further-Challenge register is then reset to Nil, and control is returned to the grammar's start state where processing of the next conversational move is commenced.

The Trace

To simulate M's challenge in lines 41–46 of the excerpt, the processor begins in the start state Produce-Next-Move. Its discourse model shows that it is in the midst of a debate and that it has a number of outstanding discourse expectations that could be executed. In particular, there are the outstanding further challenge expectations for D (or other members of his team) against R's preceding arguments.

Simulating M's conversational move, we have the processor choosing to fulfill such a discourse expectation as its next conversational move (choice A). Since challenging an issue space's support is equivalent to challenging the issue space itself, all challenge expectations cite the issue space to be challenged. As its next conversational move therefore the expectation (Further-Challenge, D, C7) is chosen—C7's Support-cs slot points to C6, the space about to be attacked. This discourse expectation was created when D, in line 27, first challenged C7. Having chosen such an expectation, control goes to the state specified in the expectation—Further-Challenge/Step 1, the state responsible for further challenges.

The first thing done is to choose M, a known team member of D, as next speaker and to generate the clue word "And." At this point the processor must update its discourse model. By M's move we have the following underlying context space structure:

C6: Lines 23–25, ". . . only one of the brothers acted that way." Goal: support; Method: modus-tollendo-tollens; Corelator: C7; Status: closed.

C7: Line 26, ". . . not blame the child's aggressive behavior on the child's home." Goal: fix claim; Method: constrainment; Corelator: C3; Support-cs: C6; Counterclaims: C8; Status: generating.

C8: Lines 27–28, ". . . nothing to do with home . . . child's environment." Goal: challenge; Method: irrelevance-by-expansion; Corelator: C7; Counterclaims: C9; Status: generating.

C9: Line 29, ". . . brothers have same environment." Goal: challenge; Method{1}: apply expansion; Corelator{1}: C8; Method{2}: derived-from; Corelator{2}: C6; Counterclaims: C10; Status: generating.

C10: Lines 30, 39, "They do not have the same environment." Goal: challenge; Method: deny-truth; Corelator: C9; Support-cs: (C11, C16); Status: controlling.

C11: Lines 32–33, "You and I . . . not same environment." Goal: support; Method: analogy; Corelator: C10; Support-cs: (C12, C13); Status: closed.

C12: Lines 34–35, "I am seeing window . . . you're not." Goal: support; Method: modus-tollendo-tollens; Corelator: C11; Status: closed.

C13: Line 36, "You are not looking at you." Goal: support; Method: modus-tollendo-tollens; Corelator: C11; Status: closed.

C14: Line 37, "Two people can't be same place." Goal: relate analogy; Method: abstraction; Corelator: C10; Support-cs: C15; Status: closed.

C15: Line 38, ". . . otherwise same space." Goal: support; Method: modus-tollens; Corelator: C14; Status: closed.

C16: Line 40, "They don't have the same friends." Goal: support; Method: modus-tollens; Corelator: C10; Status: active.

Beginning with the active context space, C16, the processor appends it, together with context spaces C10, C9, and C8, onto its intervening subarguments list. Intervening discussion contained in context spaces C15, C14, C13, C12, and C11 are not accessed in this traversal. This correctly reflects the influence of closed context spaces: they are entirely irrelevant to subsequent discourse processing (unless they are explicitly reentered). Thus the grammar's structuring and linking mechanism of partitioning discourse utterances into a hierarchical network of context spaces with varying influential roles enables it not only to identify and establish a relevant discourse context for subsequent engagement but to mark and ignore all preceding sections of discourse that need not be considered in a reestablishment.

The processor now assigns R the role of Future-Defender and chooses the further challenge option of giving a new countersupport argument to R's earlier support for her claim that one could not blame a child's home for the child's aggressive behavior. Updating actions performed include (1) setting CCS to C7, (2) setting the status assignments of C16, C10, C9, and C8 to closed, (3) setting the Type-Further-Challenge register to challenge.

The processor is now ready to begin subcategorization of the forthcoming challenge move. Since this is M's first challenge against C7 and M's challenge is not in response to a demand for support, the processor appends M onto C7's list of antagonists. It also appends onto the Expectation-List register the expectation that M may at some future point further challenge C7. Then, to generate M's utterances, the processor would take the direct challenge form of attack.

The subcategory of direct challenge chosen is the substantive form. Since M attacks C7's support space, C6, the processor reassigns C7 a generating status and reassigns C6 an active status. It then creates a new context space for the forthcoming challenging utterances—C17. C17's status is assigned active, and CCS is set to point to it. C6 is reassigned a controlling status, and Head-CCS is set to point to it. At this point the processor further subcategorizes the type of support challenge about to be generated.

R's support for her claim that one could not blame a child's home for the child's aggressive behavior rested on the fact that there were two twins from a same home who manifested different social behavior. Explication of M's challenge rests in recognizing certain presuppositions underlying R's presumed generic principle of support and the non-carry-over of these presuppositions in its current instance of use. As discussed in chapter 3, R's principle of support is basically: "If the environment is the cause of social behavior, then two people sharing a same environment would manifest similar behavior." In using this principle of support, R maps "two people sharing a same environment" onto "two twins sharing a same home." M's challenge consists in challenging this mapping. A presupposition of two people sharing a same environment is that the environment treats the two people identically; two kids in a same home are usually not treated identically, hence the inapplicability of the mapping and use of the principle for the case at hand.

Having generated these utterances and filled C17 with the argument, the processor now attempts to further link into its network of context spaces. Though C17 is a challenge of C6, C6 is a support space, and the challenge therefore is really against C7. Since Head-CCS points to C6 whose goal is "support," the processor appends C17, the new challenge space, onto the countersupports slot of the issue space that C6 supports, that is, C7. Lastly, the processor creates the discourse expectation that the Future-Defender (R) will counter-challenge the challenge given—Challenge-Choice, R, C17, is appended onto the Expectation-List register.

Features Underlying the Modeling of Discourse Resumptions

In this chapter we have illustrated what our system can and cannot do. In particular, the system does not have any extra mechanisms to direct it in generation mode to choose one path from a number of possible choice paths and in interpretation mode to know exactly where a return is being made where a number of possibilities are viable (e.g., the return could be to anyone of the generating context spaces of a subargument).

In a more complete, sophisticated system we would expect at least some triggering of memory such as "Oh, I know X. And X can be used in this argument" and then the module to be guided by that memory system. In interpretation we would want some fancy and quick matching mechanism that could match a speaker's words, perhaps with some key words associated with a given context space.

Nevertheless, the system basically can work, though in less than optimal fashion. We have been able to illustrate a number of features of the system that enable it to do context tracking and move generation and interpretation. We have in particular illustrated how it uses outstanding discourse expectations and a functional partitioning to model discourse resumptions. A discourse resumption entails reestablishment of a currently suspended discourse context, and this involves closing all intervening discussion from the current point of discussion back to the point of return. The grammar's linking mechanism of context spaces and its differentiation between various influential discourse roles that context spaces play enable it both to reestablish a current relevant discourse context and ignore all intervening discussion not relevant to this reestablishment.

We have also seen how the processor uses registers and context space values set on earlier cycles through the grammar, and on earlier transitions within a given cycle, to keep track of earlier decisions and moves in order to ensure that its subsequent discourse generation moves are maxim abiding.

Lastly, we have illustrated a number of the grammar's subcategorizations for possible categories of conversational moves. Final subcategorizations entail an abstract specification of semantic and logical connections between what is currently being said to what went on before, and these connections should be seen as system calls onto other modules of the system. We have also shown how the grammar's type of subcategorization enables it to handle by a single mechanism such diverse moves as conceding a subargument and further challenging an opponent.

Appendix 7A: Portion of the Grammar Accessed in the Trace

Produce-Next-Move:

Choose(A: If Not(Expectation-List = Nil)
         Then Expectation <- Choosed(Expectation-List)
         Go Expectation.Function

    B: If Discourse-Mode NE "Debate"
        Then Go Developmental-Choice/Step 1

    C: If Discourse-Mode = "Debate"
        Then Go Developmental-Choice/Step 2

    D: Go Nondevelopmental-Choice

    E: Go Transitional-Utterance)

Further-Challenge/Step 1:

Choose(A: Push Shift-Speaker-Expectation

    B: knownside <- Expectation.Speaker
       push Shift-Speaker-Sameside/Step 1)

Step 2:

Speaker EXPRESS "And, furthermore"/"And"/etc.

Step 3:

irrelevant-context <- CCS
Push Find-And-Delete-Expectations-Irrelevant-Contexts/Step 1

Step 4:

Future-Defender <- Oneof(Expectation.Context.Protagonists)

Choose(A: If For Some I,J
            (Expectation.Context.CounterClaims{I}
            OR
            Expectation.Context.CounterSupports{I})
            MEMBER Intervening-Subarguments
            AND
            Expectation.Context.CounterClaims/CounterSupports{I}
               .SupportCS{J}
            NE Nil
            Then HEAD-CCS <- Expectation.Context.Counterclaims/
                  CounterSupports{I}
               Expectation.Context.Counterclaims/Countersupports{I}
                  .Status <- "Controlling"
               CCS <- Expectation.Context.Counterclaims/
                  Countersupports{I}.Support-cs{J}
               HEAD-CCS DELETE Intervening-Subarguments
               CCS DELETE Intervening-Subarguments
               Type-Further-Challenge <- "Support"

        B: CCS <- Expectation.Context
            CCS.Status <- "Active"
            Type-Further-Challenge <- "Challenge")

Step 5:

REPEAT space <- Next-Of(Intervening-Subarguments)
  Push Close-Space
UNTIL space = Nil
If Update-Constraints NE Nil
THEN Push Implicit-Concessions
Intervening-Subarguments <- Nil
Go Further-Challenge-Support/Step 3

Shift-Speaker-Expectation:

If Expectation.Speaker NE Speaker
Then Speaker APPEND Participant-List
      Speaker <- Expectation.Speaker
      Speaker DELETE Participant-List
(POP)

Shift-Speaker-Sameside/Step 1:

For Some I,
Current-Side <- Side{I} S.T. knownside MEMBER Side{I}
If Current-Side NE (knownside)

Then Choose(A: Go Step 2
              B: Speaker <- Oneof(Current-Side)
                 S.T. Speaker NE knownside
                 Speaker DELETE Participant-List
                 knownside APPEND Participant-List
                 (POP))

Step 2:

Sides APPEND Oldsides
Speaker <- Choosed(Participant-List)
 S.T. Speaker NE knownside
 AND
 Not(Speaker MEMBER Current-Side)
Speaker APPEND Side{I}(Sides)
knownside APPEND Participant-List
If For Some J NE I,
 Speaker MEMBER Side{J}(Sides)
Then Speaker DELETE Side{J}(Sides)
(POP)

Find-And-Delete-Expectations-Irrelevant-Contexts/Step 1

Delete All Expectations of Expectation-List with
    Context = irrelevant-context
irrelevant-context APPEND Intervening-Subarguments
irrelevant-contexts-list
    <- irrelevant-context.Contextual-Function.Corelators

Step 2:

irrelevant-context <- Choosed(irrelevant-contexts-list)
If irrelevant-context = Nil
Then (POP)
If irrelevant-context NE Expectation.Context
 AND
 irrelevant-context.Status
 NE "Closed" OR "Superseded"
 AND
 Not(irrelevant-context MEMBER Intervening-Subarguments)
Then Push Close-And-Delete-Expectations-Irrelevant-Contexts
        Go Step 2
Else Go Step 2

Further-Challenge-Support/Step 1:

Choose(A: knownside <- Speaker
                push Shift-Speaker-Sameside

         B: Go Step 2)

Step 2:

Speaker EXPRESS "And"/"And, furthermore"/etc.

Step 3:

If Type-Further-Challenge = "Support"
Then Choose(A: Same-Principle <- True

                B: If CCS.Authority NE Nil
                        Then Same-Authority <- True

                C: If CCS.Authority NE Nil
                        Then Same-Authority <- True
                                Same-Principle <- True

                D: Same-Principle <- Nil
                        Same-Authority <- Nil)
        CCS.Status <- "Closed"
        CCS <- HEAD-CCS
        Go Support-Choice/Step 2
Else Go Challenge-Choice/Step 2

Challenge-Choice/Step 1:

Future-Defender <- Speaker

Choose(A: Push Shift-Speaker-Expectation

         B: knownside <- Expectation.Speaker
              Push Shift-Speaker-Same side)

Step 2:

If Not(CCS.Comment.Contextual-Function.Method
    = "Flat-Rejection")
  AND (Expectation.Associated-Constraints
    NE "Supply-Support-Claim"
    OR
    "Supply-Support-Rejection")
  THEN (Further-Challenge,Speaker,CCS)
    APPEND
    Expectation-List
If Expectation.Associated-Constraints
    = "Supply-SupportClaim"
  THEN Expectation.Associated-Constraints <- Nil
        Go Support-Choice/Step 1

ELSE If CCS.Goal NE "Support"
      THEN If Not(Speaker Member CCS.Antagonists)
            Then Speaker Append CCS.Antagonists
ELSE If For Some I,
      Not(Speaker MEMBER CCS.Contextual-Function.Corelator{I}
        .Antagonists)
      S.T. CCS.Contextual-Function.Method{I}
        NE "Inference-Of"/"Derived-From"
      THEN Speaker APPEND CCS. Contextual-Function.Corelator{I}
        .Antagonists

Choose(A: Push Challenge-Directly/Step 1

      B: Push Challenge-Indirectly/Step 1)

Step 3:

Expectation <- [
  Function <- Challenge-Choice
  Speaker <- Future-Defender
  Context <- CCS]
Expectation APPEND Expectation-List
Expectation <- Nil
Type-Further-Challenge <- Nil
Go Produce-Next-Move

Challenge-Directly/Step 1:

Choose(A: If Not(Expectation.Associated-Constraints
            = "Supply-Support-Rejection")
          AND
          Not(For Some I, CCS.Contextual-Function.Method{I}
            = "Deny-Truth")
          AND
          Not(CCS.Comment.Contextual-Function.Method
            = "Flat-Rejection")
          AND
          Not(For Some I, CCS.Contextual-Function.Method{I}
            = "Apply-Expansion")
          Then Choose(1: Go Emotive-Flat-Rejection
                      2: Push Irrelevance-Rejection
                      If * EQ Nil THEN (POP))

      B: If Not(Expectation.Associated-Constraints
            = "Supply-Support-Rejection")
          AND
          CCS.Comment.Contextual-Function.Method
            = "Flat-Rejection"
          Then Go Demand-Support-Rejection

C: If Not(Expectation.Associated-Constraints
     = "Supply-Support-Rejection")
   AND
   Not(CCS.Comment.Contextual-Function.Method
     = "Flat-Rejection")
   AND
   (CCS.Goal NE "Support"
   Or
   CCS.Support-Fact = Nil
   Or
   CCS.Support-cs = Nil
   Or
   CCS.Support-cs.Support-Fact = Nil)
   Then Go Demand-Support-Claim

D: If Type-Further-Challenge EQ Nil
   AND
   (CCS.Goal = "Challenge"
   Or
   (CCS.Goal = "Fix-Claim"
   And
   For Some I,
   CCS.Contextual-Function.Corelator{I}.Goal
     = "Challenge")
   Or
   (CCS.Goal = "Support"
   And
   (HEAD-CCS.Goal = "Challenge"
   Or
   (HEAD-CCS.Goal = "Fix-Claim"
   And
   For Some I,
   HEAD-CCS.Contextual-Function.Corelator{I}.Goal
     = "Challenge"))))
   Then Go Concede-Subargument

E: If CCS.Support-cs NE Nil
   Then Choose(1: No-Op
               2: space <- CCS
                  Push Generating-Space
                  CCS <- Last(CCS.Support-cs)
                  CCS.Status <- "Active")

Else If CCS.Goal = "Support"
  Then Choose(3: No-Op
        4: space <- CCS
         Push Close-Space
         CCS <- HEAD-CCS
         CCS.Status <- "Active"
         HEAD-CCS <- Nil)
If Type-Further-Challenge EQ Nil
 Then If CCS.Method
   NE Oneof("Modus-Tollens,"
    "Modus-Tollendo-Tollens*,"
    "Modus-Tollendo-Tollens")
   Then Speaker EXPRESS ("No") ("But")
   Else Speaker EXPRESS
    ("Well") ("Of course") ("But")

Choose(A: If CCS.Goal = "Support"
    AND
    CCS.Contextual-Function.Method NE "Analogy"
    Then
    Push New-Challenge-Epi
    Push Challenge-Support-Specifics

  B: Push New-Challenge-Epi
   Push New-Factor

  C: Push New-Challenge-Epi
   Push Range-Application

  D: If For Some I,
   CCS.Contextual-Function.Method{I}
    = "New Factor"
   Then
   Push New-Challenge-Epi
   Push Irrelevant-Factor

  E: Push New-Challenge-Epi
   Push Deny-Truth

  F: If For Some I,
   CCS.Contextual-Function.Method{I}
    = "Analogy"
   Then
   analogous-space <- CCS
   Push New-Challenge-Epi
   Push Challenge-Analogy-Mappings))

Step 2:

For Some I,
 (CCS
 APPEND
 (If HEAD-CCS.Goal = "Support"
 AND
 HEAD-CCS.Contextual-Function.Method NE "Analogy"
 Then HEAD-CCS.Contextual-Function.Corelator{I}.Countersupports
 Else CCS.Contextual-Function.Corelator{I}.Counterclaims)
 S.T. CCS.Contextual-Function.Method{I}
   NE "Derived-From" OR "Inference-Of")
(POP)

Generating-Space:

space.Status <- "Generating"
space.Focus.High APPEND space.Focus.Medium
space.Focus.High <- Nil
(POP)

Close-Space:

space.State <- "Closed"
space.Focus.Zero <- (space.Focus.Zero, space.Focus.Low,
  space.Focus.Medium, space.Focus.High)
space.Focus.High <- space.Focus.Medium <- space.Focus.Low <- Nil
(POP)

Challenge-Support-Specifics:

If HEAD.CCS.Support-Fact NE Nil
Then Choose (A: No-op
              B: Go Challenge-Basis-Support)
Go Challenge-Authority

Challenge-Basis-Support:

Choose(A: Go Challenge-Mappings/Step 1
       B: Go Challenge-Scope/Step 1
       C: Go Challenge-Validity/Step 1)

Challenge-Mappings:

Speaker EXPRESS some Proposition, P
S.T. For Some SA2 [Possible(Infer(Implication(P) = SA2))
 Or
 Let SA2 = P]

S.T. For Some I, For Some PR(I)
 [SA2 DENY True(PR(HEAD-CCS.MAPPINGS.X{I}))
 WHERE
 (True(PR(HEAD-CCS.MAPPINGS.Y{I}))
 Presupposition-Of
 HEAD-CCS.Support-Principle)

Step 2:

Setslots(CCS)
 Contextual-Function <- [
   Method <- "Challenge-Mappings"]
 Claim <- Epistemic-Claim(P)
 (POP)

Appendix 7B: Trace Lines 41–46 of the Genetics-Environment Debate

ENTERING: Produce-Next-Move/Step 1

CHOOSING A:
Expectation-List NE Nil THEREFORE
Choosing Expectation <- (Further-Challenge, D, C7)

ENTERING: Further-Challenge/Step 1

CHOOSING B:
[knownside <- D
pushing to Shift-Speaker-Sameside/Step 1
 current-side <- (D,M)
 current-side NE (D)
 THEREFORE CHOOSING B:
 [SPEAKER <- M
 Participant-List <- (R,J)
 Participant-List <- (D,R,·]

RETURNING TO: Further-Challenge/Step 1

Step 2:

M EXPRESS: "And"

Step 3:

irrelevant-context <- C16
pushing to Find-And-Delete-Expectations-Irrelevant-Contexts/Step 1
 no expectations on expectation-list with context = C16
 Intervening-Subarguments <- (C16)
 irrelevant-contexts-list <- (C10)

Step 2:

irrelevant-context <- C10
irrelevant-context-list <- Nil
irrelevant-context NE Nil
C10 NE C7
AND C10.Status = "Controlling" NE "Closed"/"Superseded"
AND Not(C10 Member (C16))
THEREFORE pushing to
 Find-And-Delete-Expectations-Irrelevant-Contexts/Step 1
 DELETING (Further-Challenge, R, C10) from Expectation-List
 Intervening-Subarguments <- (C10, C16)
 irrelevant-context-list <- (C9)

Step 2:

irrelevant-context <- C9
irrelevant-context-list <- Nil
irrelevant-context NE Nil
C9 NE C7
AND C9.Status = "Generating" NE "Closed"/"Superseded"
AND Not(C9 Member (C10, C16))
THEREFORE pushing to
 Close-And-Delete-Expectations-Irrelevant-Contexts/Step 1
 DELETING (Further-Challenge, D, C9) from Expectation-List
 Intervening-Subarguments <- (C9, C10, C16)
 irrelevant-context-list <- (C8, C6)

Step 2:

irrelevant-context <- C8
irrelevant-context-list <- (C6)
irrelevant-context NE Nil
C8 NE C7
AND C8.Status = "Generating" NE "Closed"/"Superseded"
AND Not(C8 Member (C9, C10, C16))
THEREFORE pushing to
 Close-And-Delete-Expectations-Irrelevant-Contexts/Step 1
 DELETING (Further-Challenge, R, C8) from Expectation-List
 Intervening-Subarguments <- (C8, C9, C10, C16)
 irrelevant-context-list <- (C7)

Step 2:

irrelevant-context <- C7
irrelevant-context-list <- Nil
irrelevant-context NE Nil
C7 = C7 THEREFORE Going Step 2

Step 2:
irrelevant-context <- Nil
irrelevant-context = Nil THEREFORE (POP)

RETURNING TO:
Close-And-Delete-Expectations-Irrelevant-Contexts/Step 2
go Step 2

Step 2:
irrelevant-context <- C6
irrelevant-context-list <- Nil
irrelevant-context NE Nil
C6 NE C7
  AND
  C6.Status = "Closed"
  THEREFORE Going Step 2

  Step 2:
  irrelevant-context <- Nil
  irrelevant-context = Nil
  THEREFORE (POP)

  RETURNING TO:
  Close-And-Delete-Expectations-Irrelevant-Contexts/Step 2
  go Step 2

  Step 2:
  irrelevant-context <- Nil
  irrelevant-context = Nil
  THEREFORE (POP)

RETURNING TO:
Close-And-Delete-Expectations-Irrelevant-Contexts/Step 2
go Step 2

Step 2:
irrelevant-context <- Nil
irrelevant-context = Nil
THEREFORE (POP)

RETURNING TO: Further-Challenge/Step 3

Step 4:

Future-Defender <- R
Choosing B:
[CCS <- C7
C7.Status <- "Active"
Type-Further-Challenge <- "Challenge"]

Step 5:

space <- C8
pushing to Close-Space
 C8.Status <- "Closed"
 C8.Focus.Zero <- (C8.Focus.Zero, C8.Focus.Medium, C8.Focus.Low,
  C8.Focus.High)
 C8.Focus.High <- C8.Focus.Medium <- C8.Focus.Low <- Nil
  .
  .
  .
 C16.Status <- "Closed"
 C16.Focus.Zero <- (C16.Focus.Zero, C16.Focus.Medium, C16.Focus.Low,
  C16.Focus.High)
 C16.Focus.High <- C16.Focus.Medium <- C16.Focus.Low <- Nil

RETURNING TO: Further-Challenge/Step 5
Update-Constraints = Nil
Intervening-Subarguments <- Nil
go Further-Challenge-Support/Step 3

ENTERING: Further-Challenge-Support/Step 3
Type-Further-Challenge = "Challenge"
THEREFORE go Challenge-Choice/Step 2

ENTERING: Challenge-Choice/Step 2
C7.Comment = Nil
AND
Expectation.Associated-Constraints = Nil
THEREFORE Expectation-List <- ((Further-Challenge, M, C7), . . .)
Expectation.Associated-Constraints = Nil
AND
(C7.Goal NE "Support" & Not(M Member C7.Antagonists))
THEREFORE
C7.Antagonists <- (M, D)
CHOOSING A: pushing to Challenge-Directly/Step 1

CHOOSING E:
C7.Support-cs = C6 NE Nil
THEREFORE CHOOSING 2:
[space <- C7
pushing to Generating-Space
    C7.Status <- "Generating"
    C7.Focus.Medium <- (C7.Focus.Medium, C7.Focus.High)
    C7.Focus.High <- Nil

RETURNING TO: Challenge-Directly/Step 1 (Choice E)
CCS <- C6
C6.Status <- "Active"]
Type-Further-Challenge = "Challenge" NE Nil
C6.Goal = "Support"
AND C6.Contextual-Function Method = "Modus-Tollendo-Tollens*"
    NE "Analogy"
THEREFORE CHOOSING A:
pushing to New-Challenge-EPI
  rcontextual-function <- [
    corelator <- C6]
  rgoal <- "Challenge"
  rmode <- "Explicit"
  pushing to Construct-EPI

    ridentifier <- C17
    setslots(C17)

RETURNING TO: New-Challenge-EPI
returned register value: * = C17
C6.Status <- "Controlling"
HEAD-CCS <- C6]
CCS <- C17
C17.Status <- "Active"

RETURNING TO: Challenge-Directly/Step 1 (Choice E/A)
pushing to: Challenge-Support-Specifics

C6.Support-Fact =
"Only one of two twins acted negatively"
NE Nil
THEREFORE Choosing B: go Challenge-Basis-Support

ENTERING: Challenge-Basis-Support
Choosing A: go Challenge-Mappings/Step 1

ENTERING: Challenge-Mappings/Step 1

M EXPRESS: "You know, to say that two kids come from
                the same family is really meaningless,
= P   because when you think of the difference
                in treatment that two kids can get in
                exactly the same family, it's incredible.
                You know, it's the difference between night
                and day."

because:
1. P = SA2
2. P1 = "treated same way"
   X1 = "two twins living in same home"
3. SA2
   DENY
   True(treated same way(two twins living in same home))
4. Y1 = "two people sharing same environment"
5. Necessary(True
   (treated same way(two people sharing same environment)))
   for
   True(
   IF
   One's social interactive behavior is influenced by
   one's environment before (& during) kindergarten
   THEN
   Two people sharing this same environment will
   manifest the same social interactive behavior)

Step 2:

setslots(C17)
Contextual/Function <- [
  Method <- "Challenge-Mappings"]
  Claim <- [
    State-of-Affairs <- Two kids living in same home are treated in the
      same way
    Epistemic-Predicate <- not true]
RETURNING TO: Challenge-Directly/Step 1

Step 2:

HEAD-CCS = C6
AND C6.Goal = "Support" AND C6.Method NE "analogy"
Therefore C7.Countersupports <- C17

RETURNING TO: Challenge-Choice/Step 2

Expectation <- [
 Function <- Challenge-Choice
 Speaker <- R
 Context <- C17]
Expectation-List <-
((Challenge-Choice,R,C17), (Further-Challenge,M,C7), . . .)
Expectation <- Nil
Type-Further-Challenge <- Nil
Go Produce-Next-Move

Chapter 8

Cognitive Processing and the Context Space Theory

The context space theory assumes that the cognitive processing of discourse overlaps with general cognitive processing abilities and thus is consistent with other current theories of cognitive operations. The particular processes employed in the discourse grammar reflect many functional abstractions or schemas: generalization, instantiation, implication, presupposition, inference, focus, and so on. Within the grammar we have specific points at which calls are made to such schemas. As Chomsky (1980) suggests, it is yet an open question as to what should fall under the language faculty and hence appear in some form in its representations of meaning. But many of these non-language-specific operations are used in the domain of the language faculty; they form the basic operations by which we can formalize the abstract language rules governing conversational speech. Though there may well be orderings of such operations specific to the fulfillment of different kinds of cognitive tasks, this sharing of cognitive structures between separate systems seems quite reasonable, since one would expect the mind to be equipped with a basic set of cognitive operations. Extended discourse is only one of the many cognitive tasks that people perform; it is not unexpected that there should be correspondences between the way people perform this task and the way they go about performing others. A nonoverlap between our linguistic and nonlinguistic functioning would be cause for alarm; if it were proposed that individuals used some remarkable, unique cognitive ability in discourse processing, we should have to wonder why they make such limited use of this ability. But this is clearly not the case. As Adams (1980) notes in her discussion of the development of children's syntactic processing capacities:

> A remarkably close temporal correlation between the development of related logical and linguistic skills is often observed (e.g., Olson 1970, Palermo and Melfese 1972, Tapin, Staudenmeyer, and Taddonia 1974). Almost certainly this is not mere co-

incidence. It would seem more likely that the emergence of both kinds of skills presupposes the acquisition of some common conceptual structures.

Hierarchical Structuring of Information

One important feature of correspondence between the context space system and more general theories of cognitive processing is reflected in the system's view of discourse structure. Its hierarchical partitioning of an ongoing conversation is consistent with cognitive theories that individuals comprehend their environment in a hierarchically structured way. Discourse utterances in this respect are but an object of perception.

Focused Processing: Selective Attention and Frames of Reference

A fundamental rule of our discourse grammar is that the generation and/or interpretation of utterances of one context space are directly related to only one preceding space. This principle reflects the kind of focused processing that we find in natural discourse. Only one of a few related items is highlighted at any given point in time. And such a mode of thinking oriented toward concentrated thought suggests that our cognitive processes are not attuned to remembering disparate entities in short-term memory and simultaneously working on them. It is the discourse correspondent of selective attention.

Among the discourse phenomena reflecting focused processing are the following facts: (1) We pursue only one discourse topic at any given point in time. (2) Though in discourse there are a number of open lines of future development, typically only one line of functional and thematic development is chosen. It is probably safe to conjecture that an attempt at simultaneous option fulfillment would be perceived either as an ambiguity or go unnoticed. (3) We update the status of preceding discourse utterances so as to highlight a specific set of utterances while deemphasizing another set, as reflected by our use of such clue words as "But," "Anyway," "Incidentally," and corresponding continued pronominalization or nonpronominalization to elements of preceding context spaces. This phenomena is further reflected when following one option of development, other options previously available no longer seem viable. (4) We usually limit discourse pronominalization to a specific single entity considered to be in the highest focus in a relevant discourse context.

In general, simultaneous achievement of more than one discourse function by a given set of utterances (i.e., by having them simultaneously directly related to varying discourse topics and serving varying conversational moves) is considered to be a "creative" use of language. It is not considered the norm or typical of how we ordinarily use language. We even have special descriptive terms for such occasions: allegory, pun, play on words, double entendre, and so on. Thus we have distinct genres, perceivably different both in form and frequency from our ordinary use of language.

However, it is questionable if we can simultaneously process creative discourse forms in terms of their multifunctionality. Consider, for instance, the allegory. The processing of the "story" of an allegory is qualitatively different than our processing of an ordinary narrative discourse. To listen to the events specified as a "real" story probably would entail losing hold of the allegory being told. At minimum, processing of such discourse forms necessitates some conscious shifting between the two modes of interpretation, similar to the "shifting" needed to see "simultaneously" the two views of a Necker cube.

The grammar's notion of focused processing and its limitation of single conversational move achievement is, as we have said, consistent with psychological research on selective attention and the notion that an individual is a "limited-capacity processor." There are even stronger correlations between the context space theory and notions such as selective attention.

As noted by many psychologists (e.g., Neisser 1967, Lindsay and Norman 1972), cognitive processing usually entails using preattentive processes to segment and distinguish elements being attended to. The discourse system presented here similarly recognizes the importance of segmentation and of subsequent processing. It is generally assumed that cues and expectations are among the primary elements directing an individual's segmentation and focusing choices (James 1890, Schutz 1970). The context space processor similarly uses cues and expectations to direct its segmentation of utterances into constituent context space constructs.

For example, "clue word" and "explicit shift mechanisms" (Cohen 1983, Goldberg 1981, Meyer 1977, Reichman 1978, Schiffrin 1980) are major features of the discourse grammar. These clue words usually preface the substantive remarks of a speaker's conversational move. They often indicate that the speaker's utterances will entail a context space shift and hence that a different segment is about to be put into the field of focal attention. In attending to the subsequent active context space, our field of local attention is limited to it and the controlling context space in direct relation to which the active space is being developed.

Selective attention is clearly a major aspect of most cognitive processing tasks and has been used in the context space theory as a means of explaining many discourse phenomena. A more specific and better concept for focused processing and the phenomena of selective attention, however, is the concept of "frame of reference" processing.

Discourse Processing and Frame of Reference Identification

Virtually everything we do and perceive is in relation to some single fixed frame of reference. For example, riding in a train, we see the train (and ourselves) as moving by viewing the landscape as standing still, or we view the train (and ourselves) as stationary while the landscape moves.

Frame of reference processing involves understanding one unit in terms of a fixed other. It therefore presupposes an ability to segment and differentiate between the unit serving as a frame of reference and the unit being analyzed in relation to the reference frame. A frame of reference provides a schematic structure in relation to which subsequent processing is performed. In discourse it provides the necessary context that directs subsequent generation and interpretation. It provides the listener with the framework by which to identify the "point" of a speaker's utterances. As noted earlier, the point of a speaker's utterances is reflected in the communicative function served by the context space containing the utterances.

A discourse reference frame governs subsequent interpretation in much the same way that an individual's choice of reference frame governs whether she or he will see the train (and herself or himself) as moving or stationary. Since the communicative function of an active context space relates to the preceding controlling context space, it follows that a frame of reference includes both the controlling and (subordinate) active context space. This is somewhat analogous to a main verb (and any adverbials processed thus far) being the frame of reference used to interpret subsequent adverbial phrases.

Developmental studies of children's discourse engagement and procedures in perception tasks (like comparing or contrasting attributes of objects) bears out the need to differentiate between a notion of "attention" and "frame of reference utilization." Young children do attend to other children's utterances; their utterances do make mention of elements mentioned by a preceding speaker. Yet their responses are somehow not "in tune" with a preceding speaker's. In both perception and language generation tasks young children use "local" rather than "wholistic" procedures (Gibson, Gibson, Pick, and Osser 1962, Karmiloff-Smith 1979); their procedures do not rely on some external frame of reference, and their objects of study and creation are disconnected islands.

As shown by Karmiloff-Smith (1979), children's models of extended discourse generation only begin to approximate the adult model when children replace their local procedures with more wholistic ones. They begin to organize and segment their utterances into larger units, and their subsequent linguistic forms, like those of adults, tend to be dependent and driven by unitization. Similarly in perception tasks we see a developmental trend away from local procedures to ones that involve processing with a fixed frame of reference.

Since wholistic organization and its use as a frame of reference, rather than selective attention, is the major factor of the developmental growth of a child's model of discourse to that of the adult model (and similarly for the child's perception procedures), it follows that wholistic organization and frame of reference processing must be a major, mandatory element governing maxim-abiding extended discourse engagement.

Frame of Reference and Point of Reference
I have already shown elsewhere (Reichman 1978) that discourse partitioning elicits Reichenbach's (1947) point of reference for the processing of tensed verbs; a major aspect of a reference frame is Reichenbach's point of reference for verbs. Hence changing a point of reference entails changing the reference frame that will be used in subsequent discussion.

To forestall unnecessary frame of reference shifts and still be able to refer to events outside of this reference frame, speakers can use certain linguistic devices, specifically the past perfect (future perfect) tense, to refer to prior (future) events. This follows from Reichenbach's observation that the future and past perfect tenses do not introduce a new reference point—hence they do not necessitate a reference frame shift.

In the following excerpt, for example, the speaker's focus is on the episode involving the speaker's discussion with Mary and not the episode in which Kurt spoke to Mary about the speaker. By citing the event in the past perfect tense, the speaker is able to introduce this event without causing a subsequent context space shift and accompanying shift of reference frame onto this prior episode.

SIMPLE PAST: "Mary's reaction this time was, um, 'Why are you doing that?' Starting to be negative, so it was clear
PAST PERFECT: that Kurt *had said* something to her.
SIMPLE PAST: And then I didn't really want to talk to him."

Notice that the time reference point for the speaker's subsequent simple past tense utterance is the same as that of the first clause in the simple past. The original time reference point has not been supplanted.

In contrast, in the next excerpt a speaker begins a new conversational move in the midst of another (i.e., an Interruption move as signaled by the speaker's use of the clue word "Incidentally") which results in a context space and accompanying frame of reference shift; the original time reference point is not immediately available and its respecification is required:

> "He made a comment to me about, uh, I'm not too sure what it was, something about the Portuguese people. *Incidentally, while I was standing there,* I noticed . . ."

Discourse Deictics

Let's now reconsider conversants' use of deictic expressions in discourse. In general, deictic referring expressions necessitate a reference system. "Close" *locative* deictics, such as "here," are used by speakers in reference to their own physical space: "far" locative deictics, such as "there," are used to refer to the listener's space. This results from the speaker's physical space constituting his or her *physical reference frame.* In the preceding excerpt, for example, the speaker uses "there" because her current physical space is not identical to the physical space being referenced in the excerpt.

However, there is another reference frame that influences a speaker's choice of deictic referring expression. I call such uses *discourse* deictics. Discourse deictics do not depend on a speaker's physical reference frame but rather on his or her discourse reference frame.[1] Examples of discourse deictics presented in chapter 5 were a speaker's use of "there," "here," "these," and "the," to refer to constituents of a preceding context space. (Other examples of such discourse deictic uses can be found in Fillmore 1975; Linde 1982; Reichman 1979, 1984; Schiffrin 1980.)

As demonstrated in chapter 5, speakers only use discourse close deictics to refer to elements of the active and controlling context spaces. This follows from the fact that a speaker's discourse reference frame is limited to these two spaces.

Selective Attention and Reference Frame Identifications

Given the importance of reference frame processing, it is possible to posit that frame of reference rather than selective attention is the primary explanation of many discourse phenomena. It simply follows from frame of reference criteria that a speaker's utterances are interpreted as communicating a single communicative act in relation to a single preceding controlling context space. Focused processing reflects this phenomenon—we can only use a single frame of reference at a time.

Let us now recharacterize our earlier analogy between discourse focused processing and possible selective attention procedures governing our single-view perceptions of ambiguous figures like the "Peter-Paul Goblet," the "Young Girl-Old Woman," and the "Necker Cube." Both are manifestations of our processing being limited to a single reference frame. As noted by Attneave (1974), each distinct view of these ambiguous figures really involves a unique reference system. As we only use one reference system at a time, we can only process one view at a time.

Thus the context space theory's emphasis on "relevant discourse context" identification can really be thought of as stressing discourse "frame of reference" processing. The claim here then is that discourse processings, like most other forms of cognitive endeavors, proceeds by individuals' understanding something in relation to some frame of reference. In discourse this frame of reference is a current controlling and active context space pair.

Formal Logic and Spontaneous Discourse

Our analysis of conversational moves and their characterizations in the context space grammar depend heavily on logical rules of inference assumed to be used by discourse participants. We have said that conversational moves represent the types of semantic and/or logical coherence relations holding between utterances of a discourse and that their formalizations can be compared in their content-free form to the formalizations of a formal logic system. Moves are described in a formal predicate-calculuslike language. Basic cognitive operations, such as "Infer," "Imply," "Instance," "Exclusive-or," and "For all" are treated as primitives of the language, and the grammar's generation/interpretation rules are written in terms of such primitive operations and the constituent elements of the grammar. Since recent work has questioned the applicability of the logician's formal logic systems to individuals' rules of inference, as exemplified by their spontaneous generation of supports and challenges of claims put forward, consideration of this issue is necessary.

Works of particular interest to this discussion are those of D'Andrade (1982), Johnson-Laird (1980), and Toulmin (1958). These works discuss the relevance and aptness of formal logic systems to "the mental processes that underlie ordinary reasoning and the question of what rules of inference they embody" (Johnson-Laird 1980). As Toulmin states, there is a tension between formal logic as a formal mathematical science and formal logic as a study of "proper, rational, normal thinking processes."

The works in essence provide a negative prognosis on the applicability of formal logic to everyday reasoning tasks. To quote Johnson-Laird, "The development of formal logic has not helped psychologists to elucidate the mental processes that underlie inference." And Toulmin, "It begins to look as though formal logic has indeed lost touch with its application." Our own analysis of spontaneous discourse, however, does not coincide with such negative rejection.

Johnson-Laird's and D'Andrade's rejection of "syllogistic inference rules" rests on their nonpredictivity of the specific conclusions generated, or lack thereof, by individuals given two propositions in an experimental environment. Johnson-Laird's replacement theory "contains no rules of inference. Its logical component consists solely in a procedure for testing mental models," where a mental model is the development of a consistent and "all combination possible" instantiated "microworld" of the assertions stated in the propositions. D'Andrade's replacement, on the other hand, is based on schemas and preexisting experience. Toulmin's rejection stems from his assertion that proofs in formal logic systems necessitate "analytic backing," something that we clearly never have sufficient evidence for in ordinary reasoning tasks.

Though these claims cannot be disputed, it is nevertheless fruitful and important to recognize that major aspects of formal logic are still quite applicable, and used, in ordinary reasoning tasks, in particular, in informal argumentation in ordinary discourse. As we have illustrated, an explication of how a statement of fact supports or challenges a preceding claim often appeals to some generic principle and logical rule of inference. In other words, people do seem to use the set of formalized syllogistic inference rules in their establishment of arguments, as strongly reflected by the fact that one's argument can be invalidated not only by an opponent's denial of the truth of one's statement of support but by an opponent's denying the validity of the inference rule used to yield the conclusion, given a principle of support and support statement.

Second, if we recognize that a formal logic system does not run ad infinitum in isolation and that it can be amended by, or at least sensitive to, probabilistic criteria and elements in focus, then the lack of correspondence between the predictions of formalized logic and what we find in actual experimentation and practice can be reduced. For example, as warranted in discourse argumentation, and characterized in this grammar, conversants use general rules of inference to establish conclusions evident to both speakers and listeners. Namely a speaker knows the claims she or he wants to prove and a listener (i.e., opponent) too is able to predict that the conclusion the current speaker is aiming at is one that challenges her or his own preceding claim or support of such.

Indeed, in the two classic cases of nonpredictivity supplied by Johnson-Laird, the valid conclusion not reached by the individuals tested was about an element that only appeared in a predicate position of a premise. For example, his studies show that people, in general, do not conclude "Some of the scientists are parents," given the two premises, "Some of the parents are drivers" and "All of the drivers are scientists." Now, it is well known that a subject of a propositional utterance is usually of higher focus than any of its other elements. As expected, therefore, a system defined in terms of drawing conclusions on elements in focus has difficulty in proving things about entities that are not of primary importance. An individual's use of formal rules of inference are goal directed, as determined by the structural nature of a preceding discourse and entities considered in focus in this discourse structure.

Analogies in Spontaneous Discourse

Analysis of our linguistic productions can thus lead to fruitful insight into the mechanisms of cognitive thought. A particularly interesting case is our treatment of analogies. Analogy construction has been a topic of much interest to cognitive researchers, and a major aspect of their investigations has been an attempt to identify those aspects of knowledge considered important in analogy (Black 1979; Carbonell 1980; Gentner 1980, 1982; Hobbs 1980; Miller 1979; Ortony 1979; Sternberg 1977; Winston 1980). Gentner's structure-mapping theory seems most compatible with our own findings. Gentner argues that analogies are based on an implicit understanding that "identical operations and relationships hold among nonidentical things. The relational structure is preserved but not the objects" (1982). In illustration Gentner presents the Rutherford analogy between the solar system and the hydrogen atom, where the relation "more massive than" holds between the corresponding magnitudes but where the absolute mass of the sun and that of the nucleus are of no relevance to the analogy.

The context space theory's contribution to this approach is its ability to characterize the relations that must remain constant between the two domains. The context space theory stresses that identification of these relations is dependent on the current relevant discourse context and on the discourse function of a speaker's conversational move. In maxim-abiding discourse only elements felt to be directly contrastive to elements in the initiating context space are discussed in the analogous space. The development of an analogous context space is thus constrained by the earlier development of the context space to which it is analogous. Analogy construction and comprehension then are not as unwieldy as has been supposed; they do not entail combinatorial measures of comparisons between two domains. Like all of discourse processing, they are focused tasks.

In their work on metaphor Lakoff and Johnson (1980) present a large set of metaphors that people use daily. Their many beautiful and phenomenologically insightful examples range from our natural equation and description of "love" in terms of "war" (e.g., "She fought for him," "He fled her advances," "He is slowly gaining ground with her," "She is beseiged by suitors") to "ideas" are "fashions" (e.g., "That idea went out of style years ago," "Marxism is currently fashionable in Western Europe," "Old fashioned notions have no place in today's society").

Many aspects of Lakoff and Johnson's analysis of how and why these metaphors proliferate in our daily lives are exceedingly compatible with the approach taken here. In particular, Lakoff and Johnson's focus on a gestalt approach to the use of metaphor, and notions of a metaphor simultaneously "highlighting" and "hiding" aspects of an object under discussion and thought, are in accord with the analysis given here. In other words, if we assume that gestalt refers to a wholistic view of relations within a given domain, then the two approaches correspond, since as has been illustrated earlier, Gentner's structure-mapping approach, used in the context space analysis, stresses the importance of a "schematization of relations" holding between the two domains under discussion. Correspondingly the "highlighting-hiding" phenomena underlying the use of analogies has been stressed in this work when, for example, it has been claimed that the acceptance or validity of an analogy is context dependent. So, for example, in the context of the conversation in which it was used, the analogy between "England" and "Syria" is valid, in that their respective situations of being an "invading side-favoring police force" is the "highlighted" feature validating the analogy. On the other hand, the analogy in this discourse context hides many of the differing features between these two domains, such as their vastly different social and cultural organizational behaviors.

Analyzing analogies found in spontaneous discourse, and rejections of them, gives clear reflections of some of our structural representations of knowledge, our notions of similarity and contrast, our ability to focus selectively on, and thereby highlight and hide, particular pieces of knowledge structures at given points in time, and our ability to integrate new knowledge into preexisting structures.

An analysis of conversants spontaneously discussing analogies is revealing of the dualistic nature of this cognitive task. On the one hand, it can be described as a noncreative, retrieval-matching task, whereas on the other, it can be described as highly creative and innovative. On the ordinary side, we have the fact that the creation of an analogy is restricted and highly predetermined by already existing knowledge structures. We know that contrary to some currently held beliefs, similarities do exist independent of metaphor, and it is precisely on such preexisting knowledge structures that we base our analogies. For example, let's consider N's initial response to M's analogy between Syria's being in Lebanon and England's being in Ireland: "I don't know enough about it to know, maybe." This response reflects that evaluation of an analogy necessitates some independent knowledge of the two domains involved. Or, for example, reconsidering M's earlier rejection of the "Ireland-Vietnam" analogy—"I mean, when you say it's like Vietnam, I can't take Vietnam. Vietnam is North Vietnam and South Vietnam"—it is clear that M bases her rejection on preexisting independently established knowledge structures of the two domains involved.

On the other hand, it is simultaneously true that given some basic structures for comparison, "metaphors can create new meanings for us" and in some cases can "induce similarities" (Lakoff and Johnson 1980). Exemplifying this later facet of analogies, we see M, in this same excerpt, trying to induce a new connection between the relations she has set up in her knowledge structure of the England-Ireland situation (i.e., England's motivation for behaving as she did) based on and induced by her earlier comparison of this situation to that of Syria and Lebanon. Thus analogy is both a "mere retrieval and matching process of already known information" and an "immediately creative" process.

A second aspect of the creativity involved in discussion of analogies is of course a conversant's insight into the aptness and relevance of an analogy to a particular point of discussion. This aspect of analogy use brings to the fore the whole question of "truth" in analogy and whether there is some fixed set of relations that must be true between two domains for an analogy between the two to be appropriate.

We would claim that, in general, there is no such fixed set of relations that must hold true between two domains. The aptness of an analogy, as it occurs in discourse, is not judged by assessing the number of relations that correspond between the two domains. Similarity and contrast do not exist in a vacuum. Rather, just as there is no set of fixed most important events to be stated each time a particular narrative is retold, so too in the case of analogies there is no set number of fixed relations that must correspond. In particular, as we have illustrated, only those relations standing in a somewhat causative nature to the relation claimed to hold in the initiating context space, which are critical for the purpose for which the analogy is being made, must hold true in the analogous context space. Thus it is linguistic context rather than existential truth that creates analogies in discourse.

The context space analysis of discourse and the grammar formulated to capture this analysis demonstrate that discourse processing relies largely on more general cognitive operations. The context space approach provides a way to understand discourse phenomena as reflective of the focused, frame of reference processing so fundamental to human cognitive capacities.

Chapter 9

The Structure of Discourse:

On the Generalizability of Discourse Theory

In chapter 1 we observed that the context space theory represents a major departure from many previous theories of discourse. We can now in the next two chapters look in some detail at a number of these approaches to discourse analysis, with a view toward understanding the major points of contention as well as of overlap and possible integration between them and the context space approach. Such comparisons will illuminate the specific contributions of our system to current attempts to understand how discourse is generated and interpreted.

We have said that the context space theory provides a structural and functional analysis of discourse. Structure and function are slippery concepts, however. To understand what structural and functional aspects of discourse the theory addresses, it will be useful to distinguish the context space theory's use of these concepts from those in other discourse analyses.

Does Genre Dictate Structure?

The context space theory purports to delineate general rules of maxim-abiding discourse processing, rules applicable to many forms of discourse engagement—teaching dialogues, therapy dialogues, narrative dialogues, informal debates—and underlying any form of coherent discourse. Much of previous text or discourse analysis, however, has been based on characterizing and differentiating between different discourse forms. Each such categorized form is treated as a distinct discourse "genre" or "schemata" with its own special and predictable structure. Various analysts have generated a profusion of genre classifications based on widely varying criteria for distinction and have delineated different conventions applicable to each type. Some classifications are based on the purpose of a set of utterances and result in classifications like "narratives," "arguments," and "descriptions." Other classifications are based on the style of presentation and result in distinctions like "poetry" or "verse." Still others are based on content and result in classifications like "drama," "fiction," and "riddles." Whatever the classification scheme this approach assumes that genre dictates structure, that shared rules of discourse development depend on these various possible structures.

Let us consider what it means to say that each discourse form has its own structure. In an article describing good writing skills, Collins and Gentner (1980) explain that "using structures that are easy to recognize, such as tree structures, lists, and tables, is one important strategy." This use of structure is general and abstract, an architectural notion of design. Later in the same article, however, the authors distinguish between another set of structures, called "forms."

> *Pyramid Form.* Any text can be structured so as to cover the most important ideas or events first and then to fill in more and more detail. . . .
> *Story or Narrative Form.* Any text can be structured according to the temporal and casual relations between the events that occurred. . . .
> *Argument Form.* . . . One version of the form is: introduction, background, definition of issues, statement of what is to be proven, . . .
> *Process-Of-Elimination Form.* This is a kind of inverted pyramid structure where the writer makes an argument by eliminating all possible alternatives.

In these descriptions structure refers to the selection and ordering of details used to develop a topic. The descriptions focus on content-relational aspects of the forms, not their abstract design features.

Some discourse analysts interchange the term "structure" with the term "schema" (or "schemata"), which is also used in divergent ways. In a common use of the term Sheridan (1978) explains that "schemata represent generic concepts which are stored in memory. These generic concepts include underlying objects, situations, events, actions, and sequences of actions." In this sense schemas refer to "scripts" of prototypical series of actions to be applied in stereotypic situations or "frames" containing prototypical descriptions that help us recognize actions or objects.[1] When discourse analysts claim that schemas are fundamental to our interpretation of a discourse, they are usually referring to these kinds of content-rich, world-knowledge schemas (e.g., Cicourel 1981, Lehnert 1981).

However, schema is also used to refer to a content-independent structure of organization. For example, Mosenthal (1978) explains that "schemata are often defined as the expectations people have concerning the parts which should occur in stories and paragraphs and the relationship which should occur among the parts." This does not contradict the previously defined notion of a schema, since the idea of, say, an "oral narrative" is just as much a generic concept in memory as in one's concept of "being in a restaurant." However, there is a qualitative difference between this structural notion of schema and the one encompassed in a notion of a content-rich script. Anderson, Picher, and Shirey (1979) have usefully distinguished between the two types of schemata as used in discourse interpretation (as summarized by Lange 1981):

> "Textual schemata" embodies knowledge of discourse conventions that signal organization, with specialized conventions characteristic of distinct text forms and other conventions common to most text forms. These organizational schemata include a story schema, a personal letter schema, a news article schema, a scientific report schema, and so on. "Content schema," embodies the reader's existing knowledge of real and imaginary worlds. "What the reader already believes about a topic helps to structure the interpretation of new messages about this topic."

Given the two basic senses of structure by Collins and Gentner (e.g., tree vs. narrative) we are in a better position to understand what it means to claim that "different discourse genres have different structures." In the content-relational or organizational development sense of structure, different genres indeed have different structures. "Setting," for instance, is a part of a "narrative genre" but not a part of an argument structure; "support" is a part of an "argument genre" but not of a narrative. Where one's goal is to account for differences in thematic developments, the idea that different genres have different structures allows us to set up specific predictions of what is to come next in a given discourse form.

However, in the sense of structure referring to trees, lists, and tables—the sense of structure as architectural design or abstract underlying form—the claim that different genres have different structures is, in light of the context space theory analysis, clearly false.

Genre approaches to discourse analysis generally ignore the more abstract, architectural principles of discourse structure. Rather, they specify components of particular discourse forms and the order in which these appear. As we shall see, this kind of structural description leads to some crucial deficiencies in the account of discourse phenomena. To illustrate, we shall look briefly at two "genre dictates structure" analyses, one by Hasan and one by Rumelhart, who base their genre distinctions on very different criteria but ultimately produce a similar characterization of discourse structure.

Hasan (1977) uses extralinguistic, situational concepts to characterize different discourse types. Using Halliday's (1970) notions of "field" (the specific situational context of an interaction), "tenor" (the kind of contact dictated by the roles and relationships of the people involved), and "mode" (the communication mode), Hasan posits that every discourse genre has its own "contextual configuration" (CC) defined by these elements. For instance, the following CC defines a genre Hasan calls the "professional consultation, client, telephone" genre:

Field: professional consultation; medical; application for appointment.
Tenor: client: patient-applicant; agent for consultant: receptionist; thus "maximum social distance."
Mode: aural channel: −visual contact: telephone conversation; spoken medium.

According to Hasan, the values in a CC determine "what elements may occur in what configuration." In the CC described, for instance, the constituents include

Obligatory Elements	*Optional Elements*
Identification (I)	Greeting (G)
Application (A)	Query (Q)
Offer (O)	Documentation (D)
Confirmation (C)	Summary (S)
	Finis (F)

Using these, Hasan offers the following text and accompanying "structural description":

—Good morning (G) Dr. Scott's clinic (I) may I help you (Q)
—Oh hello good morning (G) this is Mrs. Lee speaking (I) I wonder if I could see Dr. Scott today (A)
—um well let me see I'm afraid Mrs. Lee I don't have much choice of time today would 6:15 this evening suit you (O)
—yes, yes, that'll be fine (C)
—may I have your address and phone number please (D)
—24 May Avenue, North Clyde and the number is 527–2755 (D)

—thank you (D) so that's Mrs. Lee for Dr. Scott at 6:15 this
evening (S)
—mm yes thanks (F)
—thank you (F)

Hasan's analyses suggests that in the main it is the kind of social interaction taking place that dictates the composition of the discourse.

Rumelhart (1975), on the other hand, does not base his genre
characterizations on such external situational criteria. His work in
genre/schemata classification concerns what he calls "story grammars." Story grammars have two sets of rules: (1) syntactic rules that
specify compositional elements and (2) semantic rules that specify
their relationships.

Syntactic Rules
Rule 1:   A Story is composed of Setting and Episode.
Rule 2:   A Setting is composed of State Descriptions.
Rule 3:   An Episode is a sequence of Events and Character
          Reactions.
Semantic Rules
Rule 1': The Setting described must allow for the Episode.
Rule 2': The State Descriptions making up the Episode follow
          one another.
Rule 3': The Event must have caused the Reaction.

Rumelhart's notion of structure is thus highly specific to the retelling
of a set of events and strongly linked to relations between phenomena of the real world.

The foundations of and the criteria for genre distinctions in Hasan's and Rumelhart's analyses are thus quite different. But both
purport to be studying a discourse's structure, and both assume that
identifying this structure means characterizing a linear, sequential,
and fixed order for component constituents of this structure.

Let us compare these analyses to the context space approach. In the
context space analysis certain constituents of a discourse are identified based on their "thematic" connection with other constituents.
For instance, a debative issue context space can have several support
subconstituents. However, there is no a priori, linear characterization of where these thematically related constituents will appear in a
given discourse. This is because describing structure by a fixed
linear characterization leaves no room for the nonlinear suspensions
and resumptions of conversational development and cannot account
for the important fact of discourse flexibility (see Goffman 1974). For
example, fixed linear characterizations do not easily accommodate
interruption suspensions with subsequent returns—closing sus-

pensions with subsequent reopenings or development of a second subordinate constituent that does not relate primarily to the last preceding constituent but to an earlier one.

For both Hasan and Rumelhart discourse developments depend solely on semantic and/or temporal relations between events in the real world. But in fact discourse developments do not depend solely on these external relations. With respect to narratives, for instance, though two events may have actually occurred in a single episode, it does not follow necessarily that they both warrant mention in the telling of the episode in a given discourse context. And even if both events are mentioned, it does not necessarily follow that they will be mentioned together, or in relation to each other. In the telling of a story or episode, not all events that actually occurred are stated; the telling is limited to a specification of only those events needed to illustrate a particular point. Thus, though many events may "belong together," as they have occurred in the same time frame in the same location or even led to each other, they do not necessarily belong together in a same discourse context. What particular descriptions of a subject enhance fulfillment of a particular conversational move is determined by the discourse context in relation to which the move is being performed. It is the discourse function served by a particular storytelling that mainly determines what belongs where.

The kind of structure revealed in genre-specific analyses of discourse is intricately interwoven with the content of particular discussions and can best be thought of as "textual schemata" or "specific form" structures. The claim that "different genres have different structures" might then be clarified: different genres usually have different thematic developments.

Though the context space theory does address itself to the question of different thematic developments, for instance, in its specification of various conversational moves and the particular inferential components associated with these specific moves, the specification alone does not constitute our approach to discourse structure. Of more importance is the interaction between the specification and the dynamic flow of discourse. The crucial aspects of conversational move identification in our theory are recognizing (1) that the implicit components of a conversational move must be ferreted out, tracked, and recorded as a part of the discourse, and (2) that the standardization of the moves have different effects on the discourse structure. For example, the effect of performing a second support move closes the preceding support space, putting it in the discourse background while leaving the claim being supported in the foreground. The context space analysis has been developed to characterize both local and high level features of discourse processing. The main force of the context space approach is its identification of an underlying abstract level of discourse structure and its derivation of general rules of maxim-abiding discourse engagement from this structure. For example, we are concerned with delineating the effects of closing, interrupting, or subordinating to a context space. The theory thus addresses itself to both the content-relational forms of discourse and to its "architectural design" features. The architectural features are common to all forms of discourse, and they result in a shared set of linguistic rules.

In the conversational excerpts presented throughout our discussion, we have seen that within any single discourse many "genres" appear: one minute a narrative is being told; the next minute the conversants are arguing about the goodness or badness of an actor's action in the narrative. Within the supposed separate logical genre, for example, we have seen embedded narratives serving as supports or challenges to an opponent's claim. If all rules of discourse were genre specific, we would have to assume that conversants switched their discourse processing procedures and rules from minute to minute—a remarkably unparsimonious processing system.

On empirical grounds as well we have reason to reject the notion that all discourse processing is genre specific. We have seen, for instance, ample linguistic evidence that the same rules of reference and clue words are employed across different discourse types. Thus, though for some purposes we may want to distinguish genres of discourse, we cannot let our structural analysis of discourse depend on these distinctions.

Abstract Structure in Other Theories of Discourse

Many discourse analysts have recognized elements of the abstract structure underlying various kinds of discourse. A brief look at the similarities and differences between such analyses and the context space theory will help delineate the essential features of our system and provide support for our notion that this system is in fact generalizable across discourse forms.

The Ethnomethodologists

The ethnomethodologists share the context space theory's goal of explicating discourse rules common to all forms of maxim-abiding oral communication. As is the case for the context space system, the ethnomethodologists derive their rules from the analysis of freely occurring dialogues.[2] The analysis begins with rules for "turn taking." Why this is so should be clear: turn taking obviously occurs in all conversations, no matter what the subject or who the participants. Focusing on this content-free and (in some respects) situational context-free feature of discourse, Sacks, Schegloff, and Jefferson (1974) identify operational rules of transfer like "current speaker selects next" and address issues such as how various kinds of conversational pauses reflect the operation of various rules.

In delineating the relation between a preceding and succeeding turn and identifying legal points of transfer between speakers, the ethnomethodologists employ the notion of "adjacency pairs" as a major feature of discourse organization: pairs like greeting/greeting, offer/acceptance or refusal, question/answer. On one speaker's turn the speaker utters the first part of the pair, and on the next turn a second speaker utters the second part. Notice that not only is identification of such pairs a natural extension of the turn-taking focus, but it naturally follows the linear, sequential, temporal view of discourse resulting from this focus. This is the ethnomethodologists' primary notion of how preceding discourse context constrains and predicts succeeding conversational development.

Though the context space theory stresses the recurrence and frequency of conversational moves necessitating "discourse popping" and focuses on the mainly nonlinear and nonsequential deep structure, rather than on the superficial sequential structures of conversation, the two analyses begin to approach each other when the ethnomethodologists discuss "seeming violations" of turn-taking, adjacency pairs and sequential organization in discourse. There is recognition that interruptions occur and that linguistic markers serve as clues of these interruptions to listeners. However, though in the context space theory an interruption (with its associated markers like "Incidentally" or "By the way") is a frequent and legitimate conversational move that can occur anywhere in discourse, Schegloff and Sacks (1973) stress that interruptions are "misplacements" in discourse and that "misplacement markers . . . display an orientation by their user to the proper sequential-organization character of a particular place in a conversation." Their examples of interruption include "an utterance inserted after a question has been asked but before it has been answered" and the introduction of a new topic of discourse in "the closing section of talk."[3]

A second example of partial correspondence between the ethnomethodological and context space views of discourse is Sacks' taking note of the fact that certain ordinary rules of discourse, like turn taking, are suspended during development of discourse units such as stories, riddles, and jokes: a single speaker may retain the floor until completing one of these forms. Since the context space theory views a conversation not as a linear sequence of turns but as a forum for the functional development and fulfillment of conversational moves, it does not have to explain a speaker's holding the floor for longer than a single utterance as an exception to some rule. Rather, a speaker "legitimately" holds a turn as long as it takes to fulfill a conversational move. In telling a story in fulfillment of some move, a speaker naturally retains the floor until completion of the story (i.e., the move).

Given the notion then of a conversational move and the associated construction of a discourse unit, we can enhance the ethnomethodological analysis of turn taking. Let us recall that a discourse unit is not simply composed of a set of utterances referring to a set of events of a single time period that leads to a climax and/or punch line. Discourse units are complex structures: they have subconstituents, a culminating event, punch line, or the like. Thus, for example, in the context space theory the assertion of a claim and presentation of two separate narrative supports for the claim result in development of a single discourse unit (albeit the unit is composed of subunits). To extend the ethnomethodological analysis, we allow speakers to retain legitimately the floor for development of a context space and its subconstituents. In fact sometimes it would be inappropriate to consider a turn over before execution of a set of various conversational moves. For example, in the context space analysis, when an analogy is used for the purposes of explanation or challenge, it is mandatory for the speaker to return to the initiating space of the analogy. Though here subdiscussions and a temporary releasing of turns to coconversants is possible, the first speaker's turn is really not completed before resumption of the initiating space of the analogy is performed.

The ethnomethodologists do recognize in any case that there are content and content-free structural elements common to various forms of naturally occurring discourse, and they recognize that not all of these elements fit easily into a linear and sequential view of discourse structure. The context space theory's more abstract, nonlinear, hierarchical view of discourse structure, however, provides a more parsimonious and coherent account of relations between discourse elements.

An interesting bridge between the ethnomethodological school of thought and a more abstract structural approach is provided by Polanyi (1978). In a study of oral narratives Polanyi notes that speakers often begin a story with an abstract statement of some sort, which they immediately follow with a first event of the story event line. The

retelling of this first event, however, is more often than not interrupted in midstream by the speaker's citation of some "interesting"
background material, the relevance of which only becomes apparent
at a later point in the story's retelling. After completion of the background material, speakers resume from the point of interruption.

Polanyi claims that such "false starts" are not errors or accidental
interruptions but can be thought of as planned behavior necessitated
by rules of turn taking. To get hold of the floor, a speaker starts a
narrative with an explicit statement of its relevance to a current topic
of discourse. Beginning the narrative gives the speaker the right of
floor until the story is completed. Once having the floor, the speaker
can relax and indulge in the telling of the story, which may include
elaborating on some points of background.

Polanyi observes that such false starts and resumptions can be
thought of as "pushes" and "pops." Polanyi thus immediately focuses on the nonlinear, dynamic features of discourse engagement.
In addition Polanyi notes that false starts are regularly linguistically
resumed with the marker "so" (in the context space analysis "so" is
shown to accompany resumption of a superordinate after subconstituent building) and by repetition of the phrase interrupted (in the
context space analysis such repetition is also identified as a return
mechanism). Both the push-pop concept and the linguistic signals
observed by Polanyi complement the kind of discourse analysis offered by the context space approach.

The Tagmemic School
Unlike the ethnomethodologists, or the context space approach, the
Tagmemic school begins analysis by distinguishing between different genre forms. There are nonetheless some important similarities
between the results of the Tagmemic analysis and the context space
approach.

According to proponents of this school (e.g., Jones 1977, Pike 1967,
Longrace 1972, Longrace and Levinsohn 1977), discourse, like single
sentences, should be thought of as having an underlying "deep
structure," defined as an organization of discourse constituents and
subconstituents. Each constituent is identified by "slots" normally
associated with its presence. In the main the Tagmemic school's notion of constituent-subconstituent structure is the content-oriented
"textual schemata" structure discussed previously, a sequential representation of thematically related constituents of particular discourse forms. For example, the Tagmemicists identify a "narrative
genre" composed of slots for aperture, stage, prepeak episode, peak,
postpeak episode, closure, and finis (where aperture and finis are in

some sense outside the boundaries of the actual episode). This analysis recognizes the functional relationships of discourse elements, for instance, the importance of climax and resolution in a story. A story, to be a story, must have a climactic event. This is similar to the context space approach, which rests on viewing discourse utterances as functional in nature.

Like the context space approach, which identifies surface linguistic forms that reflect relationships between discourse elements, the Tagmemicists also attempt to identify some surface level "cohesion" devices operative across discourse genres. Many of the ties they identify, however, seem to be artifacts of the content of a current discussion. For example, Longrace and Levinsohn (1977) cite "lexical ties and paraphrase" as one form of surface structure cohesive device and, in exemplification, present sequences like, "He *shot* him and he *died*." To consider such sequences as illustrating linguistic cohesion devices is misleading because they are just epiphenomena of discussing a given discourse topic. However, Longrace and Levinsohn's list of structural cohesive devices includes some items that cannot be attributed merely to the content of discourse. In particular, they discuss the fact that certain particle and affix markers are used in the Cubeo language to distinguish a story's main character from its other protagonists. In addition Longrace and Levinsohn speculate that there is some correlation between deictic references and "paragraph breaks." For example, they have noticed that "the use of the demonstrative 'chi' (that) in Inga, to modify references to participants, partially corresponds with a new paragraph." These aspects of cohesion complement the context space's "cohesion rules," specifying that some reference forms can only be used for discourse entities in high focus and/or in the current relevant discourse context.

In addition, though not actually representing a developed theory of discourse popping, Longrace and Levinsohn recognize that pure linearity does not govern thematic development. For example, in considering the following set of sentences,

> 1. So the mother-in-law went ahead, weeping, to where she had buried the piece of wild papaya. 2. On arriving, she said, "Here is where he is buried." 3. Having said that, she fled a little way off and hanged herself.

> 4. The father dug into the grave, and on removing the earth, found just a piece of wild papaya. 5. "Oh, no!" he said. "I'm going to find out what really happened."

> 6. So saying, he followed her footprints. 7. and found her; 8. she was hanging, having strangled herself.

Longrace and Levinsohn note that "the actions of sentence 4 do follow not from that of 3, but of 2; the father dug in response to the mother-in-law's words, not her hanging herself."

Thus though the Tagmemic school's analysis of discourse does not reach the abstract level of analysis reflected in the context space theory, their work recognizes many important structural phenomena the context space theory has been developed to explain.

The Functional-Sentence-Perspective Approach

The Functional-Sentence-Perspective (FSP) (Danes 1974, Halliday 1976, Sgall and Hajičo'va 1977) or the Communicative Dynamism (CD) (Firbas 1971) school of thought is another major approach taken to text/discourse analysis. The FSP and CD approaches emanate from Marthusies's early work in the Prague school, which is based on distinguishing between the "theme" and "rheme" of an utterance. The theme of an utterance, usually called the "old" or "given" information, is what the sentence is all about; the rheme of the utterance, usually called the "new" information, is what is being added or predicated about this known information. A theme-rheme distinction is usually based on the claim that the theme of a sentence precedes its rheme.

Though most of this work centers on the analysis of single sentences, the approach has also been used to address questions of structure in more extended discourse. For example, Palkova and Palek (1977) illustrate how a theme-rheme distinction can be used to explain how and why certain "fronting" operations are more appropriate in one discourse context than another. A more comprehensive endeavor toward extended text/discourse analysis by proponents of the FSP approach is presented in a well-known work by Halliday and Hasan, *Cohesion in English* (1976).

Halliday and Hasan posit three separate elements of text analysis: (1) the texture within a sentence, (2) the texture of the whole discourse, and (3) the structure of this discourse. By texture within the sentence Halliday and Hasan refer to the structural decomposition of a sentence onto its theme and rheme; by texture of the discourse they refer to a set of linguistic "cohesive ties," which they claim reflect the "hangingness together of a text"; and by structure they mainly refer to ethnomethodological work and notions like "textual schemata." We shall see, however, that Halliday and Hasan's divorce of text structure from "texture" and their mainly linear view of a discourse's structure result in an unsatisfactory account of relations between discourse elements.

Cohesion, according to Halliday and Hasan, "occurs where the interpretation of some element in the discourse is dependent on that of another." Such cohesion is in their view the underlying element of text that makes it "hang together as a text." They identify five major cohesive devices underlying "cohesive text production," which they illustrate as follows:

1. *Reference*
   A: Wash and core *six cooking apples*. Put *them* into a fireproof pan.
2. *Substitution*
   B: I shoot the hippopotamus with *bullets* made of platinum. Because if I use leaden *ones,* his hide is sure to flatten them.
3. *Ellipsis*
   C: Does Jane sing?
       Yes, she does. (SING)
4. *Conjunction*
   D: My client says he does not know this witness. *Further* he denies ever having seen her or spoken to her.
   E: "You'll find yourself in the Fourth Square in no time. Well, that square belongs to Tweedledum and Tweedledee
       the Fifth is mostly water—the Sixth belongs to Humpty Dumpty—*But* you make no remark?"
5. *Lexical Cohesion*
   F: "Well, I'll eat it," said Alice, "and if it makes me *larger,* I can reach the *key;* and if it makes me *smaller,* I can creep under the *door.*"
       (larger—smaller; key—door)

Such examples illustrate that Halliday and Hasan's notion of cohesion and the surface linguistic phenomena reflecting such cohesion are radically different than those based on a hierarchical organization of discourse utterances. That similar words appear in a given stretch of discourse is an artifact of the content of discussion. Further divorcing lexical cohesion from structure can be misleading and can lead to a false analysis of a piece of text. For example, consider the following text presented by Grosz (1977):

P1: I'm going camping next weekend. Do you have a two-person *tent* I could borrow?

P2:   Sure. I have a two-person backpacking *tent*.
P1:   The last trip I was on there was a huge storm. It poured for two hours. I had a *tent* but I got soaked anyway.
P2:   What kind of *tent* was it?
P1:   A tube *tent*.
P2:   Tube *tents* don't stand up well in a real storm.
P1:   True.
P2:   Where are you going on this trip?
P1:   Up in the Moinarets.
P2:   Do you need any other equipment?
P1:   No.
P2:   Ok. I'll bring the *tent* in tomorrow.

As Grosz notes, in an explication consistent with the context space approach, the referent of the tent in P2's last utterance is the one that he owns and intends to lend to P1; it is not the tent owned by P1 which was the one last mentioned before P2's utterance. Grosz explains this by noting that the two tents lie in separate "focus spaces," the second space being a subordinate of the first. By the time of P2's last utterance, only the superordinate space containing mention of the tent that P2 owns is in focus; hence it is the only available referent in the current discourse context. But according to Halliday and Hasan's linear view of a discourse structure, such a hierarchical partitioning of the discourse cannot be recognized and hence, according to their analysis, the connection between all occurrences of "tent" in the dialogue are equivalent.

In addition *nonpronominalization* rather than pronominalization is a major linguistic device that reflects a discourse's structure, cohesion, and texture. Halliday and Hasan's example of pronominalization is basically no different than ordinary pronominalization found within the single utterance. It is not the use of a pronoun that gives "cohesion" to the "wash and core apples" text. These utterances form a coherent piece of text (i.e., the combination "hangs together") not because the pronoun "them" is used but because they jointly describe a set of cooking instructions.

There is, however, another work from the FSP school that does provide a more plausible structural account of relations between discourse elements: Danes's (1974) work on "thematic progression." Basing his analysis on the theme-rheme distinction, Danes posits that the following three progressions account for much if not all of discourse development:

1. Make the old rheme the new theme:

T1 → R1

T2 (= R1) → R2

2. Give a new rheme to the preceding theme:

T1 → R1
T1 → R2

3. Discuss a new rheme and theme pair that stands in the same relation to a higher level theme as does a preceding theme-rheme pair:

T1

T2 → R2   T3 → R3   T4 → R4

Though Danes's interpretation is meant quite literally—in (1) T2 is identical to R1, in (2) the second T1 is a literal remention of the first, and so on—at a more abstract level his work addresses the hierarchical nature of text structure. To see this, let's represent the three figures as

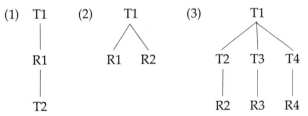

Now, if we do not limit T1, R1, and R2 to be particular constituents of two successive utterances, then (2) in the figure can represent a speaker's citation of two supports (R1, R2) for a claim, T1. Under a similar extension, (3) can be used as a representation for, say, three counterchallenges to a claim T1, each counterchallenge having its own respective cited support.

Though this is useful, it is not yet sufficient. In particular, we are immediately confronted with the dilemma of "What's in a link?" posed by Woods (1975). Though the representations depict the notion of subordination found in discourse, how do we know, for example, in (1) whether R1 is a support of or a challenge to T1? Or, in

(2) whether R1 and R2 denote two supports of T1, two challenges of T1, and/or one support and one challenge? Clearly, a more elaborate structure is required to distinguish between these possibilities. A discourse structure needs to be able to differentiate explicitly, as the context space structure does, between subordination and particular subordinating relations. Thus, though an FSP approach can recognize hierarchical structure in discourse, the context space theory provides a more complete and more accurate account of the structural basis of relations among discourse elements.

Hierarchical Approaches
There are a number of works that have explicitly recognized the underlying abstract structure of discourse: Cohen's (1984) work on argument structures, Linde's (1974) work on apartment descriptions, Grosz's (1977) work on task-oriented dialogues, Levin and Moore's (1977) work on dialogue games, Litman and Allen's (1984) work on clarification subdialogues, Mehan's (1978) work on school interactions, Linde and Gougen's (1978) work on planning discourses, Weiner's (1979) work on explanation, among others. Cohen, Grosz, Linde, and Weiner all propose an underlying hierarchical tree structure to discourse where in a conversation the "discourse focus" is on one subnode of the tree. Creation of a subnode represents further development of a given theme of discourse. Traversing up the network corresponds to a "discourse pop," wherein one resumes discussion of an earlier subject that has led to a current subordinated discussion. A brief consideration of these analyses will indicate the ways in which they support the context space approach.

Linde analyzes the ways people describe apartment layouts. Her main claim is that people do not randomly choose rooms, or parts of rooms, to describe; they structure their descriptions according to a schematic, temporal "tour-walk" through an apartment. Linde posits that describing an object, like describing an apartment, constitutes developing a single discourse unit, composed of many subnodes in a treelike representation. In the apartment situation each node of the tree corresponds to a room in the apartment, and the single relation between all nodes is "physical tour-walk sequence."

A major conceptual overlap between Linde's work and the context space approach is that both identify the important relationship between underlying discourse structure and referring expressions. For instance, Linde notes that items from one node of a tree, referenced at another node, are referred to by the far deictic "that" rather than the close deictic "this." This corresponds to the context space analysis' similar findings that (1) the far deictic "that" is used to reference an element from the preceding discourse which is no longer in the current relevant discourse context and (2) that the close deictic "this" is used to refer to elements currently in the relevant discourse context.

Grosz's discourse analysis, like Linde's, focuses on a specific domain of knowledge and some goal-directed task entered into by a conversant. In Grosz's work subjects are asked to interact verbally with an "expert" to build a pump. Grosz's dialogues and analyses support the notion that an individual's utterances can be hierarchically partitioned into a treelike network. And, as in Linde's work, the discourse structure identified closely corresponds to the structure of the object as it is considered for task purposes. In Grosz's tree representation, the single identified relation between nodes of the discourse tree is the task-subtask relation.

Grosz goes even further than Linde in identifying the correspondence between discourse structure and a conversant's pronominal reference form. Among her findings is the observation that on return from a subordinate node in a tree (where no branch crossover occurred), an individual would immediately repronominalize references to constituents at the superordinate node, despite seeming intervening semantic contenders for the pronominal reference in the subordinate discussion.

There are both major correspondences and major distinctions between the context space approach and the works of Linde and Grosz. Both Linde and Grosz emphasize a hierarchical organization of discourse utterances and the influence of such an organization on a speaker's pronominal and deictic reference forms. However, their analyses identify only a single relation between nodes of the hierarchy, based on a particular external state of affairs being described. In contrast, the context space theory has attempted to characterize a whole set of possible node relations for any given subject of discussion or task of accomplishment (e.g., challenge, interruption, support).

Another major distinction between the context space approach and Linde's or Grosz's analyses is that the relations between discourse elements identified by Linde and Grosz are only superordinate-subordinate relations. Thus in Grosz's upward treewalk along a single branch pronominalization is always allowed. However, once we catalogue the many different types of interrelationships that are possible between discourse constituents, with their varying effects on the foregrounding and backgrounding of preceding context spaces, we find a simple treelike representation of nodes and corresponding reference rules inadequate. In the context space analysis, for instance, resuming an earlier context space does not always allow for immediate repronominalization of the elements contained in that space even if the space is a superordinate (e.g., return to a generating context space). In addition lacking from both Linde's and Grosz's works is recognition or an analysis of the predominate discourse-structure role played by nonpronominalization (see chapter 5).

In Linde's and Grosz's work on "planning discourses," which centers on identifying the underlying structure of a speaker's explanation of some plan of action, once again a strictly superordinate-subordinate tree is presented. In this case, however, nonterminal nodes of the tree explicitly cite one of a number of possible node relations. In the main their representation of planning discourses is similar to the structure Weiner identifies for explanations, and we shall therefore leave exemplification of this approach to the fuller discussion of Weiner's work.[4]

Weiner posits a treelike structure of discourse. Nonterminals of a tree correspond to particular "legal" semantic/logical relationships between successive utterances, and terminal nodes of the tree correspond to the specific utterances expressed. The following thematic relationships are identified in Weiner's work:

1. The Statement-AND-Statement relation.
2. The Statement-EXAMPLE relation.
3. The Statement-REASON relation.
4. The GENERAL-SPECIFIC relation.
5. The Statement-ALT-Statement relation.
6. The IF-THEN relation.

Weiner notes that these relations often are recursive and that a discourse structure is usually some elaborate tree. For example, consider Weiner's parse of the following statements:

1. Why a person who is a financial analyst should need to go to an accountant.
2. Because uh particularly this year, he's up on taxes and otherwise I would have to go read the book, you know, Lasser's and go through that.

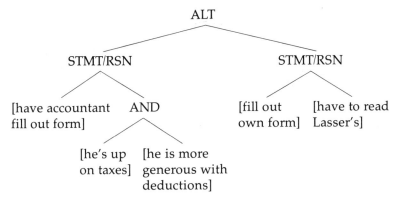

We could perhaps posit that Weiner's tree reflects the hierarchical structure underlying all forms of discourse, with only the specific functional nonterminal node relations distinguishing one discourse genre from the next. So, for example, presumably the narrative genre would have more CAUSE/ACTION relations than ALTERNATIVES relations. However, discourse production/interpretation is more complex than Weiner's structural representation suggests. The representation does not give a full account of the complex interrelationships found in a discourse or text.

For example, let's consider the occurrence of a challenge-counterchallenge move in discourse. The genetics-environment debate cited earlier began with D and R arguing whether heredity is responsible for an individual's criminal behavior or if society, the environment, is responsible for criminal behavior. R, on the side of the "heredity cause," shows that only one of two twins living at home (presumably sharing the same environment) manifested negative interactive social behavior; D, on the side of the "environment cause," claims that no two people can ever be said to be sharing the same environment. Using Weiner's structural representation of discourse, the analysis for this argument would be something like

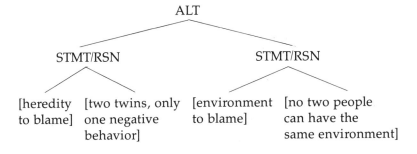

But such representation is clearly inadequate and misleading. Specifically, the claim that "no two people can have the same environment" is not a support or evidence for the claim that the "environment is to blame for criminal behavior." Its status as a support for this position is a derivative one, stemming only from the fact that it is a countersupport to the support given for the "heredity is to blame" position. This dual, inherited attribute of "no two people have the same environment" is not easily represented in a tree structure.

In addition Weiner's representation system leaves no room for the inferential components needed to explicate how one proposition can serve as support of another (i.e., the implicit support-principle underlying most statements of support) nor does it leave room for the general rule of inference being relied on in the giving of such support (i.e., to distinguish between supports relying on valid and those relying on invalid inference rules).

Therefore a much more elaborate network of concepts and differentiating connections between nodes is needed to encode the varied interrelationships that exist between a discourse's basic constituents. Nonterminal nodes of the network cannot be simple predicates like those proposed by Weiner. A much more sophisticated network construction than those so far proposed is needed. The foundations of such a network are provided in the context space grammar and the discourse ATN we have described.

The Context Space's Characterization of Abstract Structure in Discourse

At its highest (or deepest) level of characterization the context space theory addresses the most general and abstract features of discourse structure. At this level there are no designations of components particular to specific functional thematic developments. A context space is merely an abstract structure with slots for (1) a propositional representation of the discourse utterances said to lie in the space, (2) the conversational move fulfilled by the space, (3) propositional representations of the implicit components needed for the space to fulfill a move, (4) the influential status of the space at any given point in a discourse, (5) links to preceding discourse context spaces to which this space has some relation and a specification of the relation, (6) links to subconstituent context spaces, and (7) focus level assignments to constituents of the utterances said to lie in the space.

If we use this level of characterization, all discourse utterances, whether narration, discussion, explanation, description, or argument, share the same structure. After characterizing possible status and focus level assignments, and the scope and nature of change allowed at any given point, we can specify a single set of rules applicable to all discourse forms:

1. A conversation is a series of conversational moves, each move corresponding to a particular functional relation between the utterances generated and a preceding context space (if any) in the foreground of discourse.
2. Utterances in a single context space serve the same conversational move.
3. All conversational moves have an associated set of preconditions and effects that derive from, and operate on, the discourse's underlying deep structure.
4. During development of a subconstituent space, the superordinate space is assigned a controlling status.
5. At any given point the current relevant discourse context governing subsequent discussion is the active and controlling space pair.
6. Closing a context space results in all of its constituents being given zero focus level assignments.
7. Putting a context space into a generating status results in a reassignment of its high focus constituent to a medium focus.
8. A context space having an open status assignment reflects that it is expected/required that the space be resumed and completed after completion of the digressive context space.
9. Closed context spaces can be ignored in the discourse popping process.
10. Discourse popping results in the closing of all context spaces developed during intervening discussion (i.e., those not already closed).
11. Generation/interpretation rules only access context spaces in a current relevant discourse context.
12. Linguistic markers like "But" signal that an active context space should be closed and that a closed space is to be reactivated; clue words like "By the way" signal that an active context space should be reassigned an open status.
13. Linguistic markers like "Now" and "Like" signal that a subconstituent, subordinate context space is about to be developed.
14. Close discourse deictics can only be used for constituents in a controlling or active context space.

15. Pronominal reference can only be used to refer to a constituent in "high focus" in a controlling or active context space (subject to some intersentential exceptions).

Corresponding to the description of the context space theory at its most abstract level of characterizing discourse, we can identify a set of features that any grammar (processor) of discourse should possess:

1. Conversational move identification based on functionality.
2. Constraints and actions associated with these moves. Constraints are written in terms of preceding conversational development and the resulting discourse structure. Actions include the effects of the move on the underlying discourse structure.
3. List of outstanding discourse expectations to direct generation and interpretation of subsequent utterances.
4. Conversational move and clue word classification to direct generation and interpretation of subsequent utterances.
5. Methods to track the changing relevant discourse context as a conversation progresses.
6. Categorization of a set of methods for conversational move fulfillment. These methods identify the implicit components underlying a move. They should be made explicit by the grammar.
7. Context space identification and classification by slots.
8. Generation and interpretation routines should only access an active and controlling context space pair.
9. Anaphoric and deictic reference generation and/or interpretation should be guided by the active and controlling context space pair.

The context space approach identifies principles common to various forms of effective discourse, regardless of purpose or subject matter and the situational context that motivates the discourse. At this abstract level of characterization all discourses share the same structure. With this structural analysis it is possible to explain how conversants continue to share compatible models of ongoing discourse and to account for the suspension, resumption, topic shift, clue word, and reference phenomena that pervade naturally occurring conversation. The context space approach demonstrates the importance of an abstract structural account in elucidating the conventions governing the generation and interpretation of coherent discourse.

Chapter 10

Linguistic Theory and World Knowledge:
An Integration

As we noted in chapter 1, there has been a great deal of work in text and discourse research based largely on the notion that the interpretation of meaning depends on the identification of speaker beliefs, intents, goals, and plans. This trend has culminated in the view that a functional, world knowledge approach—in opposition to a linguistic or structural one—is what is required for discourse analysis. Furthermore, through interpretation of certain traditional approaches to linguistic theory (e.g., Harris 1951, Chomsky 1965, Katz and Fodor 1963, Harweg 1977), proponents of the world knowledge school often assume that any linguistic or structural theory necessarily excludes consideration of the ways non-discourse-specific information affects discourse communication. Accordingly the world knowledge theorists often claim that by definition a linguistic theory cannot accommodate the functional and contextual features inherent in extended discourse.

We have emphasized that the context space theory is not opposed to the claim that world knowledge is needed and accessed in discourse engagement any more than it opposes the claim that knowledge of the lexicon of a language is needed for such engagement. We have simply demonstrated that in addition to such knowledge, there is some discourse-specific knowledge that is needed and used in discourse processing. As we have amply illustrated, the discourse grammar developed here incorporates both a functional and contextual approach in its analysis. However, the concept of function in the context space theory does in some respects differ from that of the world knowledge theorists. In fact there is a sense of function that is vital to discourse processing which their work does not generally recognize, characterize, or deem important. In consequence the world knowledge approach is unable to account for a number of discourse phenomena which demonstrates that a purely nonlinguistic, general world knowledge approach to discourse analysis is, by itself, insufficient.

Communicative Function versus Speaker Intent

A major difference between the context space and world knowledge approaches is our distinction between the discourse function of a speaker's conversational move and underlying intent when voicing a set of utterances. To better understand this difference, let us briefly review the development of the central role given to "speaker intent" identification in discourse analysis.

In a radical departure from the traditional philosophical correlation between "meaning" and truth/falsity, Austin (1962) introduced a distinction between performative and constative utterances. Austin claimed that the notions of truth and falsity cannot be applied to performative utterances; performatives involve actions—they are not true or false. For example, stating "I name this ship Liberty" under appropriate circumstances results in the ship being so named and is not open to a true/false analysis.

This distinction in utterance type led to the well-known theory of "speech acts" described by Austin (1962) and by Searle (1969) and of "conversational implicature," described by Grice (1975).[1] Fundamental to the speech act theory is an emphasis on the "functionality" of languge and the need to distinguish between the force of an utterance and its literal content. Associated with all speech acts are a set of felicity conditions, preconditions, and effects. Felicity conditions mainly refer to a speaker's psychological state, preconditions to the functioning of the real world and a speaker's social status, and effects refer to changes in the external world, including the mental states of others, created by the speech act. For example, the "naming of ship" act can only have its intended effect of the ship being so named if its precondition that the person doing the naming has authority to do so is true.

A major felicity condition of all speech acts is the sincerity condition. As Searle states:

> . . . to assert, affirm, state (that P) counts as an expression of belief (that P). To request, ask, order, entreat, enjoin, pray, or command (that A be done) counts as an expression of a wish or desire (that A be done). To promise, vow, threaten, or pledge (that A) counts as an expression of intention (to do A).

The context space theory is also based on recognizing the functionality of discourse and the preconditions and effects associated with different communicative acts. The grammar's characterization of communicative acts, however, is specific to a maxim-abiding, structural and functional thematic development of the discourse. Its characterizations are derived from the discourse structure and certain logical and semantic rules of inference: they are not derived from access to a speaker's underlying goals, beliefs, plans, and/or social status in the real world. An act's preconditions stem from the preceding discourse structure, and its effects are on this discourse structure.

What types of communicative function rules are encoded in the grammar? Well, for example, there is the rule that in the context of an ongoing debate, the force of a speaker's "Why" question following an opponent's "So What" is a challenge whose effect is to set up the discourse expectation that the addressed conversant will replace a previous flat dismissal with a substantive challenge. There is also the contrastive rule that the effect of such a "Why," following an opponent's assertion of a claim, is to set up the discourse expectation that the addressed conversant will give some support to this assertion. There is also the rule that in discussion mode a speaker's "Why" is to be interpreted as a request for explanation. In all of these cases whether the "Why" is motivated by a desire for information, a hatred of the opponent, or an attempt to save face or to give oneself more time to think is irrelevant to the discourse analysis. No matter what psychological state the speaker or listener is in, the "Why" question in the differing discourse contexts serves the respective illocutionary forces, and each force has its own distinct set of effects on the discourse structure.

We have already illustrated the importance of the distinction between a conversant's intent for saying what she or he does and the communicative effect of the speaker's utterances in a given discourse context. We have also pointed out the logical difficulties inherent in the position that the identification of intent is the primary feature governing discourse processing. We have shown that what needs to be identified (rather than speaker intent) is the conversational move performed by the speaker—a structural connection between a speaker's utterances and the preceding discourse—and that this is usually derivable from the discourse context and conventional rules of discourse processing. For example, the context space processor uses expectations set up by preceding conversational moves, clue word indicators, and formal logical/semantic criteria to identify the force of a speaker's utterances as a challenge. In deriving such an interpretation, we (and the grammar) have no need to posit that the speaker desires or wants this challenge.

This is not to deny that a speaker's intent is often reflected in the discourse function served by her or his utterances. There usually is a correspondence between a speaker's intent and performed conversational move, probably stemming from individuals acquiring over time standardized procedures for ways in which to express underlying intentions, beliefs, and desires (similar to Lewis's [1969] and Bennett's [1976] analysis in discussing "convention").[2] If this convention hypothesis is correct, then we can understand how, rather than speaker intent identification driving the interpretation of the speaker's utterances, it is the interpretation of those utterances through conventionalized conversational move characterizations that enables us to hypothesize the speaker's underlying psychological state.

The Issue of Text Linguistics

A major argument against linguistic theories of discourse has been advanced by Morgan and Sellner (1980) who claim that discourse analysis is best subsumed under a theory of world knowledge, intention, and action, in total disregard of rules particular to discourse engagement. Morgan and Sellner's primary argument against a "linguistic" theory of discourse rests on the claim that much of discourse "coherence" merely corresponds to the "coherence" found in the external world. They begin by making a distinction between this world knowledge approach to discourse and the requirements of linguistic knowledge at the sentence level:

> Knowledge that, in English, the determiner precedes the noun (as opposed to many languages with the opposite order) seems to follow from no other fact of the psychological, culture and so on of the people who speak English. It seems to be, then, a strictly linguistic piece of knowledge and, as such, in the domain of linguistic theory.
>
> In a syntactic theory, the objects generated are strings of words, each with an associated structural description. The grammar, by virtue of its mathematical properties, makes unambiguous claims about possible strings of words and about what structural description is associated with a given sentence.

In contrast to sentences, the authors claim relations between discourse elements are not "linguistic." Resting many of their arguments on story grammar analyses (Prince 1973, Propp 1968, Rumelhart 1980), the authors dismiss discourse from the domain of linguistic inquiry:

> First and most obviously, stories have content: the facts and events that make up the "world" of the story; not functional relations, but just the kind of relations that hold between the facts

and events of the real world: temporal order, relations of causa-
tion, motivation, and so on. The most appropriate system for
describing this aspect of story content, then, is a system for describing facts and events in the world.

As to "presentation structure," which one would think has some relation to linguistic theory, the authors claim:

> A second and very different aspect of the content of a text is the
> manner in which the world is described: the storyteller's choices
> concerning which points of content to present explicitly and
> which to leave to the hearer to infer; what order events should be
> presented in and so on. . . . The most appropriate system for
> describing this aspect of story content is a system for describing
> intentions, goals, purposes, and plans; a full-fledged theory of
> acts would be a start. Note that this aspect of a story is not a
> matter of linguistic form.

In commenting on story structure they claim:

> The ability to impose some kind of organizational structure on
> the events narrated in a story is most likely the same ability one
> uses in imposing structure on observed reality.

On surface linguistic phenomena they assert:

> As far as we can see, there is no evidence for cohesion as a lin-
> guistic property, other than as an epiphenomenon of coherence
> of content.

Morgan and Sellner's argument contains a number of errors. First,
their claim that sentential linguistics is "mathematical," and not dependent on or derived from correspondences to the "real" world, is
highly unmotivated and in direct contradiction to many linguistic
pragmatic theories of sentential linguistics in the research literature.[3] As we discussed in chapter 1, it is generally recognized that a
structural analysis is often insufficient for the clear interpretation of a
sentence; such interpretation requires reference to external world
knowledge and/or to a preceding discourse context. It is also clear
that the elementary objects of linguistic analysis—nouns, adjectives,
adverbs, and verbs—directly reflect our view of our external world.
Many linguists also recognize that much of sentential construction
and interpretation is pragmatic. If a noncorrespondence to our perceptions of the real world and nonaccess to world knowledge were
necessary criteria for a linguistic study, then linguistic inquiry is a

dead field. Morgan and Sellner's distinction on these bases between sentential and discourse linguistic analysis is simply ill founded.

Of more relevance against Morgan and Sellner's claim that a linguistic, structural analysis of discourse is misguided are the many discourse phenomena that we find in an analysis of naturally ongoing dialogues—surface linguistic forms, discourse popping, the functional relation of a speaker's utterances to the preceding discourse—that simply cannot be explained by the structure of the "real" world.

We have seen that a structural decomposition of a discourse into constituent context spaces with varying influential status explains and predicts numerous seemingly uncalled for forms of reference found in spontaneous discourse. For example, when returning to an open, controlling or precontrol context space, speakers immediately repronominalize their references to entities contained in these spaces, despite potential semantic contenders for such references in intervening "talk." In contrast, in reference to an element last mentioned, in a currently closed context space speakers use full descriptors to refer to the entity in question despite the fact that no seeming semantic contenders were discussed in the interim.

We have seen also that the criteria dictating the retelling of a narrative in spontaneous discourse, and the structural decomposition of a narrative into the discourse structure, are not merely a reflection of the structure of the episode as it occurred. When the telling of different events of a single episode perform different communicative functions in the discourse, we find speakers partitioning the different portions of an episode into distinct context spaces. This structural decomposition is reflected by a speaker's surface linguistic clue words, such as "Incidentally," and respecification of portions of the orientation section just given (usually time and location orientation, e.g., "Incidentally, while I was standing there"). It would be a difficult position to maintain, or prove, that while the episode was occurring, these distinct events were separately segmented into different structural components in the teller's long-term memory. In fact it is quite possible that on one occasion events A, B, and E of an episode are put into one context space, and events C and D, of this same episode, are put into a separate context space, whereas on another occasion events A and D are put into a single context space. One's structuring of discourse utterances relating to a single episode—one's choice of which events to retell—is a dynamic process, dependent on the flow of the preceding discourse (and the intentions of the teller) rather than on some notion of "truth" in the outside world. (See Chafe 1979, McKeown 1982, and Reichman 1979, 1984 for further discussion.)

Correspondingly we have seen that in the use of analogies a speaker's choice of citation of (non)correspondences is governed by the discourse structure and the conversational move being served by the analogy. The actual structures of the respective domains and their full set of relations and (non)correspondences to each other are not the criteria governing presentation in discourse.

In answer to this, Morgan and Sellner may choose to respond, "But we allow for conversational move identification." Yes, they do, but their notion of move is of a different nature than those derivable from the discourse context—moves that they may wish to label "nonlinguistic":

> A judgment as to what the speaker is trying to do in a discourse will influence the interpretation of what he or she says. . . . This kind of relevance, then, would be most insightfully considered not as some kind of semantic entailment relation between sentences but as relations of purpose between speech acts, relative to some goal.
>
> Lacking even a partially explicit theory of plans, actions, and inference in which to state such hypotheses, though, our proposals are little more than speculation. But we think this line of research is more likely to bear fruit than that of constructing ever more exotic linguistic units and levels and accounts of discourse comprehension.

We have shown that conversational move processing is dependent on discourse analysis. To claim that the identification of underlying intent alone suffices and that linguistic units, such as the notion of a context space, are excess and nonproductive tools of analysis is merely to ignore the manifold linguistic evidence for these units in discourse processing.

The Integration of Speech Act/World Knowledge and Linguistic Theory

The context space grammar described here characterizes one set of rules operative in discourse. The rules formalized in the grammar are abstract, written as a means of characterizing that set of abstract constraints operative in conversational speech, and are independent of particular speaker/listener beliefs, world knowledge, attitudes, and personal motivations. However, though these rules are autonomous, actual use in conversations is intertwined with any given speaker's world knowledge and beliefs. In this respect the discourse grammar is analogous to sentence grammars such as Chomsky's (1965) transformational grammar. For example, though an individual may have a whole set of phrase structure rules—such as "A sentence can be decomposed into a noun phrase and a verb phrase, a noun phrase into a determiner and a noun, a verb phrase into a verb or verb and prepositional phrase, a prepositional phrase into a preposition and a noun phrase"—he will never be able to generate the utterance, "The machine is broken" if he does not have the word "machine" in his lexicon. Similarly, if R in our genetics-environment debate excerpt had not known any studies supporting the genetic side of the genetics-environment controversy, she could not have successfully presented a study supporting her side of the argument. This would not mean that she did not have this possible form of argumentation in her discourse grammar. She simply would not have had any appropriate propositions stored in memory that could fulfill the abstract constraints set on this path.

The grammar simply provides an additional level of analysis to approaches that require specifics of world knowledge and belief structures. Though in a sense written as a discourse processor, the system does not have access to all of the information necessary to process discourse: there is no incorporation of sentence level syntax, actual words (except for some discourse connectives, i.e., "clue words"), or everyday affairs. The context space system does discourse processing via calls to abstract procedures that specify sets of semantic or logical constraints that surface linguistic forms have to fulfill in order to maintain certain conversational roles at given points in the conversation. These constraints are specified in terms of slot fillers of preceding context spaces, and certain basic cognitive operations (procedure calls), such as "Infer," "Instance," "Exclusive-Or," and "Imply," which are considered primitives of the system. Presumably determining whether, for example, "A Instance B," is true would necessitate accessing world knowledge data. That level of analysis, however, is orthogonal to and separate from the endeavor undertaken here.

Thus we do not deny that frames, scripts, schema, belief systems, and semantic networks are needed and utilized by a discourse grammar. We illustrate how the complex process of discourse processing can be decomposed into a number of separate cognitive activities. Our effort has been to show that there is a characterizable set of independent discourse processing rules and to specify them in terms of an abstract grammar of discourse processing. These rules are at a level above actual production and can be specified without access to individual speaker beliefs and knowledge structures.

Furthermore there are some general beliefs about language form that we assume most participants in our language community share. It is on this basis that we can have effective communication with people of this language community that we've never met before. The assumed shared rules of language form direct, constrain, and impinge on the structures we use in conversing. So, for example, my particular beliefs about a person are not what causes me to say, "I went home at ten," rather than "Went home at ten I." Analogously the rules presented in this grammar characterize those rules of discourse form that participants in our language community share regardless of their intentions, world knowledge, and beliefs. So, for example, despite any personal beliefs that D may have about R, when in the genetics-environment excerpt R utters in line 29 "Right, but, X," D expects the utterance to be an indirect challenge to his preceding statements.

We have indicated, however, that there are clearly other sorts of rules operative in discourse processing. These include rules derived from beliefs and structures dealing with the dynamic social-psychological factors that are brought into play in the choice of what to say next. For example, issues of social peer relationships, assertive/nonassertive behavioral traits, depth of knowledge on a given subject matter, and beliefs about another conversant's attitudes and consciousness affect what a conversational participant may say and hear. These factors can be considered to be a separately operative module in discourse, or they can be incorporated in further development of the context space grammar.

From the outset the context space system has been developed with the intention of subsequent hookups to other discourse-convention modules. For example, many of the grammar's transition arcs specify possible choice paths "appropriate" in a given context. It is clear that a second mechanism, more sensitive to psychological motivation and/or the situational context, would decide which one of these paths to choose (see Schmidt 1976, 1977). For instance, we could include the probability that in argumentation a meek person would be more likely to choose an indirect rather than a direct form of challenge. Such other mechanisms should be thought of as occurring with, rather than in place of, a more structural approach; conversely, the context space processor should be thought of as operating together with such a psychological model. The role of the grammar is to express the constraints inherent in linguistic communication within which psychological and social factors may operate. The context space processor can operate in conjunction with such components to generate or interpret utterances. Neither alone is sufficient to model human discourse performance.

Let us turn then to some of the clear points at which these different models can be integrated.

A number of works on communication have made the speech act theory their cornerstone of analysis (e.g., Allen 1979, Appeit 1981, Bruce 1980, Cohen 1978, Cohen 1981, Dore 1977, Labov 1977, Litman and Allen 1984, Newman 1980, Power 1979, Pratt 1977, Sinclair and Coulthard 1975, Wilensky 1978). Many of these, like the analyses of the founding fathers, emphasize the sincerity condition and access to a speaker's pychological state as fundamental elements of analysis. The works attribute specific goals, plans, and beliefs to speakers and also reference an external state of affairs. For example, consider Allen's (1979) analysis of the "Inform Act":

INFORM(speaker, hearer, P): P is a proposition
    precondition   speaker KNOW P (= = P and speaker
                     BELIEVE P)
    effect   hearer KNOW P
    body   hearer BELIEVE speaker WANT(hearer
                     KNOW P)

Making use of such rules, Allen's system models a person B responding to a speaker A's request for information by having B infer that A wants to know the information, which can be accomplished if B informs A of the information, which thereby means that B infers that A wants B to inform A of the information. In addition for B to respond "appropriately," B has to infer some plan of A's that would require A to have this information. For example, a user asking the Allen system the departure time of a train will also get the departure gate number of the train, since the system will infer that the user needs the time information in order to meet or take this train, and to do so requires that the user not only know the time of departure but the gate number as well.

Labov and Fanshel's (1977) work on therapeutic discourse similarly derives its method of analysis from the speech act theory's notion of preconditions and effects formulated in terms of psychological states, the role status of persons involved in the interchange, and the social organization of the real world via its rights and obligations. For example, using the challenge speech act rule stated next, Labov and Fanshel analyze a child's questioning when her mother plans to return from a prolonged absence as a challenge to her mother's competence in the mother role:

If A makes a request for B to take an action in role R, based on needs, abilities, obligations, and rights which have been valid for some time, then A is heard as criticizing B's competence in role R.

Since in the context space approach, interpretation of some "speech act" stems from rules of discourse rather than from such direct rules of social and psychological convention, one could say that the context space and speaker intent theories are in conflict with one another. For example, let's consider the seemingly opposed versions of analysis the two approaches would take to interpret a speaker's utterance of "It's cold in here" as a request for a listener to "Close an open window."

In Allen's system (described earlier) the following set of inferences about the speaker's psychological state are made:

(1) the speaker wants me to know that s/he is cold; (2) and since s/he knows that I know that being cold is undesirable, (3) s/he intends me to infer that s/he does not want to be cold. Furthermore, (4) since s/he knows that I know that the open window is causing him/her to be cold, (5) s/he expects and intends me to close the window. Therefore I take the utterance as a request.

In contrast, one possible way for the context space theory to characterize the force of the utterance as a request is for it to formulate a conversational move and method for requesting performance of an action: the speaker states a "negative state of affairs" that could be altered if this action were performed.

Under the context space paradigm then listeners can simply access conventionalized discourse rules to determine the force of such indirect requests.[4] A listener's ability to infer a probable underlying speaker intent for an utterance is similarly easily explained: he or she uses knowledge of the obvious correlation between conventionalized forms of intent communication and conversational move generation (which he or she assumes is a shared convention among all participants in the language community).

Notice that even the context space processor must somehow be able to ascertain that the utterance "It's cold in here" specifies a "negative state of affairs." In general, however, this is like pointing out that in order to "understand," the system has to be able to identify word meanings. Of course it must—a database of cultural standards and world facts is as elementary to a language system as a lexicon.

More important, an individual using a context space grammar to analyze discourse must be able to ensure that there are no specific contradictory beliefs about the speaker that would warrant rejection of the conventional force of an utterance (e.g., it might be known that the particular speaker who said "It's cold in here," loves the cold; i.e., though for others the utterance would be a negative assertion, for this particular speaker it is a positive one).[5] This returns us to a point made in chapter 1: mutual or privy knowledge between co-conversants is an equally important aspect of discourse processing.

There is yet another area of interaction between conventionalized, discourse structure systems and world knowledge systems. This has to do with speaker plan attribution. As in Allen's system many speech act approaches focus on inferring underlying speaker plans (Bruce 1980, Cohen and Perrault 1979, Power 1979). It is clear that given some plan, a speaker's utterances will often reflect it. This simply follows from the fact that our utterances usually reflect what we're thinking about.[6] Of more interest, however, is how speakers' structuring of their plans are reflected in the choices of surface linguistic forms to describe the plans. We should expect in fact to find a high correlation between speakers' structuring of discourse context space structures—as reflected in their surface linguistic forms like "Now" and "By the way"—and their current structuring of the component actions involved in an underlying plan of action.

For example, in the following dialogue most of us would interpret the question about London as being independent of the earlier query about the Kentucky:

A: What time does the Kentucky come in?

B: 10:00 p.m.

A: By the way, how much is a ticket to London?

We infer this independence not because we know about or ponder on A's psychological state. Rather, A's language itself reflects for us this independence. It is A's use of the clue words "By the way" that directs our inference. These simple words help us determine that the London question is probably not a part of A's plan having to do with the Kentucky.

Most goal/plan-oriented systems take no notice of such surface linguistic phenomena—plan recognition drives linguistic interpretation, and not vice versa. At minimum, some bidirectional system is warranted. For example, by being sensitive to the clue word "Now," these systems could reasonably infer that a speaker is continuing to develop the same plan posited for his or her earlier utterances; with the clue word "Anyway," these systems should recognize that the listener may be leaving investigation of a current plan and returning to one earlier left unfinished.

Another feature of possible integration between these two approaches is on the issue of "perspective taking." In its current formulation the context space processor builds only a single discourse structure or model for a conversation. This corresponds to the assumption that our coconversants' modeling of an interaction is identical to our own; we expect them to be using the same rules that we do. If this is true, then we have no need to construct an explicit model of a coparticipant's model of a conversation. However, there is clear evidence that at times in conversations coconversants have distinct models of the discourse, so sensitivity to the discourse models of others and comparisons between these and one's own are required. Consider a brief example. We presented earlier an excerpt between conversants G and B discussing some argument that G had with her father. In our analysis of that excerpt we explained that at a certain point in the conversation G and B were focusing on different discourse elements: G shifts her focus to her mother, B continues to focus on G's father. We further showed that G and B used their own individual discourse models to guide their choices of surface linguistic referring expressions (e.g., B pronominalizes her reference to G's father, since in her model he is still in focus; G, on the other hand, follows B's pronominal reference with a full descriptor expression, since in her model her father is not in focus). A number of issues relating to perspective taking are, however, raised by this example: (1) Is B's pronominal reference "legal"? (2) If in B's model G's father is in focus ("legalizing" her pronominal reference), where/how has B integrated into her model G's succeeding utterances which clearly have G's mother in focus rather than G's father? And (3) is G's nonpronominal reference mandatory?—would we not find speakers automatically updating their models based on a coconversant's switch in focus?

In the current context space prototype the issues raised by these questions are not addressed. Incorporating some appropriate version of a speech act system into a context space theory approach could lead to fruitful resolution of such issues.

There is another aspect of the context space theory that distinguishes it from many strictly structural approaches to text linguistics and makes it particularly sensitive to "world knowledge" considerations. Many structural approaches seem to rest on the assumption that "the meaning is in the text." Consider, for example, Goetz and Armbruster's (1980) remarks:

> A common feature of the discourse structure analyses to date is
> that text structure is treated as though it were an inherent, im-
> mutable attribute of the text, interpreted in the same manner by
> all readers. Thus, the importance of an element of text is deter-
> mined by the position of that element in the structure of the
> text. . . . An alternative position is the constructivist view out-
> lined by Spiro. In the constructivist view, the emphasis shifts
> from the structure of text as an independent, immutable entity to
> structure and meaning as imposed on the text by the reader.

Though structural in nature, the context space theory is not a pro-
ponent of the notion of a "fixed meaning in text." As Spiro notes, the
fixed meaning view does not allow for inferential elaborations as part
of the process of comprehending prose, nor does it allow for contextual and functional derivations.

In contrast to the fixed meaning approach, the context space theory
stresses that inferential components of a speaker's utterances are as
important as components verbally expressed. This importance is
captured by the grammar's characterization of types of context
spaces, which are often distinguished by slots particular to implicit
components of the corresponding conversational move.

In addition the theory's notion of "meaning" is highly contextually
and functionally determined. For example, consider Brewer's (1980)
comments on the following set of utterances: "Jack made out his will.
He slipped on his 'New York is fun city' T-shirt. He gathered up his
roll of wire. Then he got into the car and drove south. He got out and
took the elevator."

> Although this is a fairly coherent piece of narrative discourse, it
> is a lousy story. It does not build up to a climax. It does not seem
> to have a natural ending. It does not seem to have a point.

The context space theory would not even find the text coherent—
precisely because it lacks a point. In the context space approach,
function and structure are not in opposition; on the contrary, discourse functionality determines the discourse structure.

The context space theory holds that the discourse flow and a
speaker's surface forms greatly constrain and predict functional dis-
cernment and interpretation. It is ironic then that proponents of the
seemingly opposed "constructivist" view (e.g., Spiro 1980, Goetz
and Armbruster 1980) present studies such as those of Lachman and
Dooling (1968) and Bransford and Johnson (1972) that show that depending on "context"—such as preceding titles—a listener will
interpret a piece of text quite differently. But this is precisely why the

context space theory was constructed—to enable identification of that preceding section of discourse providing the speaker and listener the discourse environment in which to "connect something that is given with something other than itself" (Bartlett 1932).

Antagonists of the structural view also present the Anderson and Pichert (1978) study, where subjects are asked to rate the importance of a story's idea units from the perspectives of a home buyer and a burglar, namely which parts of the story would be of more interest to home buyers and which to burglars. The study showed that depending on perspective assigned, the subjects rated different parts of the story as more important than others. In assessment of the studies Goetz and Armbruster state: "If importance is indeed an inherent aspect of text, as implied by existing text analysis systems, then assigned perspective should have no effect on rated importance."

Once again, if the piece of text were uttered in discourse, it would have been stated in some surrounding discourse context. This discourse context itself would have specified the perspective imposed in the laboratory and similarly would have led listeners within the communicative context to identify different elements as major.[7]

Finally, it is important to recognize that using the context space grammar does not dictate a unique interpretation for a set of utterances; its rules of discourse processing, in essence, correspond to function calls to procedures capable of accessing world beliefs, a lexicon of the language, and beliefs about social norms of behavior. Interpretation is not fixed. For example, since in our society aggressiveness is often considered a negative attribute diametrically opposed to one's being nice, the context space processor using as its world knowledge component the norms of our society would interpret the illocutionary force of B's utterance as a challenge:

A: I think Susan is a wonderfully nice person.

B: I think she's very aggressive.

On the other hand, the processor, using a world knowledge component of another society, could conceivably interpret B's utterances as a support. The meaning, or illocutionary force of an utterance clearly depends on both context identification and world knowledge beliefs.

Note, however, that semantic interpretation and conversational move identification are not arbitrarily contingent on a particular listener's mental model of the world. In the context space grammar there are many rules particular to conversational move identification that are not open to arbitrary assessment on the part of a listener. In other words, assuming the hearer is a competent speaker of the language, a speaker's repeated nonpronominalization of an entity under discussion, nonpronominalization to an entity just referenced pronominally, and use of such clue words as "It's like," "Incidentally," and "But, anyway" must convey to the listener certain structural attributes of the discourse as well as aspects of the force and underlying point of the speaker's utterances.

To posit a diametric opposition between a speech act-world knowledge theory of discourse and a linguistic structural one is inappropriate and unnecessary. Clearly both types of analyses are relevant and necessary for a full analysis of the dynamic and complex communicative process of discourse engagement. The context space theory of discourse can encompass both.

Notes

Chapter 1

1. Though theorists debate whether or not people actually employ these rule systems, such systems are generally regarded as adequate for describing the composition of sentences from their basic constituents and for modeling their underlying structure.

Chapter 2

1. This of course does not apply to elliptical utterances and the like.

Chapter 3

1. See Cohen (1980, 1983), Hobbs (1976), Levin and Moore (1977), Lockman (1978), McDonald (1983), McKeown (1982), Mehan (1978), Pitkin (1977a, 1977b), Phillips (1977), Prince (1973), Reichman (1978), Sadock (1977), Wilks (1972, 1981), and Wilson and Sperber (1979).
2. Cohen 1983 distinguishes between cases where clue words are obligatory and cases where they are not. We have not made that distinction. Rather, as discussed in Reichman (1978), our position is that if there is not at least one surface indication of a context space shift (e.g., clue word, tense shift, far deictic, or a switch to a nonpronominal form), hearers will first attempt to integrate a succeeding utterance into the current context space before considering a context space shift.
3. Notice that some rules involve negation whereas others do not. In choosing which particular rule schema fits an incoming utterance, we must attend to this aspect of the utterance. So, for example, if the incoming utterance includes a "not," Modus-Tollens is a much more likely candidate than Modus-Ponus.
4. In a full analysis of the excerpt many more context space structures would be identified; only those relevant to the current point are specified here. For a more detailed analysis of the excerpt, see Reichman (1978).
5. While speaking, M draws a pictorial representation of a steam plant, and some of his deictic references in the excerpt refer to elements of this diagram.

Chapter 4

1. The grammar's formalization of this move allows for the fact that sometimes a conversant will explicitly state the generic principle underlying the support while leaving the particular state of affairs implicit. For example, it is quite acceptable for a speaker to support a claim that "Alaska is depressing" by saying that "All cold

places are depressing," leaving one to infer (or retrieve from knowledge) that "Alaska is a cold place."

2. Lines 15–16 of this excerpt, "Well, of course, that's where he learns his behavior, in kindergarten," support this analysis: the child is referred to pronominally, while his behavior is named; also the deictic "that" is corrected to name "in kindergarten," which is in low focus.

3. Reassignment of the preceding active context space usually results in the reassignment of the status values of the context space to which it is subordinate. In general, then, these superordinate spaces are reassigned a closed or generating status from an earlier controlling one. In special cases (such as analogy or interruption) the superordinate space may be assigned instead a precontrol status.

4. This analysis assumes prior statement of the issue to be supported. In debates, however, we can have the case where the support move is made without explicit statement of the issue to be supported. Here we would first infer some issue to be supported, and then create an issue context space to hold the implicit issue. We then have an issue context space to support. The inferred issue is constructed by negating the opponent's claim which is under current attack. Cohen (1983) allows for the general case of supports preceding a claim to be supported.

Chapter 5

1. See Chafe (1973, 1975, 1976), Grimes (1978, 1980), Grosz (1977), Hirst (1983), Kantor (1977), Kuno (1977), Karmiloff-Smith (1980), Linde (1974, 1979), Longrace and Levinsohn (1977), Reichman (1978), Sgall and Hajičo'va (1977), and Sidner (1979).

2. This is similar to Longrace and Levinsohn's 1977 report about deictics in the Inga language and the noun particle and affixes in the Cubeo language.

3. This type of pragmatic approach to discourse reference is compatible with Hankamer and Sag's (1976) distinction between "deep" and "surface" anaphors. "Deep anaphora," Hankamer and Sag tell us, allows for "pragmatic control and has other properties indicating that the anaphoric relation is determined at an essentially presyntactic level," and it is "sensitive to the coherence of semantic units that are not directly represented in the superficial syntactic structure." An example of a deep anaphora occurs in the following scenario: Mark and Tim are studying a portrait in an art museum, and Mark exclaims, "It's stupendous." The type of pragmatic control allowing for these deep anaphors, I believe, is the focus of attention notion running through the cited works. In fact, using these works, we can take deep anaphora control even further than do Hankamer and Sag. It seems warranted to claim that pragmatics not only governs unexpected deep anaphora pronominalization but, more important, that it dictates *nonpronominalization* to many syntactically "legal" anaphors. Thus, though in a vacuum pragmatic control may allow a speaker to reference many different sorts of elements pronominally, for smooth, maxim-abiding, effective communication only corresponding elements in a listener's focus of attention—*as determined by the discourse structure*—should be so referenced.

4. We can delineate Olson's set of contenders for a pronominal or close deictic reference. We have yet, however, to include in this system what Webber (1978) has called "evoked entities," which result largely from quantification, nor have we included Vendler's (1971) "invoked" entities—for example, "the engine" of a car when a car is mentioned.

5. Other than focus level criteria there are of course some other causes of choosing one mode of reference over another. For example, we usually refer to individuals

by name (rather than description) to a listener who is quite familiar with the person under discussion even if our story does not center around this individual. Implicit reference occurs when, for example, in back reference to a preceding cited event, we only reference some of its components.

6. In the spontaneously generated elliptical examples on which this analysis is based, the utterance containing the elliptical reference entailed a return to a previously closed context space. In essence the topic of the resumption was a somewhat more generalized version of the initial topic of the closed space. These cases then are not the usual cases of ellipses discussed in the literature, wherein a preceding utterance suffices for the elliptical expansion.

7. See Langacker (1982) for the import of dative shift.

8. The analysis is actually somewhat more complicated. For further details see Reichman (1978).

9. Though here we go directly from descriptor to pronoun, this excerpt should not be seen as a counterexample to the rule that usually an intervening name specification is required. One rarely refers to parents by name.

10. It has been brought to my attention that a "Between X and Y," where Y is pronominal, may be awkward. In any case we often do find such constructions, so I do not believe that it provides a complete explanation for G's nonpronominalization.

11. The "local" versus "global" shift distinction made here is related to the distinction made by Grimes when he considers a subsection of a narrative that focuses on a minor character to be a local and temporary shift from the global topic that concerns a major character of a story.

12. For particulars of the formal analysis of "analogous" utterances, see Reichman (1981).

13. The term "that potential" would have been a far definite reference (see Reichman 1979, 1984).

14. M is challenging the mapping between "two twins at home" and "two people sharing a same environment." Her challenge is a generic one in that she is not asserting that she has particular knowledge about these particular two twins. Her claim is that, in general, two children at home are usually treated differently. R could have countered that in this particular situation, these two particular twins did not receive differential treatment. Since M's claim is generic, "two kids" (or "two twins") is the appropriate referent rather than "they." This is in contrast to D's assertions which make claim to the two particular children under discussion, though he, like M, only has generic support for his assertions.

Chapter 6

1. For a complete review of ATNs, see Bates (1980).

2. Though there are many actions associated with each of the states in the figure, for clarity, only "push" and "go" actions are cited.

3. Some registers function much like local variables of an ordinary programming language in that they are not used in transition tests but rather merely as temporary placeholders. These registers therefore are not included here and are not capitalized in the figures.

4. In recognition mode of course the updatings performed along the path to final recognition of the utterances are tentative until such an end state is reached. Conceptually one should think of the grammar's paths being tested in parallel until one path (or several) shows success; others fail due to precondition tests encountered along the way.

5. Expectations involving context spaces whose statuses are either open or precontrol should be considered nonoptional; expectations involving generating status context spaces should be considered optional.
6. Clearly when we say that the processor chooses a next speaker, we are generally referring to the way we are using the grammar to simulate generation of existing dialogues. In independent generation of discourse, speakers select themselves as the next speaker for a number of varied reasons. Such reasons, like those determining a particular choice path out of a number of suitable ones, we leave to another module of the system.
7. In addition to the constraints presented here, these transitions are also blocked by an antagonist's preceding conversational move of demanding a protagonist to give supportive evidence of a claim just made. In such cases transition to this state is itself forestalled by a preceding transition test.
8. Similarly flat rejections do not result in reestablishment of a relevant discourse context. They do, however, result in the creation of a comment "space," which will temporarily fill the slot of the active space's claim slot. The comment space is not a full-fledged context space as it does not have an associated status slot, any slots corresponding to implicit components of a move, or any subconstituents. In fact, when a substantive challenge is given in place of the flat rejection, we undo the status of the comment lying in a separate subordinate space, by transferring the comment onto a list of all comments given to the space in an "old comment" slot. This enables the grammar to distinguish comments just stated from ones stated a while ago in the discourse.

Chapter 7

1. During argumentation Head-CCS points to a support context space being challenged, an issue space being challenged, or to a counterclaim/countersupport issue space for which support has just been given. In the two former cases the speaker's flawed space is pointed to by Head-CCS. In the latter case a corelator of the Head-CCS space is the speaker's flawed space.
2. A debative-issue context space is one that has a counterclaims slot and a countersupports slot and can only be created once in the midst of argumentation.
3. All claims of the opposition, bypassed on the way up the context space discourse model to the claim to be salvaged, are considered implicitly accepted by the speaker's side.
4. An open question of course is how the choice is made. At this point let's assume another higher level module makes this choice. Control is actually passed to step 3 of this routine.
5. This routine is also responsible for further challenges that do not entail fixing one's subargument. Many of the same procedures are applicable to the two situations, though they differ in two respects: (1) in the latter case, if a support option is chosen, it is thought of as further support rather than replacement support, and (2) intervening implicit concessions are noted on the Domain-Constraints register only in the event of preceding concession.
6. Recall that since further testing was appropriate to distinguish between flawed issue and supportive spaces, this space has not yet been closed.
7. When the claim concession option is taken in the Concede-Subargument routine and a Further-Challenge expectation is chosen, control passes to this state of the grammar.

Chapter 8

1. However, the locative/physical frame can overrule the discourse reference frame rules. Specifically the use of "here" cannot be used by a speaker in reference to any other physical location than the one where the speaker is presently.

Chapter 9

1. For instance, the restaurant script described by Schank and Abelson (1977), the "face" and "room" frames described by Minsky (1975), and semantic networks described by Collins and Quillian (1969).
2. The ethnomethodologists' analysis is also like the context space theory's analysis in its effort to provide a methodology that can delineate an individual's process of interpretation without having to claim that only one interpretation of an utterance is viable. This is in contrast to the many approaches to text analysis in which a fixed coding scheme is sought and optional interpretations are in theory ruled out.
3. Jefferson (1979), however, does recognize that "off development" can occur anywhere in a discourse, and she discusses speakers' surface linguistic forms signaling and/or excusing this (e.g., use vs. nonuse of repetition in a story's preface).
4. The major difference is the names of the relations at nonterminal nodes.

Chapter 10

1. There are of course major distinctions between Austin's and Searle's works. In particular, Searle's use of Grice's notion of speaker intention depends on psychological motivation as determining the force of an utterance, whereas Austin's forces stem more directly from social organization rules.
2. Though like Austin, both Lewis's and Bennett's notion of convention focuses on organizational rules of society rather than on conventional rules of discourse engagement.
3. Their use of this argument is odd; in another article Morgan and Green (1980) explicitly note that "it is slowly becoming clear that there are a number of kinds of correlations between pragmatic and syntactic form."
4. We're proposing something similar to Bennett's notion of "dullard" operation: "Hear S, infer P, purely through the generalization that when S is uttered, P is true" (p. 195). Bennett, however, committed to retaining some form of the Gricean conditions in utterance generation/interpretation, claims that people do not really function as dullards, they just believe that everyone else does. Using such an analysis, he posits a set of "sub-Gricean" conditions.
5. Similar to Scribner's (1977) claim that empirical biases enter a problem solution process as a "selector" and "editor" of the evidence—that is, a possible solution is first generated via general rules of inference and is *later* possibly rejected due to some specific world knowledge beliefs.
6. Bruce, analyzing children's fox fables, adds an interesting twist to plan analysis by focusing on situations where a speaker purposefully hides underlying intent from coparticipants in the situation.
7. Of more interest, in the retelling of a story, one usually only states those events and orientation pieces needed for the story to fulfill a single conversational move. It is therefore unclear whether such a neutrally biased story, serving two separate perspectives, would occur in discourse without some extra structuring devices, such as an "Incidentally" subspace.

References

Adams, M. Failures to comprehend and levels of processing in reading. In R. Spiro, B. Bruce, and W. Brewer (eds.), *Theoretical Issues in Reading Comprehension*. Erlbaum, Hillsdale, N.J., 1980, 221–237.

Allen, J. A plan-based approach to speech act recognition. Ph.D. Thesis. University of Toronto, 1979.

Appelt, D. Planning natural language utterances to satisfy multiple goals. Ph.D. Thesis. Stanford University, 1981.

Anderson, R. C., and Pichert, J. W. Recall of previously unrecallable information following a shift in perspective. *Journal of Verbal Learning and Verbal Behavior* 17 (1978):1–12.

Anderson, R., Picher, J., and Shirey, L. Effects of the reader's schema at different points in time. R-119. Bolt, Beranek and Newman, Inc., Cambridge, Mass., 1979.

Attneave, F. Multistability in perception. In R. Held (ed.), *Image, Object, and Illusion*. W. H. Freeman, 1974, 91–99.

Austin, J. L. *How to Do Things with Words*. Oxford University Press, 1962.

Bartlett, F. C. *Remembering*. Cambridge University Press, 1932.

Bates, M. The theory and practice of augmented transition network grammars. In L. Bolc (ed.), *Natural Language Communication with Computers*. Springer-Verlag, 1978.

Bennett, J. *Linguistic Behavior*. Cambridge University Press, 1976.

Black, M. More about metaphor. In A. Ortony (ed.), *Metaphor and Thought*. Cambridge University Press, 1979.

Bobrow, R., and Webber, B. PSI-KLONE—Parsing and semantics interpretation in the BBN natural language understanding system. *CSCSI/CSEIO Annual Conference*, 1980.

Bobrow, R., and Webber, B. Knowledge representation for syntactic/semantic processing. *Proceedings of the First Annual National Conference on Artificial Intelligence*, 1980.

Bransford, J. D., and Johnson, M. K. Contextual prerequisites for understanding: some investigations of comprehension and recall. *Journal of Verbal Learning and Verbal Behavior* 11 (1972):717–726.

Brewer, W. Literary theory, rhetoric, and stylistics: implications of psychology. In R. Spiro, B. Bruce, and W. Brewer (eds.), *Theoretical Issues in Reading Comprehension*. Erlbaum, Hillsdale, N.J., 1980, 221–237.

Bruce, B. Discourse models and language comprehension. *American Journal of Computational Linguistics* (1975):19–35.

Bruce, B. Analysis of interacting plans as a guide to the understanding of story structure. *Poetics* 9 (1980):295–311.

Carbonell, J. Metaphor—a key to extensible semantic analysis. *Proceedings of the 18th Annual Meeting of the ACL,* 1980.

Chafe, W. Language and memory. *Language* 49, 2 (1973):261–281.

Chafe, W. Structures and human knowledge. In J. B. Carrol and R. O. Freedle (eds.), *Language Comprehension and the Acquisition of Knowledge.* Books Demand UMI Publications, Charlotte, N.C., 1975.

Chafe, W. Giveness, contrastiveness, definiteness, subjects, and topics. In C. Li (ed.), *Subject and Topic.* Academic Press, 1976.

Chafe, W. The flow of thought and the flow of language. In T. Givøn (ed.), *Syntax and Semantics* 12. Academic Press, 1979, 159–182.

Chafe, W. The development of consciousness in the production of narrative. In W. Chafe (ed.), *The Pear Stories: Cognitive and Linguistic Aspects of Narrative Production.* Ablex, Norwood, N.J., 1980, 9–50.

Chomsky, N. *Aspects of the Theory of Syntax.* The MIT Press, 1965.

Chomsky, N. Rules and representations. *The Behavioral and Brain Sciences* 3 (1980): 1–61.

Cicourel, A. Hearing is not believing: language and the structure of belief in medical communication. *Studia Linguistica* 35 (1981).

Clark, H., and Carlson, T. Hearers and speech acts. *Language* 58 (1982):2.

Clark, H., and Marshall, C. Definite reference and mutual knowledge. In A. K. Joshi, I. Sag, and B. Webber (eds.), *Linguistic Structure and Discourse Setting.* Cambridge University Press, 1981.

Cohen, P. On knowing what to say: planning speech acts. Ph.D. Thesis. University of Toronto, 1978.

Cohen, P., and Perrault, R. Elements of a plan-based theory of speech acts. *Cognitive Science* 3 (1979):177–212.

Cohen, P., Perrault, R., and Allen, J. Beyond question-answering. In W. Lennert and M. Ringle (eds.), *Strategies for Natural Language Processing.* Erlbaum, Hillsdale, N.J., 1981.

Cohen, R. Understanding arguments. *Proceedings CSCSI,* Canadian Society for Computational Studies of Intelligence, 1980.

Cohen, R. A computational model for the analysis of arguments. Ph.D. Thesis. CSRG-151. University of Toronto, 1983.

Collins, A., and Loftus, E. F. A spreading-activation theory of semantic processing. *Psychology Review* 82 (1975):407–428.

Collins, A., and Quillian, M. Retrieval time from semantic memory. *Journal of Verbal Learning and Verbal Behavior* 8 (1979):240–247.

Collins, A., and Gentner, D. A framework for a cognitive theory of writing. In L. W. Gregg and E. Steinberg (eds.), *Cognitive Processes in Writing: An Interdisciplinary Approach.* Erlbaum, Hillsdale, N.J., 1980.

Collins, A., Warnock, E., Aiello, N., and Miller, M. Reasoning from incomplete knowledge. In D. G. Bobrow, A. Collins (eds.), *Representation and Understanding.* Academic Press, 1975, 383–415.

Comerie, B. *Aspect.* Cambridge University Press, 1976.

D'Andrade, R. Reason versus logic. *Proceedings of the Ecology of Cognition: Biological, Cultural, and Historical Perspectives,* N.C., 1982.

Danes, F. *Papers on Functional Sentence Perspective.* Publishing House of the Czech Academy of Sciences, 1974.

Dore, J. Children's illocutionary acts. In R. Freedle (ed.), *Discourse Production and Comprehension.* Ablex, Norwood, N.J., 1977, 227–244.

Fillmore, C. J. The case for case. In E. Bach and R. T. Harus (eds.), *Universals in Linguistic Theory*. Holt, Rinehart and Winston, 1968.

Fillmore, C. J. Discourse deixis. *Lectures on Deixis*. Indiana University Linguistics Club, 1975.

Firbas, J. On the concept of communicative dynamism in the theory of functional sentence perspective. *SPFFBU* 19 (1971):135–144.

Gentner, D. The structure of analogical models in science. R-4451. Bolt, Beranek and Newman, Inc., Cambridge, Mass., 1980.

Gentner, D. Metaphor as structure preserving mapping. *Proceedings American Psychological Association*, 1980.

Gentner, D. Are scientific analogies metaphors? In D. Miall (ed.), *Metaphor—Problems and Perspectives*. Humanities Press, Inc., Atlantic Highlands, N.J., 1982.

Gibson, E. J., Gibson, J. J., Pick, A. D., and Osser, H. A developmental study of the discrimination of letter-like forms. *Journal of Comparative and Physiological Psychology* 55 (1962):897–906.

Goetz, E., and Armbruster, B. Psychological correlates of text structure. In R. Spiro, B. Bruce, and W. Brewer (eds.), *Theoretical Issues in Reading Comprehension*. Erlbaum, Hillsdale, N.J., 1980, 201–221.

Goffman, E. *Frame Analysis*. Harper and Row, 1974.

Goldberg, J. A. Track that topic with Y'Know. *Proceedings of Summer Conference on Conversational Interaction and Discourse Processes*, University of Nebraska-Lincoln, 1981.

Goodman, B. A model for a natural language data base system. R-798. University of Illinois, Urbana, 1977.

Goodman, B. Communication and miscommunication. Ph.D. Thesis. R-1. University of Illinois, Urbana, 1984.

Grice, H. P. Utterer's meaning, sentence-meaning, and word-meaning. In J. R. Searle (ed.), *Oxford Readings in Philosophy*. Oxford University Press, 1971, 54–70.

Grice, H. P. Logic and conversation. In P. Cole and J. Morgan (eds.), *Syntax and semantics*. Academic Press, 1975, 41–58.

Grimes, J. Topic levels. In *Theoretical Issues in Natural Language Processing* 2. Association for Computational Linguistics, 1978.

Grimes, J. E. Context structure patterns. *Proceedings of Nobel Symposium on Text Processing*, Nobel Symposium on Text Processing, 1980.

Grosz, B. The representation and use of focus in dialogue understanding. Ph.D. Thesis. University of California, Berkeley, 1977.

Halliday, M. A. K. Some aspects of the thematic organization of the English clause. RM-5224-PR. The Rand Corporation, Los Angeles, 1967.

Halliday, M. A. K. Functional diversity in language as seen from a consideration of modality and mood in English. *Foundations of Language* 6 (1970):322–361.

Halliday, M. A. K. *Language and Social Man*. Longman, London, 1975.

Halliday, M. A. K. Text as a semantic choice in social contexts. In T. A. van Dijk and J. S. Petofi (eds.). *Grammars and Description*. De Gruyter, Berlin, 1977.

Halliday, M. A. K., and Hasan, R. *Cohesion in English*. Longman, London, 1976.

Hankamer, J., and Sag, I. Deep and surface anaphora. *Linguistic Inquiry* 7, 3 (1976): 391–426.

Harris, Z. *Methods in Structural Linguistics*. The University of Chicago Press, 1951.

Harweg, R. Substitutional text linguistics. In J. Petofi (ed.), *Current Trends in Textlinguistics*. De Gruyter, Berlin, 1977.

Hasan, R. Code, register and social dialect. In B. Bernstein (ed.), *Class, Codes and Control*. Vol. 2. Routledge and Kegan Paul, London, 1973, 253–292.

Hasan, R. The place of stylistics in the study of verbal art. In H. Ringbom (ed.), *Style and Text*. Skriptor, Stockholm, 1975, 49–63.

Hasan, R. Text in the systemic-functional model. In W. Dressler (ed.), *Current Trends in Textlinguistics*. De Gruyter, Berlin, 1977.

Hein, U. Interruptions in dialogue. In D. Metzing (ed.), *Dialogmuster und Dialogprozesse*. Helmut Buske, Hamburg, 1980.

Hirst, G. Semantic interpretation against ambiguity. Ph.D. Thesis. CS-83-25. Brown University, 1983.

Hobbs, J. A computational approach to discourse analysis. City University of New York, 1976.

Hobbs, J. Metaphor schemata, and selective inferencing. Stanford Research Institute, Palo Alto, 1979.

Hobbs, J., and Evans, D. Conversation as planned behavior. *Cognitive Science* 4 (1980):317–345.

Hymes, D. The ethnography of speaking. In T. Gladwin and W. C. Sturtevant (eds.), *Anthropology and Human Behavior*. Anthropological Society of Washington, Washington, D.C., 1962, 13–53.

James, W. *The Principles of Psychology*. Holt, Rinehart and Winston, 1980.

Jefferson, G. Sequential aspects of storytelling in conversation. In J. Schenkein (ed.), *Studies in the Organization of Conversational Interaction*. Academic Press, 1979.

Jefferson, G. Some sequential negotiation in conversation. In J. Schenkein (ed.), *Studies in the Organization of Conversational Interaction*. Academic Press, 1979, 134–155.

Johnson-Laird, P. N. Mental models in cognitive science. *Cognitive Science* 4 (1980): 71–115.

Jones, L. K. *Theme in English Expository Discourse*. Jupiter Press, Lake Bluff, Ill., 1977.

Kantor, R. N. The management and comprehension of discourse connection by pronouns in English. Ph.D. Thesis. Ohio State University, 1977.

Karmiloff-Smith, A. Language as a formal problem space for children. *MPG-NIAS Child Language Conference: Beyond Description in Child Language*, 1979.

Katz, J., and Fodor, J. The structure of a semantic theory. *Languages* 39 (1963):170–210.

Kinstch, W., and van Dijk, T. A. Comment on se rappelle et on résume des histoires. *Languages* 40 (1975):98–116.

Klappholz, D. A., and Lockman, A. D. The use of dynamically extracted context for anaphoric reference resolution. Unpublished Manuscript. Columbia University, 1977.

Kuno, S. Empathy and syntax. In S. Kuno (ed.), *Harvard Studies in Syntax and Semantics*. Harvard University Press, 1975, 1–73.

Kuno, S. Gapping: a functional analysis. *Linguistic Inquiry* 7, 2 (1976):300–318.

Kuno, S. Generative discourse analysis in America. In J. Petofi (ed.), *Current Trends in Textlinguistics*. De Gruyter, Berlin, 1977.

Labov, W. *Language in the Inner City*. University of Pennsylvania Press, 1972.

Labov, W., and Fanshel, D. *Therapeutic Discourse*. Academic Press, 1977.

Lachman, R., and Dooling, D. J. Connected discourse and random strings: effects of number of inputs on recognition and recall. *Journal of Experimental Psychology* 17 (1968):517–522.

Lakoff, G., and Johnson, M. *Metaphors We Live By*. The University of Chicago Press, 1980.

Lakoff, R. Remarks on this and that. *Proceedings of the Tenth Regional Meeting of the Chicago Linguistic Society*, 1974.

Langacker, R. Foundations of cognitive grammar. Chapter 1, Orientation; Chapter II, Semantic structure. Indiana University Linguistics Club, Bloomington, 1982.

Lange, B. Making sense with schemata. *Journal of Reading,* 24, 5 (1981):442–445.

Lehnert, W. A computational theory of human question answering. In A. Joshi, B. Webber, and I. Sag (eds.), *Elements of Discourse Understanding.* Cambridge University Press, 1981.

Levin, J., and Moore, J. Dialogue-games: metacommunication structures for natural language interaction. *Cognitive Science* 4 (1977):395–421.

Levinsohn, S. H. Progression and digression in Inga (Quechuan) discourse. *Forum Linguisticum* 1 (1976):122–147.

Levy, D. Communicative goals and strategies: between discourse and syntax. In T. Givøn (ed.), *Syntax and Semantics* 12. Academic Press, 1979.

Lewis, D. K. *Convention.* Harvard University Press, 1969.

Linde, C. Information structures in discourse. Ph.D. Thesis. Columbia University, 1974.

Linde, C. The organization of discourse. In T. Shope, A. Zwicky, and P. Griffen (eds.), *The English Language in Its Social and Historical Context* (forthcoming).

Linde, C., and Gougen, J. Structure of planning discourse, *Journal of Social and Biological Structure* 1 (1978):219–251.

Linde, C. Focus of attention and the choice of pronouns in discourse. In T. Givøn (ed.), *Syntax and Semantics* 12. Academic Press, 1979.

Lindsay, P., and Norman, D. *Human Information Processing.* Academic Press, 1972.

Litman, D., and Allen, J. A plan recognition model for clarification subdialogues. *Proceedings Coling 84,* 1984.

Lockman, A. D. Contextual reference resolution. Ph.D. Thesis. Columbia University, 1978.

Longrace, R. E. *Hierarchy and Universality of Discourse Constituents in New Guinea Languages: Discussion.* Georgetown University Press, 1972.

Longrace, R., and Levinsohn, S. Field analysis of discourse. In J. Petofi (ed.), *Current Trends in Textlinguistics.* De Gruyter, Berlin, 1977.

Mandler, J. M., and Johnson, N. S. Remembrance of things parsed: story structure and recall. *Cognitive Psychology* 9 (1977):111–151.

McDonald, D. Natural language generation as a computational problem. In J. M. Brady and R. C. Berevick (eds.), *Computational Models of Discourse.* The MIT Press, 1983.

McKeown, K. R. Generating natural language text in response to questions about database structure. Ph.D. Thesis. University of Pennsylvania, 1982.

Mehan, H. Structuring school structure. *Harvard Educational Review* 48, 1 (1978):32–64.

Meyer, B. J. F. Following the author's top-level structure. In R. Tierney, J. Mitchell, and P. Anders (eds.), *Understanding Reader's Understanding.* Erlbaum, Hillsdale, N.J., 1977.

Meyer, B. J. F. A selected review and discussion of basic research on prose comprehension. Arizona State University, 1979.

Miller, G. A. Images and models: similes and metaphors. In A. Ortony (ed.), *Metaphor and Thought.* Cambridge University Press, 1979, 202–250.

Minsky, M. A framework for representing knowledge. In P. Winston (ed.), *The Psychology of Computer Vision.* McGraw-Hill, 1975.

Montague, R. *Formal Philosophy: Selected Papers of Richard Montague.* Yale University Press, 1974.

Morgan, J., and Sellner, M. Discourses and linguistic theory. In R. Spiro, B. Bruce, and W. Brewer (eds.), *Theoretical Issues in Reading Comprehension.* Erlbaum, Hillsdale, N.J., 1980, 165–201.

Morgan, J., and Green, G. Pragmatics and reading comprehension. In R. Spiro, B. Bruce, and W. Brewer (eds.), *Theoretical Issues in Reading Comprehension*. Erlbaum, Hillsdale, N.J., 1980, 113–141.

Mosenthal, P. Three types of schemata in children's recall of cohesive and noncohesive text. *Proceedings of the AERA*, 1978.

Neisser, U. *Cognitive Psychology*. Meredith Publishing Company, 1967.

Newman, D. Children's understanding of strategic interaction. Ph.D. Thesis. City University of New York, 1980.

Olson, D. Language and thought: aspects of a cognitive theory of semantics. *Psychological Review* 77, 4 (1970):257–273.

Ortony, A. Beyond literal similarity. *Psychological Review* 86, 4 (1979):161–180.

Palkova, Z., and Palek, B. Functional sentence perspective and textlinguistics. In J. Petofi (ed.), *Current Trends in Textlinguistics*. De Gruyter, Berlin, 1977.

Phillips, B. Discourse connectives. Technical Report KS-11. Department of Information Engineering. University of Illinois at Chicago, 1977.

Pike, K. *Language in Relation to a Unified Theory of the Structure of Human Behavior*. Mouton, The Hague, 1967.

Pitkin, W., Jr. Hierarchies and the discourse hierarchy. *College English* 38, 7 (1977): 648–659.

Pitkin, W., Jr. Some basic strategies of discourse. *College English* 38, 7 (1977):660–672.

Polanyi, L. The American story: cultural constraints on the meaning and structure of stories in conversation. Ph.D. Thesis. University of Michigan, 1978.

Polanyi, L. False starts can be true. *Proceedings BLS*, Berkeley Linguistic Society, 1978.

Power, R. The organization of purposeful dialogues. *Linguistics* 17 (1979):107–152.

Pratt, M. L. *Towards a Speech Act Theory of Literary Discourse*. Indiana University Press, 1977.

Prince, G. *A Grammar of Stories*. Mouton, The Hague, 1973.

Propp, V. *Morphology of the Folktale*. University of Texas Press, 1968.

Reichenbach, H. *Elements of Symbolic Logic*. Macmillan, 1947.

Reichman, R. Conversational coherency. *Cognitive Science* 3 (1978):283–327.

Reichman, R. Conversational coherency in technical conversations. Institut pour Les Études Semantiques et Cognitives, Geneva, Switzerland, 1979.

Reichman, R. Analogies in spontaneous discourse. *Proceedings of the 19th Annual Meeting of the Association for Computational Linguistics*, 1981.

Reichman, R. Modeling informal debates. *Proceedings of the Seventh International Joint Conference on Artificial Intelligence*, 1981.

Reichman, R. Technical discourse: the present progressive tense, the deictic "that," and pronominalization. *Discourse Processes* 7, 3 (1984):337–369.

Reichman, R. Extended person-machine interface. *Artificial Intelligence* 22 (1984): 157–218.

Rumelhart, D. Notes on a schema for stories. In D. Bobrow and A. Collins (eds.), *Representation and Understanding*. Academic Press, 1975.

Rumelhart, D. E. Schemata: the building blocks of cognition. In R. Spiro, B. Bruce, and W. Brewer (eds.), *Theoretical Issues in Reading Comprehension*. Erlbaum, Hillsdale, N.J., 1980.

Sacks, H., Schegloff, E., and Jefferson, G. A simplest systematics for the organization of turntaking for conversation. *Language* 50, 4 (1974):696–735.

Sadock, J. Modus brevis: the truncated argument. *Papers from the 13th Regional Meeting of the Chicago Linguistic Society*, Chicago, 1977.

Schank, R., and Abelson, R. P. *Scripts, Plans, Goals, and Understanding*. Erlbaum, Hillsdale, N.J., 1977.

Schegloff, E., and Sacks, H. Opening up closings. *Semiotica* 8 (1973):289–327.

Schiffer, S. *Meaning.* Oxford University Press, 1972.

Schiffrin, D. Meta-talk: organizational and evaluative brackets in discourse. In D. Zimmerman and C. West (eds.), *Studies in Language and Social Interaction.* Jossey-Bass, San Francisco (to appear).

Schmidt, C. F. Understanding human action: Recognizing the plans and motives of other persons. In J. Carroll and J. Payne (eds.), *Cognition and Social Behavior.* Erlbaum, Hillsdale, N.J., 1976.

Schmidt, S. Some problems of communicative text theories. In J. Petofi (ed.), *Current Trends in Textlinguistics.* De Gruyter, Berlin, 1977.

Schutz, A. *Reflections on the Problem of Relevance.* Yale University Press, 1970.

Scribner, S. Modes of thinking and ways of speaking: culture and logic reconsidered. In P. N. Johnson-Laird and P. C. Wason (eds.), *Thinking: Readings in Cognitive Science.* Cambridge University Press, 1977, 483–500.

Searle, J. R. *Speech Acts.* Cambridge University Press, 1969.

Searle, J. R. What is a speech act. In J. R. Earle (ed.), *Oxford Readings in Philosophy.* Oxford University Press, 1971, 39–53.

Sgall, P., and Hajičo'va, E. Focus on focus. *The Prague Bulletin of Mathematical Linguistics* 28 (1977).

Sheridan, M. E. A review of research on schema theory and its implication for reading instruction in secondary reading. Indiana University at South Bend, 1978.

Sidner, C. Towards a computational theory of definite anaphora comprehension in English discourse. Ph.D. Thesis. Massachusetts Institute of Technology, 1979.

Sinclair, J. M., and Coulthard, R. M. *Towards an Analysis of Discourse—The English Used by Teachers and Pupils.* Oxford University Press, 1975.

Spiro, R. Constructive processes in prose comprehension and recall. In R. Spiro, B. Bruce, and W. Brewer (eds.), *Theoretical Issues in Reading Comprehension.* Erlbaum, Hillsdale, N.J., 1980, 245–278.

Sternberg, R. J. Component processes in analogical reasoning. *Psychological Review* 84 (1977):353–378.

Tennant, H. Evaluation of natural language processors. Ph.D. Thesis. University of Illinois, 1980.

Thorndyke, P. W. Cognitive structures in comprehension and memory of narrative discourse. *Cognitive Psychology* 9 (1977):77–110.

Toulmin, S. *The Uses of Argument.* Cambridge University Press, 1958.

van Dijk, T. A. *Macrostructures: An Interdisciplinary Study of Global Structures in Discourse, Interaction and Cognition.* Erlbaum, Hillsdale, N.J., 1980.

Vendler, Z. Singular terms. In D. Steinberg and L. Jakobovits (eds.), *Semantics.* Cambridge University Press, 1971.

Webber, B. A formal approach to discourse anaphora. Ph.D. Thesis. Harvard University, 1978.

Weiner, J. The structure of natural explanation: theory and application. System Development Corporation, 1979.

Wilensky, R. Understanding goal-based stories. Ph.D. Thesis. Yale University, 1978.

Wilks, Y. Grammar. *Meaning and the Machine Analysis of Language.* Routledge and Kegan Paul, London, 1972.

Wilks, Y. Some thoughts on procedural semantics. In W. Lehnert and M. Ringle (eds.), *Knowledge Representation for Language Processing Systems.* Erlbaum, Hillsdale, N.J., 1981.

Wilson, D., and Sperber, D. On Grice's theory of conversation. *Communications* 30 (1979):80–94.

Winston, P. H. Learning and reasoning by analogy. *Communications of the ACM* 23, 12 (1980):689–702.

Wittgenstein, L. *Philosophical Investigations.* Blackwell, Oxford, 1953.

Woods, W. A. Transition network grammars for natural language analysis. *Communications of the ACM* 13 (1970):591–606.

Woods, W. What's in a link? In D. Bobrow and A. Collins (eds.), *Representation and Understanding.* Academic Press, 1975, 35–82.

Woods, W. Cascaded ATN grammars. *American Journal of Computational Linguistics* 6, 1 (1980):1–12.

Wooton, A. *Dilemmas of Discourse: Controversies About the Sociological Interpretation of Language.* Allen and Unwin, 1975.

Index